F
B

NOT FOR MOTHERS ONLY:
CONTEMPORARY POEMS
ON CHILD-GETTING & CHILD-REARING

edited by
CATHERINE WAGNER & REBECCA WOLFF

NOT FOR MOTHERS ONLY:
CONTEMPORARY POEMS
ON CHILD-GETTING & CHILD-REARING

Front cover image by Cody Rose Clevidence

Back cover erasure by Gillian Conoley, from "Dr. B's Poof and Dare"

Cover and text design by Rebecca Wolff

Library of Congress Control Number: 2007922314

ISBN 0-9771064-8-9
ISBN-13: 978-0-9771064-8-6

Printed in the United States by United Graphics

Distributed by University Press of New England (upne.com)

Please direct inquiries to:

Fence Books
Permissions
Science Library
University at Albany
1400 Washington Avenue
Albany, NY 12222

Fence Books are published in affiliation with the New York State Writers Institute

NEW YORK STATE **riters** INSTITUTE
———————————————— State University of New York

and the University at Albany

UALBANY
State University of New York

and with help from the New York State Council on the Arts

State of the Arts

NYSCA

CONTENTS*

* Contributors are in order of date of arrival of their first child

** Bibliographic information has been omitted from contributors' notes
as it is included in full here

FOR AMBROSE CORLESS-SMITH
FOR ASHER WOLFF & MARGOT SHER

BY WAY OF PREFACE

PARTURITION

I am the centre
Of a circle of pain
Exceeding its boundaries in every direction

The business of the bland sun
Has no affair with me
In my congested cosmos of agony
From which there is no escape
On infinitely prolonged nerve-vibrations
Or in contraction
To the pin-point nucleus of being

Locate an irritation   without
It is   within
                             Within
It is without
The sensitized area
Is identical   with the extensity
Of intension

I am the false quantity
In the harmony of physiological potentiality
To which
Gaining self-control
I should be consonant
In time

Pain is no stronger than the resisting force
Pain calls up in me
The struggle is equal

The open window is full of a voice
A fashionable portrait-painter
Running up-stairs to a woman's apartment
Sings

    "All the girls are tid'ly did'ly
     All the girls are nice
      Whether they wear their hair in curls
        Or—"

At the back of the thoughts to which I permit crystallization
The conception   Brute
Why?
      The irresponsibility of the male
Leaves woman her superior Inferiority
He is running up-stairs

I am climbing a distorted mountain of agony
Incidentally with the exhaustion of control
I reach the summit
And gradually subside into anticipation of
Repose
Which never comes
For another mountain is growing up
Which   goaded by the unavoidable
I must traverse
Traversing myself

Something in the delirium of night-hours
Confuses while intensifying sensibility
Blurring spatial contours
So aiding elusion of the circumscribed
That the gurgling of a crucified wild beast
Comes from so far away
And the foam on the stretched muscles of a mouth
Is no part of myself
There is a climax in sensibility
When pain surpassing itself
Becomes Exotic

And the ego succeeds in unifying the positive and negative poles of sensation
Uniting the opposing and resisting forces

In lascivious revelation
Relaxation
Negation of myself as a unit
      Vacuum interlude
I should have been emptied of life
Giving life
For consciousness in crises   races
Through the subliminal deposits of evolutionary processes
Have I not
Somewhere
Scrutinized
A dead white feathered moth
Laying eggs?
A moment
Being realization
Can
Vitalized by cosmic initiation
Furnish an adequate apology
For the objective
Agglomeration of activities
Of a life.
Life
A leap with nature
Into the essence
Of unpredicted Maternity
Against my thigh
Touch of infinitesimal motion
Scarcely   perceptible
Undulation
Warmth moisture
Stir of incipient life
Precipitating into me
The contents of the universe

Mother I am
Identical
With infinite Maternity
   Indivisible
   Acutely
   I am absorbed
   Into
The was—is—ever—shall—be
Of cosmic reproductivity

Rises from the subconscious
Impression of a cat
With blind kittens
Among her legs
Same undulating life-stir
I am that cat

Rises from the sub-conscious
Impression of a small animal carcass
Covered with blue-bottles
—Epicurean—
And through the insects
Waves that same undulation of living
Death
Life
I am knowing
All about
    Unfolding
The next morning
Each woman-of-the-people
Tip-toeing the red pile of the carpet
Doing hushed service
Each woman-of-the-people
Wearing a halo
A ludicrous little halo
Of which she is sublimely   unaware

I once heard in a church
—Man and woman God made them—
                    Thank God.

MINA LOY
1914

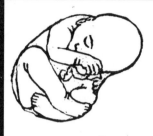

BORN IN 1882 IN LONDON, THE POET, artist, actor, playwright, and iconoclastic feminist Mina Loy was a controversial, charismatic figure in European and American modernist circles. During her varied career, she lived in Florence (where she had an affair with the Futurist Filippo Marinetti), Paris (where she designed and sold lampshades in a business backed by Peggy Guggenheim), New York, and Mexico. Though Loy's importance to the modernist movement was nearly forgotten for years, her reissued writings have received significant critical attention, and a biography by Carolyn Burke, *Becoming Modern,* appeared in 1997.

Loy's daughter Oda, born in 1904, died on her first birthday. A second daughter, Joella, arrived in 1907, and a son, Giles, in 1909. Fabienne, a third daughter, was born in 1919. Said Loy, "My conceptions of life evolved while . . . stirring baby food on spirit lamps—and my best drawings behind a stove to the accompaniment of a line of children's clothes hanging round it to dry."* Loy lived for the last dozen years of her life with her daughters in Colorado, where she died at the age of 84.

Unlike the other poets appearing in this anthology, Loy is neither North American nor living; her poem "Parturition" is included here to launch what we intend not as the usual "celebration" of poetry by mothers but as a conflagration "exceeding its boundaries in every direction."

---

*Quoted in *The Last Lunar Baedeker* by Mina Loy, edited by Roger Conover, The Jargon Society, Highlands, NC, 1982. Introduction, p. lxvi

FOREWORD

WE WERE IN ENGLAND that year, living in a semi-detached house with a nice English garden out back, and a stove that required me to shovel coal. In fact, the whole house was heated by coal, of three different sorts (for stove, boiler, fireplace) that I had to shovel. Though the garden was nice, we didn't use it much. Some months averaged three hours of sunlight a day, according to my husband's calculations. To augment depression, the house was furnished with the ugliest, heaviest, most depressingly brown furniture I have ever seen.

This was 1964-5, and we were post-docs in Cambridge traveling everywhere by bicycle. That is to say, my husband biked to the Institute for Applied Mathematics, while I biked with my big belly to market, or to a friend whose baby son liked to play with my baby daughter. It was a lonely, difficult stretch of life. When I found myself writing an experimental sequence of poems based on my first two pregnancies and births, I was startled.

Poetry, according to my professors, was supposed to be "universal." I had read thousands of love poems and thousands of death poems. These were "universal" themes. Yet I had never read a poem about pregnancy and birth. Was birth not universal? It took me a while to realize that the topic was taboo. One did not mention female physical experiences in mixed company, much less try to make literature out of them. Pregnancy and childbirth in particular were taboo, I decided, because men were unconsciously jealous of women's reproductive capacities, and women had to protect them from consciousness. The best way to do this, of course, was to be sex objects. Breasts were okay in pornography, but you couldn't nurse a child in public. So I finished the poem sequence, called "Once More Out of Darkness," fondly dubbed by friends "A Poem in Nine Parts and a Post-Partum." To see myself as an accidental taboo-breaker was exciting. When I read the finished poem in performance and some men walked out, that was exciting too. Five years later, when my son arrived in the middle of the Vietnam War, I thought I understood the reason for the taboo a little better: mothers are supposed to be quiet while fathers send sons to war. Hence the genesis of "The Mother/Child Papers."

The loneliness of the long-distance mother who is also a poet has been broken. Even when I began, it was already being broken by Mina Loy, H.D., Gwendolyn Brooks, Muriel Rukeyser, Plath, Sexton, Rich and others. But I had not read these poets. I was unaware that a women's poetry movement had begun, and that the ice of four thousand years of frozen silence was cracking, melting, breaking up. Mina Loy's "Parturition," which begins "I am the center/ of a circle of pain/ Exceeding its boundaries in every direction," was in no anthology. Anne Sexton's mantra from Kafka, "a book should be an axe for the frozen sea within us," loomed over the horizon. Since then, much has changed. Women poets write with a freedom that would be unthinkable to any past generation on earth. Poets who write as mothers are thick on the ground now. Yet fathers still send sons (and now daughters) to war, and nursing mothers are still supposed to be invisible.

The poets in this anthology have been ravished, whacked, illuminated, blown away by the experience of motherhood. The thousand experiences. The thousand interruptions. The fact that it is never what we expected, and that it is overwhelmingly intense. The intensity of the poems here bespeaks both the power of maternity in bending us to its will, and the power of the artist to resist-while-submitting. Nobody here plays a standard mom role, although there are numerous gestures in the direction of things moms do, like nurse babies and persist through exhaustion.

The poetry makes the difference. This is a book of *experimental* poetry, poetry that experiments with how it sits on the page, and with diction, syntax, location and dislocation, and with emotion and intelligence, with elements of language at peace and at war. Grace under pressure, maybe, and maybe not. Comedy, brutality, farce, mystery, ecstasy, reality. Details. Abstractions. Much attention to what Caroline Crumpacker calls "the louche interior life," and also to the opacity of words, as when Sharon Harris riffs wittily on the nuances of "mama," "mother," "mom," "mommy" or Christine Hume meditates on how "lullabye" is "porous, scabby," or "Lullabye wants you dead, and lullabye fears your death . . . Lullabye looks ahead by listening back." Nothing is taken for granted. No rules, no predictability to these poems. Often they are bizarre, surreal, because that's what it feels like to be doubled. "Zombie drinks tea! Zombie writes poems!" cries Maureen Owen, whose stream of consciousness can also include these lines on "BEDTIME":

I have this power At night
I kiss three people minutes later
they are all asleep the bizarre
& the miraculous are the same thing

For the essence of routine, read Susan Holbrook's "Nursery," composed one line at a time when the poet nursed, each line methodically and hilariously marked "Right" or "Left." I didn't count, so I don't know how many times Holbrook fed her hungry baby, but the poem is wonderfully entertaining, as if to say: see what a little inventiveness can do? If the medium is the message, and in poetry it always is, the message of all these poets is that motherhood in our time has become an immense, far-out experiment.

ALICIA OSTRIKER

INTRODUCTIONS

I.

In Alexander Tsiaras's *From Conception to Birth,* there's an astounding image of a baby emerging from a mother's body.[1] The baby appears almost to zoom out of the mother downward and toward the viewer, head first; it has pink, fragile-looking skin and flesh and is trailed by the umbilical cord. The mother, however, has no flesh or skin; the off-white bones of the pelvis and lower spine are all we see of her. The artifice, which makes visible the baby's passage through the pelvic ring, is easy to defend: the image's didactic purpose demands a flesh-free mother. (I saw the image before I went into labor and it helped me to visualize my son's departure from my body.) Nevertheless, its implication that the mother is less person than passageway is disturbing. The baby has the flesh and skin we associate with living personhood; the mother, as conduit, does not.

The image aligns with other evidence that we tend to value mothers as a kind of negative space, a container that does and should empty itself out in nurturing. At one point while seeking work for this book, I did a Google search for "mother poems." The following two were among the first that came up:

> A Mother's love is something
> that no one can explain,
> It is made of deep devotion
> and of sacrifice and pain,
> It is endless and unselfish
> and enduring come what may
> For nothing can destroy it
> or take that love away . . .

> —*Helen Steiner Rice*

---

1   Tsiaras combines and recolors MRI, ultrasound, CT and other medical images to create recognizable likenesses of the human body that make its complicated interior visible. Alexander Tsiaras, *From Conception to Birth: A Life Unfolds* (New York: Doubleday, 2002), 275.

When you have a mother
who cares so much for you
that anything you want
becomes her desires
When you have a mother
who actively pursues her goals in life
but includes you in all her goals . . .
you are very lucky indeed
Having a mother like this
makes it easy to grow up
into a loving, strong adult
Thank you for being this kind
of wonderful mother.

—*Susan Polis Schutz*[2]

In these poems, the wonderfulness of the mother depends on the degree to which she submerges herself in her relationship with the child. Even the apparently mother-centered middle item in the list of ideals enumerated by the second poem—the mother who "actively pursues her goals in life / but includes you in all her goals"—creates the sense that the mother who is wonderful pursues nothing unconnected to her child. Rice and Schutz write in praise of mothers, but their salutes to motherly self-sacrifice reveal a narcissism that exalts not the mother but the result of the mother's work: the self. Similarly, June Cotner's anthology *Mothers and Daughters: A Poetry Celebration* implies, through its organization (its sections, ordered by child's age, include "Babyhood," "Toddlerhood," "Adolescence," and "Leaving Home") that a mother is defined by her observation of and relationship with her child.[3] Cotner's anthology is fairly representative of other anthologies of writings on motherhood, all of which seem to contain the word "celebration" either in the title or on the back cover and most of which, curiously, are about mothers and daughters.

Though my relationship with my son is the most important (and pleasurable,

---

2   Both poems can be found at "Mothers Poems: Poem for mothers and about mothers [sic]," http://www.indianchild.com/mother1.htm.

3   June Cotner, ed., *Mothers and Daughters: A Poetry Celebration* (New York: Harmony, 2001).

and satisfying) part of my life, *Not for Mothers Only* is not a celebration of the mother-child relationship. That relationship is already consecrated in candied style in advertisements everywhere. Instead, in their bulk, the poems here are ruinous to assumptions that motherhood is obedient and passive in its encounter with cultural expectations for self-sacrifice, and they make it clear that mothers' creative acts—in this case, their writings—participate in a large discursive field. Rebecca Wolff and I chose not to organize poems around subject matter; you will find poems on toddlers and on miscarriage here, but they're not lumped together. We have ordered the anthology by the date of the writer's entry into motherhood (the date of her child's arrival) in order to locate the mother in a chronology of writers, among mothers who precede them and accompany them on the page. We are hoping to make manifest a poetic tradition that gives mothers increasing permission to write on motherhood and to understand such writing as part of an important historical and contemporary conversation.

The younger poets in this anthology owe a debt to the poets included here who were writing and caring for children in the sixties and seventies, women who had less support for either undertaking than poets do today. Alice Notley, in the note on her work in this book, says "I began writing poems saturated with the details of pregnancy, childbirth and motherhood sometime in 1972. I had no models for my subject—I worked entirely in isolation, in Chicago and in England. As far as I was aware, I was the first one to write such a poetry." Others were, in fact, writing of motherhood, but they tend to echo Notley's sense of isolation. Alicia Ostriker writes that as she tried, in 1965, to "discover a poetic form which could . . . convey the extraordinary sense of transformation from being a private individual self to being a portion of something else," she wondered why, if "other women knew what [she] knew . . . where were the poems?"[4] The daring poems on motherhood by the poets who appear early in this book opened a field of possibility to younger writers in this anthology. Sometimes writers' debt to them is obvious: Lee Ann Brown and Hoa Nguyen owe something to Bernadette Mayer, for instance, and Rachel Zucker to Sharon Olds; others—see Jean Donnelly—explicitly express gratitude. The poetic legacy is conspicuous, and makes me wonder at the critic Helen Vendler, who, according to a recent *New York Times* article, "has noted the lack of great poetry

---

4   Because it was out of print from the early twentieth century until 1982, Notley and Ostriker likely did not know Mina Loy's "Parturition," reprinted as preface to this book.

about motherhood."[5] *NFMO* witnesses both to a historical community of the page and to contemporary networks of mother writers across North America, notably exemplified by the Poet-moms listserv that was part of the impetus for this anthology.[6] For me, engagement with the writing mothers on the list has been a sustaining reminder of the possibility of creative activity despite and by means of the situation of motherhood.

2

Not for Mothers Only is neither impartial nor representative of its impossibly wide field; it registers Rebecca's and my overlapping (and occasionally separate) pleasures and interests and goals.[7] We became interested, reading for this project, in what would come of a new experiment in editing for us; we sought challenging, off-center depictions of the power struggles and politics involved in motherhood, investing consciously in content.

Some years ago, the poet Jennifer Moxley called for a reconsideration of content in poetry: "To my mind the debate must needs include not only how a poem is constructed, but what it is saying as well. To return to [Robert] Creeley again, 'form is never more than an extension of content'—not the other way around. Content is the great unspoken issue, possibly because once addressed our true passions will be exposed . . . '"[8] Odd as it may sound to readers not familiar with debates and trends in recent poetry, Moxley does not overstate the case: for avant-garde "language" and "post-language" poets and traditionalist "New Formalists" alike, concerns with form over content have been dominant since the 1980s (the trend might be compared to the sometime absence of figurative art from New York galleries). 9/11 speeded up a swing of the pendulum in the other direction; nevertheless, anthologies based on subject matter are the object of mild derision among my friends in poetry. The editors of such anthologies, it is assumed, must not have particularly discriminating taste, or they would not use subject matter as a measure of a work's appeal.

5   Susan Donadio, "The Closest Reader," *The New York Times*, December 10, 2006, *Sunday Book Review.*

6   The Poet-moms listserv was founded by poet Arielle Greenberg in 2005.

7   To locate contributors for this anthology, we relied on the usual calls for work on listservs, our own knowledge and networks, and word of mouth. I'm still discovering—in some cases, smacking my forehead—poets I would have solicited had I known they were mothers.

8   Jennifer Moxley, "Notes to Poetry" IV.4, *Third Factory*, posted January 9, 2001, http://www.umit.maine.edu/%7Esteven.evans/3F-4 (accessed March 31, 2007).

Subject-matter snobbery, however, runs the risk of defanging poetry, inhibiting its contribution to crucial debates. I'm as bored as anyone by poetry that fixates on subject matter to the exclusion of the resistant and protean qualities of language; but there's nothing about topicality that necessarily makes for a trivial poetics. Unexpected swerves and hinges in thought result from poetry's profound investment in its materiality. It's this transformative aspect of poetry that convinces me it can valuably address the subject of motherhood. It also reassures me that the writing in this anthology will resonate beyond any attempts I might make to direct or contain its effects.

I hope this book acts as a comforting corrective to those who feel isolated as mother-artists, and it should give a shock to anyone dubious of its appeal to non-mothers. Represented here are some of the most influential American poets now living, a short and incomplete list of whom would include Rae Armantrout, Mei-mei Berssenbrugge, Toi Derricotte, Fanny Howe, Bernadette Mayer, Alice Notley, Sharon Olds, and Adrienne Rich. The anthology also represents poets just beginning to publish, such as Amy Sara Carroll and Karena Youtz; emerging poets such as Sasha Steensen and Danielle Pafunda; and distinguished mid-career poets such as Claudia Rankine, Elizabeth Robinson, and Eleni Sikelianos. Along with the Bay Area Canadian Norma Cole (who permitted a brutal splice-and-dice of her subtle long poem "Spinoza in Her Youth"), it includes a trio of fierce Canadian poets who were new to me: Susan Holbrook, Margaret Christakos, and Sharon Harris. It includes mothers who have adopted children—Susan M. Schultz, Marie Howe, and Claudia Keelan—and three women whose poems on their experiences of non-motherhood moved us to include them: Ann Lauterbach, Marge Piercy, and Molly Peacock.

Some poets approach the topic intimately (Olena Kalytiak Davis, Beth Ann Fennelly, Notley, Jean Valentine), some historically (Gillian Conoley's witty Dr. Spock erasures, Caroline Knox), some through fictional explorations (Kathleen Fraser, Carla Harryman, Rankine), some through investigations of the power structures and economics inherent in the domestic (Wanda Coleman, Carolyn Forché, Hoa Nguyen, and, via wordplay, Susana Gardner's provocative visual lyricism). In her foreword to Patricia Dienstfrey's and Brenda Hillman's inspiring prose collection *The Grand Permission,* Rachel Blau DuPlessis notes that the essays are "in general about 'good enough' motherhood . . . and not really about <u>motherhood that,</u> for one reason or another, blows up in your face."[9] In this

9   *The Grand Permission: New Writings on Poetics and Motherhood* (Middle-

anthology, you will find writing in which motherhood does blow up in your face, amusingly or terrifyingly (see Mairéad Byrne, Lara Glenum, Miranda Field, Akilah Oliver, Maureen Owen, and many others). Many of these mothers have faced economic and domestic demands that leave little space for art-making. These poems do not, together or separately, assert an uncomplicated political desire or goal such as "We want paid parental leave,"[10] but they are hefty, heartening evidence of time spent not entirely subsumed into the workplace and the corporate media that batters (and fries) us.

I see *NFMO* as an introduction to a continuing poetic discussion of motherhood, so I will close by quoting a recent poem not included here. Rae Armantrout's "Versed" ends with the following comical and discomfiting lines: "Mother yells 'Good job!' / when he drops the stick, / / 'Good job!' / when he walks in her direction."[11] The dog-training metaphor casts "Mother" as fascist praiser. I do not want to mimic this mother by assuming the world will be a better place if everyone who reads this book "walks in my direction" to share my endorsement of the poems in it. I do want to emphasize the "self-monitoring function" art provides culture. "Metaphor," writes Armantrout, "forms a crust, / beneath which the crevasse / of each experience."

Dig in.

CATHERINE WAGNER

---

town, CT: Wesleyan University Press, 2003), x.

10   Though we do; or I do, anyway. If mothers in our country must work, and almost all of them must, why is the US one of only seven countries in the world that do not require companies to provide any paid parental leave? Why is it still difficult, in most workplaces, for women to make public their pregnancies or to take time to pump their milk without risk to their positions and reputations? Why are politicians still trying to pass laws against public breastfeeding? Such messages are still instructing mothers (despite economic imperatives) to remain invisible, to stay home and be quiet.

11   All quotes in this paragraph are from Rae Armantrout, "Versed," *Poetry Daily*, http://www.poems.com/versearm.htm (accessed March 31, 2007). Reprinted from *American Poetry Review*, July/August 2006.

SUBJECT MATTER'S NOT EVERYONE'S CUP OF TEA, aesthetically speaking. We shirk it; we do. Even the most product-centric (as opposed to those who favor process) poet will allow that formal considerations, of every sort, take precedence in and define the poem, and their experience of writing it, over those of "about." *What's the poem about?* is a neophyte's question. The potentially baffling answer is, usually, *the poem.*

So why did I leap at the chance to edit and publish this anthology when the idea presented itself to Catherine Wagner and to me as an obvious and immediate response to our experience as mothers, as poets, and importantly as members of the intimate, beset, brainiac, Poet-Moms listserv? There are not many subjects I would choose to anthologize; no other subjects, in fact, though one has learned by now never to say never. Not even death, though there is great use in a big doorstop volume of poems to be read for comfort and company in grief.

Plainly put, I was horrified to be confronted by, and to confront in myself, the sense that these poems, growing like wild, thorny, rose tattoos out of the dense, durational, contentious, irreplaceable organic material of child-getting, child-raising, were somehow *less than:* less "universal" than, less communicable than any other poem on earth—than poems about text; poems about learning; poems about cars. Poems about sound, poems about song, poems about color and space and time.

BULLSHIT! Everyone gets born, and everyone has a mother, or at the very least knows someone who does. I suppose most people have cars, too, but most people do not emerge from between their car's legs, or out of their car's belly, naked and squalling. At least not as a newborn.

As with every one of my publishing projects, my impulse is reformative. Like some kind of daft, unrenumerative union organizer, I am intent on improving material conditions for these poems that arise out of the experience of mothering. Let's not simply make a venue for these poems; let's make a gorgeous, hospitable, unapologetic venue, one that is the literary equivalent of a bathtub full of Calgon.

Cathy and I, good friends since graduate school, bore our first children within seven months of each other. Cathy, in fact, conceived her child on the weekend of my wedding party, at which I was six months pregnant. The periods after the birth of our sons proved to be ones of great productivity on the page for both of us: these unprecedented, overwhelming events and shifts in identity in me provoke the kind of loud-but-mute thinking that result in an outpouring of text. Cathy wowed me constantly with her bold and witty investigations of herself in the economy of the pregnant and nursing and needed woman. It is my one great regret, in editing this anthology, that her own wisdom prevents us from including her brilliant poems on the subject. The subject!

The dreaded subject. Some of these are poems "about," and some of these are poems "not about." Some are included here for their innovation/bravery/cunning in including children in poems that are not "about," much as children MUST be included in days and hours and thoughts that are not about children.

An alarming number of poems in this anthology exemplify the tragicomic dilemma of the poet-who-is-a-mother/mother-who-is-a-poet. Since the birth of my two children in the early part of this century, that well-meaning question dreaded by every poet—*are you finding time to write?*—has taken on awesome proportions; as Cathy asserts in her introduction (whose comprehension allows me to here take the road upon which I am most comfortable, the low one), that these poems by mothers are written at all is nothing short of a miracle. Mothering, goddammnit, is a full-time job on top of every other job we do. I will attest to it, if not assert it.

Here's the other question mothers who are poets/poets who are mothers get asked a lot: "So, how has being a mother changed your writing?" Here is my brutally literal answer, pragmatic as a peanut-butter-and-jelly sandwich on allergen-free bread: "My poems are a lot shorter now." God bless them, every one.

Here's birth, and what follows. Here's what has, at times, defined women; certainly at times exploited them; now, we hope, illuminates them. Here is what is a prerequisite for every other subject under the sun, and maybe for the sun, too.

REBECCA WOLFF

ADRIENNE RICH

was born in 1929, her three sons in 1955, 1957 and 1959. She is a recipient of the MacArthur Fellowship, the Wallace Stevens Award, the Bollingen Prize in Poetry, and the National Book Foundation's 2006 Medal for Distinguished Contribution to American Letters, among other awards.

NIGHT-PIECES FOR A CHILD

The Crib

You sleeping I bend to cover.
Your eyelids work. I see
your dream, cloudy as a negative,
swimming underneath.
You blurt a cry. Your eyes
spring open, still filmed in dream.
Wider, they fix me—
—death's head, sphinx, medusa?
You scream.
Tears lick my cheeks, my knees
droop at your fear.
Mother I no more am,
but woman, and nightmare.

Her Waking

Tonight I jerk astart in a dark
hourless as Hiroshima,
almost hearing you breathe
in a cot three doors away.

You still breathe, yes—
and my dream with its gift of knives,
its murderous hider and seeker,
ebbs away, recoils

back into the egg of dreams,
the vanishing point of mind.
All gone.

But you and I—
swaddled in a dumb dark
old as sickheartedness,
modern as pure annihilation—

we drift in ignorance.
If I could hear you now
mutter some gentle animal sound!
If milk flowed from my breast again . . . .

1964

JEAN VALENTINE

is the author of nine books of poetry. She was born in 1934. Her daughter Sarah Chace was born on July 12, 1958, and her daughter Rebecca Chace was born on February 25, 1960. The poems published here are written about them and about other children and friends, real and imagined.

from "THE CHURCH"

Alcohol alcohol alcohol
two children   hungry

depression's lead box
no air to breathe

Our therapist:
"You're married to a brilliant man,
you just have to accept it."

+ + +

I was dark and silent.
The therapist said,
"Why don't you wear lipstick?"
To J: "Does she lie on top?" To J:
"Don't *play her role*.
Don't give the children their baths
or feed them."

THE LOCKED WARD: O.T.

Poster paints, big brushes
like my girls' kindergarten brushes:
I make a big picture, primary colors:
the social workers come like kindergarten teachers
and ask me to explain it. I do, they say,

You don't need to be here.

—Where should I be?

+++

On the mental floor
 I painted a picture of the children
irreducible   altered
the MISSING children
but it was me missing.
Chewing up the mirror   the mother
was not someone else.

+ + +

To the half-way house.
Protestant. I made
maple syrup. My friend moved in
with my husband and children.
The Methodist minister: How many men
do you have in your life.
—Sir   none.

SINGLE MOTHER, 1966

No money
—the baby birds'
huge mouths
huger than themselves
—and God making
words
words

ABORTION CHILD

I thought:
You live somewhere
deeper than the well
I live down in.
Deeper than anything from me or him.

No but it took me
time to see you, thirty earth years.

HER DREAM: THE CHILD

It stared and stared
right through them to the world.

But it better come in said
a quiet man and she said Look
and took it into bed.

They lay closer
in the pale morning. Three flat white ducks
on the wall woke up and took off.

In the morning
he woke them up humming.

DEAREST,

                    this day broke
at ten degrees. I swim
in bed over some dream sentence lost
at a child's crying: the giant on her wall

tips the room over, back:
I tell her all I know,
the walls will settle, he'll go.

Holding her fingers, I watch the sky rise, white.
The frost makes about the same lines
on the same window as last winter,
quicker, quieter . . . I think how nothing's happened,

how to know
to touch a face to make a line
to break the ice to come in time
into this world, unlikely, small,
bloody, shiny, is all, is God's good will
I think, I turn to you,
and fail, and turn,

as the day widens
and we don't know what to do.

AT THE DOOR

Seeing my daughter in the circle of lamplight,
I outside:

It is not *I*,
it is *Mother.*
(But it is *I.*)

It is the first tableau, the first
red wellspring of *I.*

Chimpanzee of longing,
outside the light,

wrap your long arms
around the globe of light,
hold your long haunches
wide open: be
ungodly I.

YOU ARE NOT ONE IN A SEQUENCE

Here
Child
who is to die
take this breast
this rattle this dress
don't listen to your friends
on the other side . . .

Child who is dead:
you are not one in a sequence.
Don't come back,
blush on your cheek,
do not push your white boat up to our dock.
Let you: stay over there, with your heaven-dog and your friends,
and we: drop back down into our intents.

MARIA GRAVIDA, MARY EXPECTANT

Maria Gravida

Then the gold mother began her touching me
With her long brown face & hands
She tickled me & told me I was beautiful
She held me in the ikon & we gazed

We had a pretty goldfinch   death   salvation
Love was strong as death   Peacocks walked by
Blue immortality   Finches played in black branches
Souls around the cross   It was death in life

Our gold earth gravida
Not a casket but a darkroom for our love
The herma wrought of silver, gilded in fire
Gold mother around me inside me gravida

Eye of water

I have nay ben nn
To keep nn safe
I cannot keep them safe

If nn tway
If nn thee

Keep them
Eye of water

Moose and calf

Moose and calf eat the shoots of the willow trees
along the Alaska highway
looking for you

thirsting after don't know
before I can't remember you any more
Call to me!   friend

whose heart in your side is broken in two
just by a chance comma of time,
still, within the wound in your side

is *a place*
inviting fair—large enough (I saw)
to offer refuge for all.

To my soul (2)

Will I miss you
uncanny other
in the next life?
And you & I, my other, leave
the body, not leave the earth?

And you, a child in a field,
and I, a child on a train, go by, go by,

And what we had
give way like coffee grains
brushed across paper . . .

The Rose

a labyrinth,
as if at its center,
god would be there—
but at the center, only rose,
where rose came from,
where rose grows—
& us, inside of the lips and lips:
the likenesses, the eyes, & the hair,
we are born of,
fed by, and marry with,
only flesh itself, only its passage
—out of where? to where?

The god the mother said to Jim, in a dream, Never mind you, Jim,
come rest again on the country porch of my knees.

MARGE PIERCY

lives on Cape Cod. She has been active in feminist organizations since the late 60's. She is childless by choice, since the women in her family get pregnant if someone looks at them too long. Her partner and her cats are not her children, but maybe her 40 books are.

DIVIDING THE ROOM

When I was starting consciousness raising
groups in the 70s, when we came to talk
about children, always a crevasse opened
in the middle of the floor out of which

steamy vitriol rose in thick yellow gouts
and hot rocks hurtled across the room.
We had trusted and shared about lovers,
partners, parents, sex, jobs, rape,

abortion, harassment, but here we broke
into yes and no, having and choosing
not to have, and suddenly the air yowled
and spat and bit like a terrified cat.

Neither choice condemned the other
but felt like a blow to the belly. We could
no longer see each other through smoke
and debris. We should have defended

each other's way but never could. To
this day, when an interviewer asks,
Do you have children? And I answer
No, out trots the porcupine of silence.

TOI DERRICOTTE

born 1941, is the author of a memoir and four books of poetry. She has received numerous awards, including fellowships from the Rockefeller Foundation (2006), the Guggenheim Foundation (2004), two fellowships in poetry from the National Endowment for the Arts (1985 and 1990) and two Pushcart Prizes (1989 and 1998). Her memoir, *The Black Notebooks*, received the Anisfield-Wolf Book Award, the Black Caucus of the American Library Association Award in nonfiction, and was nominated for the PEN Martha Albrand Award for the Art of the Memoir. It was a *New York Times* Notable Book of the Year. A new essay, "Beginning Dialogues," appears in *The Best American Essays of 2006*. She is co-founder of Cave Canem, the historic first workshop/retreat for African American poets, and professor of English at the University of Pittsburgh.

"I wrote *Natural Birth* seventeen years after the birth of my son, in 1961. Before that time I had not wanted him to learn that he had been born in a home for unwed mothers. I thought it would make him feel—because I had been less than a perfect mother—that something was wrong with him. After I wrote the main sections of the book I worked for years to try to make them into traditional forms and to take out the "secrets" about my son's birth. But every time I did those things, I killed the life of the book. Finally I understood that I had to take the book as it was—not that I couldn't shape it into a work of art—but that I had to first accept the basic truth of the book. The main point was to show that my love was not "perfect," that motherhood for me, and I was sure for many other women, was not the motherhood of a Hallmark greeting card. At that point I could begin to really work with the book and shape it into a work of art. I wanted to create a beautiful gift for my son, and for others who would read the book, to say that all love, even mother's love, is human. And not to be ashamed."

from NATURAL BIRTH

transition

the meat rolls up and moans on the damp table.
my body is a piece of cotton over another
woman's body. some other woman, all muscle and nerve, is
tearing apart and opening under me.

i move with her like skin, not able to do anything else,
i am just watching her, not able to believe what her
body can do, what it will do, to get this thing accomplished.

this muscle of a lady, this crazy ocean in my teacup.
she moves the pillars of the sky. i am stretched into
fragments, tissue paper thin. the light shines through
to her goatness, her blood-thick heart that thuds like
one drum in the universe emptying its stars.

she is
that heart
larger
than my life
stuffed
in
me
like sausage

black sky
bird
pecking
at the bloody
ligament

trying
to get
in, get
out
i am

holding out with
everything i
have
holding out
the evil thing
when i see there is
no answer
to the screamed
word
GOD
nothing i can do,
no use,

i have to let her in,
open the door,
put down the mat
welcome her
as if she

might be the
called-for death,
the final abstraction.
she comes
like a tunnel
fast
coming into
blackness
with my headlights
off

   you can push . . .

i hung there. still hurting, not knowing what to do.
if you push too early, it hurts more. i called the
doctor back again. *are you sure i can push? are you sure?*

i couldn't believe that pain was over, that the punish-
ment was enough, that the wave, the huge blue mind i
was living inside, was receding. i had forgotten there
ever was a life without pain, a moment when pain wasn't
absolute as air.

why weren't the nurses and doctors rushing toward me?
why weren't they wrapping me in white? white for respect,
white for triumph, white for the white light i was being
accepted into after death? why was it so simple as saying
you can push? why were they walking away from me into
other rooms as if this were not the end the beginning of
something which the world should watch?
i felt something pulling me inside, a soft call, but i
could feel her power. something inside me i could go
with, wide and deep and wonderful. the more i gave
to her, the more she answered me. i held this conversation
in myself like a love that never stops. i pushed toward
her, she came toward me, gently, softly, sucking like a
wave. i pushed deeper and she swelled wider, darker when
she saw i wasn't afraid. then i saw the darker glory
of her under me.

why wasn't the room bursting with lilies? why was
everything the same with them moving so slowly as if
they were drugged? why were they acting the same when,
suddenly, everything had changed?
we were through with pain, would never suffer in our
lives again. put pain down like a rag, unzipper skin,
step out of our dead bodies, and leave them on the
floor. glorious spirits were rising, blanched with
light, like thirsty women shining with their thirst.

i felt myself rise up with all the dead, climb out of
the tomb like christ, holy and wise, transfigured with
the knowledge of the tomb inside my brain, holding the
gold key to the dark stamped inside my genes, never to
be forgotten . . .

it was time. it was really time. this baby would be
born. it would really happen. this wasn't just a
trick to leave me in hell forever. like all the other
babies, babies of women lined up in rooms along the halls,
semi-conscious, moaning, breathing, alone with or without
husbands, there was a natural end to it that i was going
to live to see! soon i would believe in something larger
than pain, a purpose and an end. i had lived through to
another mind, a total revolution of the stars, and had
come out on the other side!

one can only imagine the shifting of the universe, the
layers of shale and rock and sky torturing against each
other, the tension, the sudden letting go. the pivot of
one woman stuck in the socket, flesh and bones giving
way, the v-groin locked, vise thigh, and the sudden
release when everything comes to rest on new pillars.

+++

delivery

i was in the delivery room. PUT YOUR
FEET UP IN THE STIRRUPS. i put them up, obedient,
still humbled, though the spirit was growing larger
in me, that black woman was in my throat, her thin
song, high pitched like a lark, and all the muscles
were starting to constrict around her.
i tried to push just a little. it
didn't hurt. i tried a little more.

ROLL UP, guzzo said. he wanted to give me
a spinal. NO. I DON'T WANT A SPINAL. (same
doctor as ax handle up my butt, same as shaft
of split wood, doctor spike, driving the
head home where my soft animal cowed and prayed and
cried for his mother.)

or was the baby
part of this
whole damn
conspiracy,
in on it with
guzzo,

the two of them
wanting to shoot
the wood
up me for
nothing,
for playing
music to him
in the dark
for singing
to my round
clasped
belly
for filling
up with

pizza on a cold
night, dough
warm.

maybe
he
wanted
out,
was saying

give her
a needle
and let me/the hell/
out of here
who cares
what she
wants
put her
to sleep.

                    (my baby
                    pushing off
                    with his black
                    feet
                    from the dark
                    shore, heading
                    out, not
                    knowing
                    which way and trusting,
                    oarless and eyeless, so
                    hopeless
                    it didn't matter.)

no. not
my baby.
this
loved
thing

in/and of
myself

so i balled up
and let him
try to
stick it in.
       maybe
something was
wrong

       ROLL UP
he said
       ROLL UP
but i don't want it
       ROLL UP ROLL UP
but it doesn't hurt

we all stood,
nurses, round the white
light
hands
hanging
empty at our sides
       ROLL UP IN A BALL
all of us not
knowing
how
or if
in such a world without
false promises
we could say
anything
but, *yes,*
yes.
come take it
and be quick.

i put my belly in my hand
gave him that
thin side
of my back
the bones
intruding on the air
in little knobs
in joints
he might
crack
down my spine
his knuckles
rap
each twisted
symmetry
put me on
the rack,
each nerve
bright
and stretched
like canvas.

he couldn't get it in!
three times, he tried
ROLL UP, he cried, ROLL UP
three times
he couldn't get it in!

dr. y (the head obstetrician)
came in

"what are you
doing, guzzo,
i thought she
wanted
natural . . .

(to me) *do*
you want

a shot . . . no? well,

PUT YOUR LEGS UP,
GIRL, AND
PUSH!"

and suddenly, the light
went out
the nurses
laughed
and nothing
mattered
in this 10
a.m. sun
shiny morning
we were well
the nurses and the
doctors cheering
that girl
combing hair
all in one
direction
shining
bright as water.

       i
grew deep
in me
like fist and i
grew deep
in me
like death
      and i
grew deep
in me
like hiding in the sea and
i was
over me
like

sun and i
was under
me
like sky and i
could look
into myself
like one
dark eye.

       i was her
and she was me
and we were
scattered round
like light
       nurses
       doctors
cheering

            such waves

my face
contorted,
never
wore
such mask, so
rigid
and so dark

     so
bright, un-
compromising
brave
no turning
back/no
no's.

i was so
beautiful. i
could look

up in the
light and
see my huge-
ness,
arc,
electric,
heavy, fleshy, living
light.
no wonder they
praised me,
a gesture
one makes
helpless and
urgent, praising
what goes on
without our praise.

when there
was nowhere
i could go, when i
was so deep
in myself
so large
i had to
let it out
they said
        drop back. i

dropped back
on the table
panting,
they moved
the head, swiveled
it correctly

      but i

          i

was

losing
her. something
       a head
coming through
the door.
NAME PLEASE /
PLEASE / NAME / whose

head / i
don't know / some /
       disconnection

           NAME PLEASE /

and i
am not ready:

the sudden visibility—
his body,
his curly wet hair,
his arms
abandoned in that air,
an arching, squiggling thing,
his skin must be
so cold,
but there is nothing
i can do
to warm him,
his body clutches
in a wretched
spineless way.

they expect me
to sing
joy joy
a son is born,
child is given.
tongue
curled in my head

tears, cheeks
stringy with
damp hair.

this lump
of flesh,
lump of steamy
viscera.
      who

is this child

      who

is his father

      a child
      never having
      been seen
      before,
      without
      credentials
      credit cards without
      employee
      reference or
      high school grades or
      anything
      to make him
      human make
      him mine but
      skein of
      pain to
      chop off
      at the navel.

           while they could
           they held him down and
           chopped him, held him up
           my little fish, my blueness

swallowed in the air
turned pink
and wailed.

no more. enough.
i lay back, speechless, looking
for something

to say to myself.

after you have touched the brain,
that squirmy
lust of maggots,
after you have
pumped the heart,
that thief,
that comic, you
throw her in the trash.

and the little one
in a case
of glass . . .

he is not i
i am not him
he is not i

. . . the stranger.

blue
air
protects us from each other.

here.
here is the note he brings.
it says, *mother.*

but i do not even know
this man.

CAROLINE KNOX

Currently the recipient of a Massachusetts Cultural Council Individual Artist Grant, Knox is completing her sixth collection, *Quaker Guns*. She has received awards from the National Endowment for the Arts, the Ingram Merrill Foundation, the Massachusetts Cultural Council (1996, 2006), the Fund for Poetry, and the Yale/Mellon Visiting Faculty Program. She was a Visiting Fellow at Harvard in 2003–2004.

"My husband and I were both born in 1938. About 'The Fat Baby': our children were born in 1961, 1964, and 1967. Each baby filled me with delight and inarticulate wonder. Each baby was in her or his own thought—nothing to do with me. So new, a baby couldn't have any self, or anything to hold, so must rock on the self, and be the basket. I could only imagine, or couldn't imagine, how the baby could conceive of fuzzy or milk or a stuffed animal. My husband revealed that he felt the same awe by spending minutes and hours staring dumbly at the beloved ones.

"About 'Thérèse Levasseur': The impetus for the poem was Rousseau's curious and lifelong relationship with his housekeeper and girlfriend—such a strong bond, and yet how ghastly for the mother to have their children swept off to the Foundling Home—five times. Is this Enlightenment/Romantic idealism in practice? I don't know what it is, so I wrote the poem."

THE FAT BABY

the fat baby is in her own thought
she is rocked on her self
she is her basket

her fingers make a star for themselves
around anything.

a rabbit is inside her   or is that milk.
if milk   how fuzzy

THÉRÈSE LEVASSEUR

This waitress, this laundress
from the Hôtel San Quentin,
this Thérèse Levasseur is,
says the philosopher,

"someone with whom I can
identify myself: an auxiliary of my own flesh."

She is twenty-two, pretty, and a figure of scorn
to all at the hotel—unlettered, untaught,
a waitress, a laundress.

"When I first saw her shyness and sweetness,"
confesses Jean-Jacques Rousseau,
"I told her I would never abandon her.
I told her I would never marry her.
She bestowed on me a tenderness,
and Pleasure became Happiness."

Now Thérèse is no longer a sweetheart,
but a resident mistress, a settled
companion. In all but name, a wife.

"Our affection," writes Rousseau,
"grew with intimacy,
and every day we felt more keenly
we had been made for one another:
our walks in the country, our tavern
suppers, the window-seat meals;
at home, bread, cheese, fruit, wine,
chestnuts, salad, coffee.
We have a spinet, a canary
in a cage, beds covered with
striped cotton. A blanket chest and chairs."

"I tell you, she has a store of common sense
and keeps me and leads me
and protects me from my dangerous
and passionate compulsiveness.
She has the heart of an angel,"
says Rousseau, doing up her corset stays.

This is a French poem, so it has a refrain.
"He put our five children in the Foundling Home.
He gave the money for the education.
The midwife took them to the orphanage."

"Please borrow my Plutarch, countess, but do not lend it.
Please send me a dress for Mlle. Levasseur."

In Switzerland, a dignified and symmetrical
house, with good-sized gardens, The Hermitage;
fields and orchards, walks, the forest.

"She is happier than she has ever been.
The day we were united was the day
I chose my moral being. But I have never felt,"
says the Citizen of Geneva,
"the least glimmer of love for Thérèse Levasseur.
When I die, all my property belongs to her."

"What excellent coffee I drink at the chateau
with my Thérèse in the peristyle,
my cat Minette and my dog Sultan in company.
Oh, lovely dog Sultan, sensitive, disinterested, and good-natured."

This is a French poem, so it has a refrain.
"He sent our five children to the Foundling Home.
He gave the money for the education.
The midwife took them to the orphanage."

"A little, lively, neat French girl," opines James
Boswell of the forty-three-year-old
Thérèse. "A heart like mine," opines
Rousseau, as he and Boswell dine on succulent
vegetables, gigot of lamb, with thyme,
fresh trout from the river Arneuse,
quail, woodcock, the flinty white
wine and the Spanish red.

"My heart," Rousseau declares, "has always
been hers, and this will not change.
We will share our sorrows,
and if Mlle. were not here, M. Boswell,
I would tell you my opinions of women."

James Boswell in bidding farewell:
"I shall never forget your accomplishments.
You weave. You cook. You sit at the table.
You make jokes. You get up; you clear
the table; the dishes are washed; all is
tidy and Mlle. Levasseur is with us again."

As Boswell disappears, she says,
"M. Boswell, shall you see M. de Voltaire?"

+++

The voice of Jean-Jacques is aging and infirm:
"We carry rabbits in the rowboat to the little island
to renew the vanishing wildlife. Here at Môtiers,
I make silk ribbons on a little machine
with the women, my new entertainment,
and with Minette my cat and Sultan my dear old dog.
I reside with my nurse Thérèse, of honest and upright heart.
These ribbons I bestow on the country brides,
who must promise me to breast-feed their children.
Man is born free, but everywhere he is in chains."

> This is a French poem, so it has a refrain.
> He took our five children to the Foundling Home.
> He gave the money for the education.
> The midwife took them to the orphanage."

ALICIA OSTRIKER

was born in 1937, and is the mother of Rebecca (1963), Eve (1965), and Gabriel (1970), as well as grandmother of Abigail (1993) and Naomi (1998). She has published eleven volumes of poetry and is the author of several books of criticism. She considers the experience of motherhood to be like the experience of sex: it involves ecstasy, agony, and she wouldn't like to have gone to her grave without it.

from THE MOTHER/CHILD PAPERS

I: CAMBODIA

My son Gabriel was born on May 14, 1970, during the Vietnam War, a few days after the United States invaded Cambodia, and a few days after four students had been shot by National Guardsmen at Kent State University in Ohio during a protest demonstration.

On May 1, President Nixon announced Operation Total Victory, sending 5,000 American troops into Cambodia to destroy North Vietnamese military sanctuaries, in a test of "our will and character," so that America would not seem "a pitiful helpless giant" or "accept the first defeat in its proud 190-year history."
He wanted his own war.

> The boy students stand in line
> at Ohio State
> each faces a Guardsman in gasmask
> each a bayonet point at his throat.

US air cavalry thrusts into Kompong Cham province, seeking bunkers. Helicopters descend on "The Parrot's Beak." B-52's heavily bomb Red sanctuaries. Body count! Body count high! in the hundreds. The President has explained, and explains again, that this is not an invasion.

Monday, May 4, at Kent State, laughing demonstrators and rock-throwers on a lawn spotted with dandelions. It was after a weekend of beerdrinking. Outnumbered Guardsmen, partially encircled and out of tear gas, begin to retreat uphill, turn, kneel, in unison aim their guns. Four students lie dead, seventeen wounded. 441 colleges and universities strike, many shut down.

> The President says: "When dissent turns to violence, it invites tragedy."

> A veteran of the Khe Sanh says: "I saw enough violence, blood and death and I vowed never again, never again . . . Now I must protest. I'm not a leftist but I

can't go any further. I'll do damn near anything to stop the war now."

A man in workclothes tries to seize an American flag from a student. "That's my flag! I fought for it! You have no right to it! . . . To hell with your movement. We'll have to kill you." An ad salesman in Chicago: "I'm getting to feel like I'd actually enjoy going out and shooting some of these people, I'm just so goddamned mad."

One, two, three, four, we don't want! your fucking war!
They gathered around the monument, on the wet grass, Dionysiac, beaded, flinging their clothes away. New England, Midwest, Southwest, cupfuls of innocents leave the city and buy farmland. At the end of the frontier, their backs to the briny Pacific, buses of tourists gape at the acid-dropping children in the San Francisco streets. A firebomb flares. An electric guitar bleeds.

Camus: "I would like to be able to love my country and still love justice."

Some years earlier, my two daughters were born, one in Wisconsin at a progressive university hospital where doctors and staff behaved affectionately, one in England where the midwife was a practical woman who held onto my feet and when she became impatient with me said: PUSH, Mother. Therefore I thought I knew what childbirth was supposed to be: a woman *gives birth* to a *child,* and the medical folk assist her.

But in the winter of 1970 I had arrived five months pregnant in Southern California, had difficulty finding on obstetrician who would take me, and so was now tasting normal American medical care. It tasted like money. During my initial visit to his ranch-style offices on a street where the palm trees lifted their heads into the smog like a row of fine mulatto ladies, Dr. Keensmile called me "Alicia" repeatedly, brightly, benignly, as if I were a child or a servant. I hated him right away. I hated his suntan. I knew he was untrue to his wife. I was sure he played golf. The routine delivery anesthetic for him and his group was a spinal block, he said. I explained that I would not need a spinal since I had got by before on a couple of cervical shots, assumed that deliveries were progressively easier, and wanted to decide about drugs myself when the time came. He smiled tolerantly at the ceiling. I remarked that I liked childbirth. I remarked that childbirth gave a woman an opportunity for supreme pleasure and heroism. He smiled again. They teach them, in medical school, that pregnancy and birth are diseases. He twinkled. Besides, it was evident that he hated women. Perhaps that was why he became an obstetrician. Just be sure and watch your weight, Alicia. Smile.

I toyed, as I swelled and bulged like a watermelon, with the thought of driving out into the Mohave to have the baby. I continued my visits to Dr. Keensmile. I did not talk to Dr. Keensmile about Cambodia. I did not talk to him about Kent State. *Sauve qui peut.* You want a child of life, stay away from psychic poison. In the waiting room I found pamphlets which said that a newborn baby must be fed on a strict schedule, as it needed the discipline, and that one must not be moved by the fact that it would cry at first, as this was good for it, to start it out on the right foot. And my daughters were laughing at me for my difficulty in buckling their sandals.

In labor, I discovered that I could have an enjoyable time if I squatted on the bed, rocked a little while doing my breathing exercises, and sang songs in my head. The bed had muslin curtains drawn around it; nobody would be embarrassed by me. So I had settled into a melody and had been traveling downstream with it for some long duration, when a nurse came through the curtains, stork white, to ask if I was ready for my shot. Since the pains were becoming strong and I felt unsure about keeping control through the transitional stage of labor, which is the hardest, I said fine, expecting a local. This would temporarily alleviate the pain of the fast-stretching cervix, leaving other muscles free.

Of course, it was a sedative. I grew furry. They lay me down. I was eight fingers dilated, only five or seven minutes away from the final stage of labor, where a woman needs no drugs because she becomes a goddess. Then Dr. Keensmile appeared to ask if I was ready for my spinal. A faint flare of "no" passed, like a moonbeam. Because of the Demerol, if they had asked me whether I was ready to have my head severed, I probably would have said yes. Drool ran from my mouth. Yes, I said.

When they wheeled me to the delivery room, I fought to maintain wakeful consciousness despite the Demerol, and fought to push, with my own body, to give birth to my child myself, despite the fact that I could feel nothing—nothing at all—below the waist, as if I did not exist there, as if I had been cut in half and bandaged.

A stainless place. I am conscious, only my joy is cut off. I feel the stainless will of everyone. Nothing red in the room. I am sweating. Death.

The black-haired head, followed by the supple limbs, emerges in the mirror. The doctor says it is a boy. Three thoughts fall, like file cards. One: Hooray! We made it! Finito! Two: YOU SONOFABITCHING BASTARD, NEXT TIME I'M GOING TO DO THIS RIGHT. Three: What next time?

Our bodies and our minds shoot into joy, like trees into leaves. Playfulness as children, sex, work with muscles, work with brains. Some bits survive, where we are lucky, or clever, or we fight. The world will amputate what it can, wanting us cripples. Cut off from joy, how many women conceive?

Cut off, how many bear? And cut, how many give birth to their children? Now I am one of them. I did not fight. Beginning a day after my son's birth, and continuing for a week, I have swordlike headaches, which I attribute to the spinal. I am thirty-three. In the fall I will be back at work, back East. My husband and I have two daughters, both all right so far, and now the son for whom we are hoping. There will never be a next time.

What does this have to do with Cambodia?

II: MOTHER/CHILD

was dreaming *be*

water *was* *multiply*

dreaming *water* *inherit*

in *earth*

+++

The guards kneeled, they raised their weapons, they fired
into the crowd to protect the peace. There was a sharp orange-red
explosion, diminished by the great warm daylight, a match scratching, a
whine, a tender thud, then the sweet tunnel, then nothing.
Then the tunnel again, the immense difficulty, pressure, then the head
finally is liberated, then they pull the body out.

+++

was dreaming
water was
   falling and
   rising all
     along could
     not see then
       a barrier a
       color red then
         cold and
         very afraid

+++

They hold it, shining, they support it, under artificial lights, under
the neck and knees, it is limp as a glove, a handful of tendrils,
the mother watches it inhale and flex, the bloodclot over the navel
already brown, the father is blushing, he notices how the genitals
nod and bob, ornamental and puffy, mushrooms and ladyslipper,
do you hear this fellow yell now, smiles the doctor, he'll be a soldier.

They have wiped the flesh, it becomes a package, they wheel it away, clean
and alone, the mother rests on a plump pillow and is weeping
in the pretty room, her breasts are engorged, she is filling with desire,
she has thrown a newspaper to the floor, her television is dark, her
intention is to possess this baby, this piece of earth, not to surrender
a boy to the ring of killers. They bring him, crying. Her throat leaps.

+++

and sleep

and cry

la la

and cry

and sleep

+++

Nothing is changed. The sun beats
down, the traffic moves

Highly piggledy, pumpkin and pine
nobody's baby is prettier than mine

The husband and the daughters go away
and we forget them

We open all the windows
the sunlight wraps us like gauze

+++

it hurts   it is impossible
to stop the pain
it is impossible
come when it happens

please come when it happens

please

+++

I come the way that
moon comes, stars, the tides,
it is involuntary, only

God knows what elastic
pulls me to his hunger, what laws
make me gaze at that pink

forehead as if it were quite
transparent, as if I could see
what is happening daily, the way

everything is getting attached, getting
hooked up there
in his head, the way they are throwing

a settlement together, with real streets,
a marketplace, buying and selling, and outside
the town the ground to break,

the people sowing and harvesting,
already planning a city, and I
want to see it, I want to.

+++

                    one   is   inside

                but things take shape

                        vanish but reappear

                    that is   beautiful

+++

Greedy baby
sucking the sweet tit
your tongue tugging the nipple tickles your mama
your round eyes open appear to possess understanding
when you suckle I am slowly moved
in my sensitive groove
you in your mouth are alive, I in my womb
a book lies in my lap I pretend to read
I turn some pages, when satiated
a moment you stop sucking
to smile up with your toothless milky mouth
I smile down, and my breast leaks
it hurts, return
your lashes close, your mouth again clamps on
you are attentive as a business man
your fisted fingers open relaxing and
all rooms are rooms for suckling in
all woods are woods for suckling in
all boulevards for suckling
sit down anywhere, all rivers
are rivers for suckling by—
I have read that in all wars, when a city is taken,
women are raped, and babies stabbed in their little bellies
and hoisted up to the sky on bayonets—

+++

Here is the lady, here is the lady who makes

> *peace*
>> *suffering*
>>> *bliss*
>>>> *suffering*
>>>>> *peace*

+++

The door clicks. He returns to me.
He brings fresh air in.
We kiss, we touch. I am holding the flannel-wrapped baby.
The girls run to him.

He takes his jacket off and waltzes
the weightless
bundle over his shoulder.
We eat dinner, and evening falls.

I have bathed the girls. I walk by our broad bed.
Upon it rests a man
in a snow white shirt, like a great sleepy bird.
Next to him rests his seed, his son.

Lamplight falls on them both. If a woman looks, at such
a sight, is the felt pang
measureless pleasure?
Is it measureless pain?

+++

Here is the strong one, the other   *one*
Here is the strong one, the other   *after the other*

Here is the strong one, the other   *after the other*
Here is the strong one, the other   *after*

+++

Hour after beastly hour.
                    I swear I try.
You claw my skin, my nipple.
                    Am a witch. Am dry.
Cannot endure an existence
                    chained to your cry.
Incubus.   Leech.   Scream.
                    You confine me. Die.

+++

                    I can   *do what*   *I want*

                              Overturn
                                   this body

+++

A glass pane toward the spectral, mysterious garden,
a Santa Ana wind through the live-oaks,
ammonia pungent in the nostrils,
no sunrise yet. You lay on the changing table,
meowing, wet. I made you naked, laying
nightgown fabric aside, kissing your neck,
your feet, your ribs, the powdery skin-creases.
You kicked and waved your thin arms, randomly.
I whispered and blew into your stomach, to tickle.
My face being down, then, while I was blind,
somebody's hand quietly grasped my hand.
When I looked up
it was you, laughing
laughing!
              a power
such as flew out
                    and nearly knocked me over
through your staring eyes
intense, impersonal, like icy dawn
        like the son of beauty, the bow bent, and the arrows drawn—

                as once in midday three white clouds raced
                right across the zenith of the bright blue sky
                a wild west wind
                ripped at their edges like cotton, and they flew—

                outside a white cat jumps
                from a garden fence, glides
                through the yellow grass

yet but a naked, helpless kicking one—

                you were those things
                I saw! and I have seen.
                I shall be singing this
                when all the forests you have burned are green.

+++

These are my hands
I seize what I want
you bars
you who interrupt me
I will eat you

+++

Damn, it's late, I
  have an appointment, where
    the hell is my briefcase, girls,
get going to school, honey,
  wait in the car, I'll be right
    with you, okay, the formula
is in the fridge, it isn't
  necessary to heat it, just
    feed him around every three
or four hours, I'll nurse
  him tonight, he likes the radio
    and dancing around to pop
songs, and you also might
  take him outside in the morning
    before the smog hits
give him here a minute

I hold you, boy, I leave you
        here a minute

        like jewelry
        like grapes
        like perfume
        like a music box
        like silky
        many nice things to touch

        I love   I love

Higgledy piggledy my blue pig
You're not very little and not very big

The Guard kneeled
The Guard kneeled.

+++

and bright
    and warm
        la la
            and loud
                and sweet
one
after the other

after the other
after

PARAGRAPHS

If you look at a mother with a newborn infant, you see not two animals but one. They are placed in a kind of trance together, so that even when separated, a fleecy mesh connects them. The mother seems sleepy. She acts in a dream. She has little conversation, but shines at people, and wants to show them the baby, soft in its soft clothes and blankets. We see this also among the great sociable apes: when a new chimpanzee is born, the mother shyly exhibits it. Females, males, even dominant males, as well as older juveniles, come to look and fondle it.

That fondling, touching-activity, vocalization: these are to teach, they rise from the forest like birds, so that beyond the sleeping, crying, feeding, shared by the mother and child, is pride of accomplishment. It kicks, it waves wild arms, it holds up its head up on its stem. It will roll over, crawl, grow teeth. At the same time, anger. This is a prison. It exhausts the sap, the very juice. It does nothing but open its mouth. Can she never regain her autonomous self, her sunny wind-drenched leaves? She wants to kick—get off me, parasite. To kill it. To go mad.

All that is weak invites the brute. If I fail to acknowledge   my will
To murder the child, to wipe him like spill from a counter—
Then all that I call my love will evaporate, will choke.

When the mists lift, there are images. What the mother sees is the divine infant, showing where they come from, Eros, Jesus, Krishna, Blake's boy on the cloud commanding song. What does the child see, when he smiles at her as if he would be happy forever? As in the chapel ceiling, in the creation: the aged and youthful heroic figures recline amid clouds, their forefingers just parted. Michaelangelo as an artist would have known: that which was once within you, life of life, you create in freedom. You release it, you open your hand, you let it go. In a few weeks that particular smile will pass, from the mother, to the father, to others.

MOTHER CHILD: CODA

Fear teaches nothing
                    that is my message
          but O to grow means pain
          means division
          the crust cracks and the open
                         organism faces danger
              the grass plant bladed and seeded, the forked spruce
                  burst from the mountain's northern side, that never
                  asked to breathe, here in this cold, but must.

          It is the oldest, saddest story.
          The oceans were ebbing.
          The climate was chilling.
          Anyone who had a lung was forced
          to live, not die.
          Anyone who had a leg was forced
          to leap. The driven soldiers of the cause.

March. Think. Pay no attention to
the corpses. Do not attempt to join them.
March. Your task is to survive. You
are permitted to feel triumph.

Here is water, here is dry land,
up there is the kingly sky and queenly moon,
a desire to turn back and a desire
to go on are the permanent
instructions, and we know that this has something
to do with our souls, also that "go on"
for any individual thing or creature
at first means "play," "multiply," "strike
deep, aim straight" and "trust," but that
later this changes and means "it is too late,"
"take your last journey," "we love you, but goodbye."
We do not know yet what the instructions signify
for an entire species, a muddy ooze,
and we cannot make any prognosis on those levels
or answer the intimate question
                                        shall all life
          perish like us, the perfect crest subside?

I am glad and sorry to give you this information.
I see you know it already.
I want to tell you it is not your fault.
It is your fault.

So from now on you are responsible.
This is what we mean when we say
consciousness is a curse.

   Meanwhile we are looking into
   each other's eyes, windows of homes,
   and touching, with sweet pleasure,
   each other's downy surfaces.
   You will never forget this,
   will always seek, beyond every division,
   a healing of division, renewed touch.

You see the silver bridge
spanning a flood?
This is what we mean when we say
consciousness is a blessing.

MAUREEN OWEN

was born in 1943 in Graceville, Minnesota, is the author of eleven books of poetry and editor of Telephone Books Press. She currently teaches at Naropa University in Boulder, Colorado. She has been the recipient of a Poetry Fellowship from the NEA and a grant from the Foundation for Contemporary Arts, Inc.

She is also "the mother of three wonderful sons: Ulysses Dorje Owen born in 1965, Patrick Iasion Owen Brenner born in 1967, and Kyran Janos Owen-Mankovich born in 1977. Being a mother, a parent, is a full-time life-time labor of love. The returns and rewards, however, go beyond any earthly comparisons. My children have given me true participation in the meaning of life. They have kept me on my toes, focused, and paying attention. I am more grateful to them than to the air I breathe."

from ZOMBIE NOTES

Bump through 6AM Rookie lightness
Care & Feeding of baby & small children
Drive 150 miles to read poems
Do it   with feeling!
Drive 150 miles back
Get on train   Go 80 miles to work
work 48 hours straight
Retrace trajectory
Enter jeep   drive home
Sleep 3 hours

Now Friday morning!
Lunge upward
care & feeding of baby & children
Go into small study w/many books
Sit in front of typewriter
                          A Zombie!
                   Zombie drinks tea!
                   Zombie writes poems!

+++

for Bill Kushner

When he said   "petit air"   I thought the translation
would be   "little fart"   Some mornings it is cleansing
to lean from bed   lift the window   and scream   I HATE CHILDREN
into the lovely green yard.   It makes it possible   to
go downstairs   & answer Kyran's   "Mom!   mom   mom moms!" Lovingly
one thousand   one million   one hundred & forty four times   & Not
think the orange juice   suffers   in its fall   Just another
winter scene   in August   Like Ed's card   where   rouge   has been added
to the sky's cheeks   & the snowball queen   is wearing turquoise "pumps"
& embracing a bundle of cotton   shaped like snowballs   because it
is easy to write   easy poems   but more difficult   to write   more
difficult poems   which is not quite the same as saying   I'm not
interested in sex   unless I'm doing it   & not the same as
Kyran saying   "I like TV dinners   better'n I like TV"   But
somewhere in between the two   & why   this poem is titled

GRACE NOTE STUDY

On such a morning   you can wade through the bodies   of tiny khaki
army men   carrying   massive artillery   place your coffee beside
your typewriter   & begin a poem   No one
will leave you alone   because you are a mother   & When
you open the book on Calamity Jane   the first sentence   of the preface
will say   "No career is so elusive to the historian   as that of a
loose woman."

                              Reminds me of a story   on the radio
in Minnesota this summer
                        the song   it seems   was actually written about   a
                        boy   young heir to a supermarket chain   But they
                        made it a much more marketable item   by changing
                        the gender   Causing it to be about a   spoiled
                        & willful debutante

                              this is a true story
                              this is how they got a hit   45

+++

Tutankhamun's coffin weighed 2,448 pounds and 2 ounces
Searching the original letters behind museum glass   I
noticed that Van Gogh had neglected   to cross
his t's
Do you remember saying   you dreamed you had shoes
inside your shoes?   I don't know why you stay by me
My straw   my sunny blond on blue   now pink to
the color of almond flowers   as the baby climbs out
of bed   announcing   "I got dreams   all over me
got to wash them off!"   Matter-of-factly he goes
throws water at his neck and arms . . . . misses . . . .
Outside   frizzled silhouettes poke the light   So
green   with a grey mist rising   in pointless
cloud disguise.   I plan not to move   the baby
thinks I'm still asleep   through slits I track
the know-it-all birds   actually they seem to.   As
for the rest of the philosophers   ". . . . . . . nothing,"
Flannery O'Connor once wrote,   "produces silence
like experience . . . ."

+++

Because   Therefore   So

 If You Wear A Hat In The House
You Are Warmer Than If You Don't

Because   it must be the baby speaking   petitioning
Jack's Mom   "But Mom . . . these beans are good beans
They're magic! . . . the old woman gave me . . . magic beans!"   It
is radiant   on his head   Apparently the heat in
the body slips through the holes in the skull   & Rises
that's why Sean O'Casey is always photographed   with
a hat on   But O Science   You ventriloquist!   Paroxysms
of sunlight   ignite   this blond mist of curls   & I

have to weep   for the sentimental   and maudlin   one last time!
tho the Southern New England Telephone Company   has delivered
a message   "That lucky ol' sun just rolls around heaven all
day   but now it will be followed   every second
by a big silver saucer!"   Therefore by reflection
each shape completes itself   continues   along the
Silver Ridge Trail   traceable through the woods   by
the circular lids of tin cans   nailed to the trunks of the
Hemlocks   & Tulip.   So   I want to thank   the sheep
who has eaten all the maroon   & adjectival   the white
pine for not being white.   Now that I am master of the
dotted quarter note   preceding the eighth note   I thank
the baby   for pouring   into the small popsicle mold   the
large pitcher of grape juice   & Patrick   dressing
singing

        "I know a woman   named Lucky Pierre   she
        used to   cut   my hair."

+++

for Ulysses on his high school
graduation

Just come home when you need to   or how does light get
between the stars   if there's no electro magnetic forces
in space

A small roaring in the foliage   of poplar   &
reed   heat throbbing upward over the damp gravel
the last clump of tulips falls apart   Grey Tropical . .
. . . Yes   it's true!   Basically   you have
to learn what life is about   from the vertebrae pattern
of a frog!   all that remains is to be mentioned   or
don't put cast iron   in a sink full of suds overnight   &
if you can't speak to them in real language   always

use code.   Suppose this mist centered on stage left &
demanded our attention   because when everything was finally
settled   one of the dates got switched   & it all had to be
rearranged again   But O you are so beautiful   staring
out the train window   Saying
                                  "I hate Liza Minnelli!"

+++

BEDTIME

I have this power   At night
I kiss three people   minutes later
they are all sound asleep   the bizarre
& the miraculous   are the same thing.

+++

from "LETTERS TO THE LETTERS S AND F"

            for Sukey and Fanny

Tuesday   the first letter

Dear S

Today I didn't agree with what I said yesterday   to you
about having children   or not having children   Except
that I love these three   Even as   she will always sing
the praises of every tiny horrible aspect of being a mother   that I
hate   Sometimes I think I've learned   everything I know
Kyran explained at breakfast   how if you have a diaper on   you
don't need to wear underwear   & WCBS New York told about a man
completely on fire   who was rescued by his wife   She

put out the flames   with a garden hose   Now & then   a spouse
comes in handy   The air is full of light   & today I

received mail from   The Blinded Veterans Association, The American Lung
Association, Connecticut Light & Power, Bob Holman, DISCOVER (the news
magazine of science) sub titled "Can A Heart Attack Be Stopped," Katharine
Hepburn, The Abortion Fund, Wausau Underwriters Insurance Company, Ronald
Reagan, National Women's Health Network, The Print Center, Manuscripts from
Albany, Lynn, MA, Columbia, & Atlanta,   a card from Helen Adam just back
from Germany en route to Arizona   & another graced package from Tom
Weigel w/a note   Bob's card is a Winter Sunrise in the Grand Tetons   tho
it is August here . . . .

She taught herself   how to draw   in this garden   that summer.

from HEARTS IN SPACE

for Kyran at 6 months

All That Glitters . . . .

Here the picture is less gloomy.   Rumpled
sunrise on the snow   the baby wakes   and fills
the room with awkward battering
                    O Uncomplicated One!
        littlest fat face amid the sheets   a commotion
of arms   flapping   palest rouge of flippers crazily rowing
When I simply say   "Good Morning."   Who would have even
suggested   the shore life was trivial?   Last night
on the phone   I realized practically everyone is
a manic depressive   of sorts   With up   and down movements
Unlike the baby   who thinks he's a Trolley   singing Gong
Gong   Gong   He's testing his elbows   & humming.
Five minutes
into the chapter   I noticed that   males were
referred to as men   but females were referred to as wives
I remember blurting out at the party   "I have no father"
With a tremendous sense of relief!   From Grandmother   to

mother   I have passed down. Born of and through women alone.
We have   crawled under the barbed wire   & sat
on our own   sacred land!
                O Lug
                little lug
                & Oggie   when the wind
blows over the stubbles   it's fall   meaning   some things
make themselves obvious by repetition.

       And
            Tu Fu!   Always shaking your head   when
you look my way   Don't give up on me!
             I know the moon bobs in the Great River's flow
             I know about Fame   & Office!
             I have taken   this moment   to celebrate leisure!
             To contemplate
    laziness   as a goal   And Schubert himself
who had a streak of it   an incurable sponge   But loved
by all   his friends   who were fiercely loyal
                      & called him Tubby   He
was barely five feet tall   & a bloom   as from a Spanish balcony
                     was in both his cheeks.

+++
            "To be without humor is to be
               without intelligence."

                     — *Tadeusz Kantor*

Kyran smashed a dozen eggs this morning   with
one quick yank of his baby wrist   he sent them all
flying   while I was speaking to him about   yogurt.   It's
another example of   Just because you're funny . . . .
. . doesn't mean you're joking.   Last week this perfectly
well-dressed businessman   carrying a briefcase   behind me
on the ramp at Grand Central   without warning
began unabashedly intoning   "Calling Green Lantern"

"Calling Green Lantern"   "Calling Green Lantern!"   George
Sand abandoned by her lover   wrote in her journal
"thank god I have heart disease!"   It is possible
to develop   permanent grooves   in the space   between
your eyes   without even realizing it's happening.   Ulysses
pointed out to me at dinner   "You're the only person I know
who frowns while they're eating."   All I know is   Once
Long Island was so dark   & had forests   Now when that hardy
group of locals   that literally break the ice   on the Sound   to
go sailing   held their annual   "Glug Party"   to elect a new "king"
A fight broke out   somehow   between the two top candidates
  — one the principal of the grade school here in town —
Details are lacking but   in the scuffle   the converted trophy was
demolished   the irate citizens   apparently bashing one another
over the head with it   during the fray.
                              Then
as though burlesque couldn't teach us all we need to know   we
are shown the tanks blotting the quiet asphalt swerve of the drive
the civilian prostrate   at the brink of the tip of the combat boot
the bulky khaki uniform of the guardsman   who as calmly as
picking his teeth   merely tilted the long weapon   & Fired.
the man on the ground jerked so   a squadron of gnats was flung up
from the garbage lining the streets   & it seemed loose petals
bolted from the mums   in the bottle   on the table.
                         Have you seen my heart?
                         who used to go out everyday
                         alone!
It was last glimpsed   riding   on a sleeve   a grove
of Beech trees in autumn depicted   mute grey & Palest orange
fleeing the 11 o'clock news!
                    The heart   tries so hard
to do some business
                         it sallies forth each day
                         into the voyage
                    of Bill & Monty   two crumpled forms   rowing
                    through hail & violent weather   emerging
                    triumphant!   waving the mallards at B in his
                    kitchen   who roared   "Jesus Christ! There's
                    white caps on the toilet bowl   and you two
                    are out on the lake   shooting ducks!"

THERE ARE TOO MANY OF ME

lying on the bluff
naked in the local sun

it's so perfect here

no radio
     no mail
  no papers delivered

groggy

                    drifting out
                    an amorphous mind
                    over the hardly moving river

I feel like a thick   steamy   morning fog

my body rising up

a thousand microscopic beads of water.

Ulysses bobbing along the top of the stone wall
so full of questions
tiny bare feet at my elbow asking:
            "Does the government go poo poo?"

We go out to fly the kites. Where is the wind
that we need? I lift the great ruby-eyed bat kite
&   the little striped fish from the Orient   &
we run!   over the grassy strip
tiny stars jump from the knees of our dark corduroy
in bracing ochre air the kite goes up   & comes down
the children shout & cheer   we do it again & again!
I am thinking of my cheek in the soft flesh of
your shoulder. I am thinking of Afghanistan!   lips
of the fierce mountain fighters
The dust of Khyber pass   on my silver toe ring
Our long limbs resting against denuded cliff   tan
& gleaming   I will borrow N's pack   and
handy Coleman   will you trust me   just once more?

Passports drop from ornate rooftop molding
stone drapery for the gala reception.   Architecture
filling up the space
                    & Edifice
        Raised ornaments who are a part of looking up
Here I am!   across the street   A gaudy parallel of
your white tiles   but both shining   in the clear
    for one more afternoon.

+++

Yes I got the card from Spain with the little
donkey and the oranges
and the one with the translucent waters of the
blue gulf sparkling in the sun
tips of the submerged cliff coming through like
miniature craggy islands above the glimmering golden sand.
I put on the little rose carved from the angel skin coral,
my sandals slapping the dusty marble steps
and I think of you   climbing the Tuscan hills
as I go down to get the mail.

R sends me the Blue Mosque at sunset
just last week D sent me an interior of the same building.
I often have a mad desire to pee on the floor of such
places. I don't know what it is   Something
wrong with me I suppose . . . . . .   I suppose you can
catch a glimpse of vineyards and stone barns from
the three-room villa   It's still spring
here in New York   everyone is out   on the stoops
& in the street   flaunting their haughty charms
Yesterday in the park the children built a sand castle
medieval with crenelated walls   like the Chateau de Marcues
you saw   on the road to Biarritz,   overlooking the lovely
Lot River Valley   and near the prehistoric caves of
Lascaux!   and last night M asked Patrick   if he knew
where babies came from   and Patrick answered   "Paris!"

+++

I go up on the roof of the half-collapsed barn
A Hamm's in my hand   a suntan on my mind.
Over the protruding shingle nails   the broken beams
the splintered rafters   come small hands with saws
and hammers
we're going to build a clubhouse up here! they say
and build and bang and cover me with wood chips
clouds burst into white lace flowers
sawdust floats in the hot still air
some bridges are going up beside the club-house
the noise becomes tremendous
Well   I've seen America first
and now I'd like to try some airplanes, yachts,
and fast European cars   private Lear jets and
Ferraris   the sapphire waters off St. Lucia
some nice peaceful jaguar shooting in Mexico
the black volcanic sands of St. Vincent
I'd like to show this shocking pink bikini
    the lavender shores of the Mediterranean.

TOPOGRAPHY

for Meenah Abdus-Salaam & her children, Zainab, Hussein, Amna, Askia, and Fatima
& for all mothers & children who are being allowed to sink like stones through this economy

A woman throws her children
A woman throws her children from a high window
A woman rushes forward   toward her children
a woman is throwing her children   she throws them out
through a window   a woman is rushing forward
with her children in her arms   she is tossing
them one by one   tossing them into the air an
airiness that greets them but they   they
begin to fall   falling they slip from her hands
her body slams the windowframe

a woman is screaming   her children are raining
her children are raining   she has watered our dreams
with children   her babies falling toppling over
sliding down a long transparent rope   she reels in
until her hands are full of rope   and rope is coiled
where she stands   naked except for rope

Perhaps she has taught them to fly   & so flung
them from her   to set them free   to raise them
from dreariness   to encounter them in another place
she was aiming at a target placed high up
the dream opens with the dreamer standing in
the upper rooms   a point of fixation at the top

a woman throws her children   she has pushed them back
wards   or forwards   or
lifted them bodily   & shoved   or grappled in
hands arms & hair   and wrenched them from the floor
& bumped   or held them tenderly for just
a second   in her arms   the sky is full of children
she teaches them travel   the one final move
the upward maneuver

a woman is throwing her children from
a fear of heights   climbing up a bank & becoming
paralyzed by fear to look back at the story below
she invents a perilous position   she is so heavy by then
she is in search of what is hiding   & wants to
know   closer to the ground the scene changes
becomes more subtle   more mysterious   & more defined

she was aiming at a target
it was placed high up
the dream opens with the dreamer
standing in an   upper room   the figure
at the top of the cliff is a symbol of the
outcome of 2 forces   & represents the most suitable
compromise   one thinks to condense its meaning
into symbols   but the resistance of the dream
seeks to satisfy its own demands
Descent

these children were coming down
vertical wheels of baptism   without the weight
lessness of astronauts without the tops of Acacia
trees woven into rainforests   without the imaginary
nets of molecules   with only the anchor of gravity

in one lump sum they divided it
they dreamed their mother catching them up
pulling them back through windows
into rooms furnished by their terror   walls
touched by birds   silken feathers of sounds
to fill their ears   like rushing traffic

in an amphitheater tiers   &
tiers of seats rise sleepily
to a considerable height
in a seat high up watching   a child has drawn
a house   the dream always opens with the dreamer
standing in the upper rooms   a point of fixation
at the top

often they stared at the blue ceiling
often the colors of the windows floating by
often their parched throats mistook the shimmering
of the glass for waters   tears flattened their cheeks
eyes blurred & wet   who wants to see the ants getting
larger   wearing pants & skirts   hats & shoes checkers
spill light over the ruins   the missing diamonds
perched like a soul under a floor lamp

a woman throws her children from a fifth floor
window   from a sixth floor   seventh   eighth floor
window   she says it's about angels   or about
the longing to be   a trapeze artist   the
circular dance
to say exactly where the fall   begins
where can it end then   exactly
the rain hammers down   but they walk

Verlaine   La Loca   Neruda   Tu Fu   Janine
Pommy Vega   Cesar Vallejo   Gertrude Stein
O lonesome Feldspear!   the outcome of 2 forces
Ride 2 horses at the same time
cross 2 rivers   drive 2 cars   Sing
2 songs Follow   2 dreams   A woman has thrown
her children away   She laid down in her life
& looked up   her arms ache   She cannot
account for misconduct   remorse   or   eventual
scandal   she canceled future

Buy 2 of everything in case
1 gets lost   ripped off or
damaged
Live in 2 houses   two apartments   Have
2 bathtubs
2 cats
2 ways of looking at things
see 2 counselors
Enjoy 2 lovers
visit 2 friends

understand twice as much
Know 2 routes to the destination
2 ways to put your foot down
2 ways to be standing
2 ways to pronounce "no"
2 ways to dress for walking
2 walks to take
2 kinds of exercise
Have 2 different saws   2 kegs of nails
2 hammers hanging   in 2 places
discuss 2 definitions of "Post Modern"
You can do twice as much
You can be in 2 places at the same time   A
woman   suddenly alone   in an empty room
walking   & falling   walking & falling   Now
with a floor   now without one.   Her scream
descending in her throats   all the way   to the street

Headlines read   "Mom suspends time"
no one knows what to do with it now   Now
that we know   a woman throws her children
Imaginer of what this momentum influences   this
strain of unraveling fragments   bent by calls
These children with the heavens for a parachute
Children of Alto-cumulus   Nimbo-stratus
Cirrus

this woman she left it for us   Her
coating of unresolved   her study of falling
the everlasting long depth   From the top you
are below   associated by miraculous timing
the shape of the yellow curtains blown inward
behind her eyes the pure geometry of horses graze
soft coats in winter static straight out   like
strings   holding them up in the world   level
in any direction

Because a child has drawn a house   with two windows
because the child has painted a house   a woman is

calling the names and the names of names   she is
calling through her teeth   her sleep   her dream to
undream the dream she is   The outline
of altitudes

Because a woman is throwing her children into outer
space   into other galaxies   anonymous solar systems
she removes them from chaos   into the lyric of motion
transfers them from seizures of terror to the oblivion
of spinning   something else   is on her mind

She thinks the air is liquid   she
dreams her children swimming   she dreams herself
dreaming   holding the hand of the swimmer
she dreams herself swimming with the dreamer
poised   at a great height
where the dream opens   the silence she is
after   the transmogrifying wind

What billows inflating sacks full of air
incomprehensible torrents of injustice flapping
which were you going   to remember at the moment
of your escape   she said she was   "Giving them
to God"   uncoined and shimmering   a river between
friends she was remarkable portraying the iconoclast
future of la iglesias white stucco   a cross of thick
pink and leaded blue   imitation emerald and jewels
banging the long sides   of telescopic nightmare

the table of that sleep   a cartoon likeness
posing star buckets   of hair of   burning glass.
Mom   of hair of logs and timbers   she's got hair
of burning glass
hysterical dogs and feathered beings swept about
silken air flowed internally where once a river
hesitated   stone space flung   this woman who is
falling backwards into time   who has forgotten
to dress

The unconscious motive   behind the dream
compares to the   conscious motive behind
an action   a means of escape

Waterfalls appear to her
a million tiny silver fish come flying
out of the jungle   aviaries full of pins
dropping   there is a contest of stillness then
in the trees   of who can move the least
Green fruit toppling   off a dish
port of force   or bias   Motive is
significant to the dreamer   representing a
tendency   constellations drip over the
low hem   of tunnels   stacked on end
slender escapements   spinning upward
small hands slipping from her shoulders
like a shawl

Neighbors say a Queens woman's life was unraveling

because a mom threw her children   out of their
10th floor apartment   yesterday   in Far Rockaway

because in the photo   Police investigators are
shown taking measurements   of the window   because

firefighters had to guess which apartment the children
were falling from   because "she was the last one

you would expect this of"   because "she was mumbling
Mohammed Elijah & she   was going to jump also"

because a neighbor looked out in time to see the girl slide
& fall   "The mother pushed her"   he said

Woman with a vision   Who
can say enough to you now
the entrance to your grammars   scorched desert
Because you are mad   you can rejoice in it!

ear to the floor rattling   you hear
the circle scraping   the pounding door
a madwoman can't blame anyone   can't plan
an escape   because you are mad
fibers sigh for them   O Children
your mother is mad   is
this dark wing   this intrusion.

How do you feel   Mother
they've   plunged

the event occurs in the vision of itself
consequence waits in the wings   broader
wider than anything

Woman with a jungle in the shape   of a blouse
furious outposts   are the tale of the dream
wherein the tissue   of the dreamer is woven
as though the artist forgot to stop drawing
a woman is throwing her kids   she touches them
forces them out "Go, go, God's
waiting for you."

there is a window in the wall of a building
a building made of many floors   many floors up
room after room above   A woman is throwing
her children from   out of a high   window
Mother & children appear   lugging an anchor
no father in the cards
she takes   the neighbors by surprise

O kids
in positions of exile   the
nature of which is a mystery to you
the point of application   has shifted
inwards   the dream offers a kind of criticism
Our journey was strange   much
of the ground lay on the surface

the air is cool now   coming with the tourmaline
destiny of loops   the somersaulting vagrancy of
closing eyes   she handed that to them   the soft dark
to hide in   Can we say   she flew into a rage   or   they
soared into the air   there is some relationship
between the kind of accident the rider experiences and
the accident that forms the nucleus of the dream
the horse appears black   because of so much pigment
Nothing reflects that saturation   no one   no one
children absorbed into a color   until she throws them
one by one   into the light

WANDA COLEMAN

Her honors include fellowships from the John P. Guggenheim Foundation and the NEA.
She received the 1999 Lenore Marshall Poetry Prize presented by the Academy of American
poets, the New Hope Foundation, and *The Nation* magazine—the first African-American
woman to receive the award. She was C.O.L.A.'s first literary fellow, Department of Cultural
Affairs, Los Angeles, 2003-04.

GIVING BIRTH

against bone. rubbing. pressure against bladder
i pee and pee and pee
and drink water and more water. never enough water
it twists in my womb
my belly a big brown bowl of jello quakes
twenty pounds and climbing
eat eat eat. milk. got to have ice cold milk
vitamins and iron three times daily
cocoa butter and hormone cream
infanstethoscope
sex sex sex. can't get enough of that funky stuff
bras getting too small. is that me in the mirror?
it bucks/brings belches
smooth skin. glossy hair. strong nails
i'm 99% body. my brain has dissolved into
headaches tears confusion
my navel sticks out/eye of cyclops
my life for an apple fritter
snipping the elastic in panties, another pair ruined
nausea. vomit. muscle strain
"they" tell you to eat fresh fruit and lots of
vegetables. eating fresh fruit and lots of vegetables
afraid of what it will/won't be
anxious. it's got to look like him
it's got to look like me. be healthy. be live. be all right
why doesn't it hurry up and come
read books. more books. know the tv program by heart
fantasies about returning to slim
the ass sleeps. tingles when wakened
walking is hard. sitting is hard. sex, an effort

he stands in lines for me
thirty pounds and climbing
people smile, are sympathetic
will it be capricorn or aquarius?
can't drive. too big to get behind the steering wheel
ice cream cone jones
(out of three hundred deliveries this year, ours
is his third legitimate, says doc, "it's what
they are doing to the black community")
daily reports to the grandmothers
is that me in the mirror?
he worries. i worry. we worry together
more hugs and affection
i can't reach my feet
more calcium and iron
wow. my gums are bleeding. scurvy?
it rubs. twists. kicks. moves
sex? it takes too much out of me
the flu. food poisoning. cold
too tight pants bite me
preparation: pelvic spread. vaginal walls widen
forty pounds and climbing
showers. no more long hot luxury baths
muumuus and mules. naked = relief
his ear to my stomach to hear the heart beat
emergency cookies
it presses against my diaphragm. it's hard to
breathe. can't sleep good. dreams
more dreams. it's a boy. it's a girl
backaches. swollen feet
refrigerator lover, clandestine rendezvous at 2 am
advice from the experienced, questions from the barren
the planets are lining up in scorpio
suitcase packed and ready
names for him. names for her
(everybody-else-we-know-who's-pregnant-is-having
a-perfect-baby pressure)
sex? oh yeah. used to be fun
it turns. kicks twists

that's me in the mirror, definitely
why doesn't it hurry up and come
crying jags. throbs of false labor
will he be there
when it's time?

'TIS MORNING MAKES MOTHER A KILLER

mean

day grinds its way slowly into her back/a bad
mattress stiffens her jaw

it is the mindless banalities that pass as conversation
between co-workers

her paycheck spread too thin across the bread of
weeks; too much gristle and bone and not enough

blood

meatless meals of beans and corn bread/nights
in the electronic arms of the tube

mean as a bear

carrying groceries home in the rain in shoes
twice resoled and feverish with flu

it is the early dawn

mocking her unfinished efforts; unpaid bills,
unanswered letters, unironed clothes

tracks

of pain in her face left by time; the fickle high of it
facing the mirror of black flesh

mean as mean can

pushed to the floor but max is not max enough
no power/out of control/anxiety

it is the sun illuminating cobwebs

that strips her of her haunted beauty; reveals
the hag at her desperate hour

children beware

KATHLEEN FRASER

(b. 1935), one child (David Marshall, b. 1966). First marriage to poet, Jack Marshall (1961–68). Second marriage to philosopher, Arthur K. Bierman (1984). Fraser worked in the Sixties as a writer for *Mademoiselle* (NYC), after winning a poetry prize in their annual college contest. This overlapped with her first teaching job via the Academy of American Poets "Poetry in the Schools" project (NYC, 1964–66). Her teaching career continued at The Iowa Writer's Workshop (1969–71) and Reed College (1971–72), moving to San Francisco State University (1972–92) to direct the Poetry Center and found the American Poetry Archives (1973). From 1975–92, she began teaching full-time at SFSU as professor of Creative Writing in the MFA Writing Program. She currently works with poets in the grad writing program at California College of the Arts in San Francisco each fall and lives in Rome in the spring.

Fraser published and edited HOW(ever) from 1983 to 1992, now on the web as How2, www.How2journal.com. She is winner of two NEA writing grants and a Guggenheim Fellowship in poetry. Early in her publishing career (1964) she was winner of the Frank O'Hara Poetry Award and the Discovery Award. She is currently collaborating with NY painter Hermine Ford on a text/image exhibit of large-scale wall pieces to be shown at Pratt Institute of Architecture in Rome, in April of 2007.

On motherhood, in tandem with the making of poetry, she writes: "it completely changed my perception of time, from continuous to discontinuous. I was forced from the naive expectations of a learned formal art to a far more improvised necessity involving interruption, error and negotiated compromise with private workspace. Once another struggling human arrived under my care, my capacity for attention, compassion, invention and thought changed radically. For this—and for my son—I am grateful."

CHILD INSIDE OF AIR AND LIGHT, NOT SPEAKING

I cannot think how it looked—my room before this one—except that it was upstairs and big enough for everything. The new room belongs to grownups and is outside my body which keeps being hot. The new room is tall with lots of dark blue air around me stretching to all four walls. It is the outside coming in through the window. Out there it is snowing, they keep saying that's why the air is so white, it's why I can't breathe.

I think it's because all the leaves fell off the trees and there was no place to stop the light. I try to remember the color of branches without leaves, but I only see heat running up the walls breathing in and out.

They pat me up and sit me at the end of the bed every morning against a pile of white pillows that get crumpled with sweat. At night I get lost somewhere outside in the snow, or I forget when it is night and when it is day because I don't do anything but look out and there is no other place except in the space that comes after the curtain hanging across the doorway where everyone else lives. They keep the curtain closed so my eyes won't hurt. The doctor's voice passes through the material of the curtain like a radio voice and so does my father's.

+

There is a big stack of folded white diapers belonging to my brother on the nightstand next to the island where I live. They are for blowing my nose on, instead of handkerchiefs. The nightstand floats around in the water and if I run out of space on one diaper then I call out for another and she comes in and unfolds a fresh one and hands it to me. I like it when it is new and clean. I hold it to my cheek and pretend it is a tablecloth. Once when they thought I was getting better it was because I called it my flag. The larger ones last longer than little pieces of cloth with flowers on them.

All week I've been sitting here for a day as long as a year except when someone rushes in or when my father comes home for lunch smelling of his wool coat and the coldness on his skin. He gives me my medicine made into a kind of scratchy pill that he presses down on until it becomes white powder in the teaspoon of maple syrup.

I try to remember the other rooms in the house and what each person does out there. Drinking coffee. Singing. Radio programs while ironing. My brother crying out from his crib up the stairs. She brings me a bowl of something on a tray. It smells like a bad thing will happen if I put it in my mouth. The new bed is wide and long. I shouldn't spill anything on the spread. Sometimes it stretches like a park or a sidewalk, or there are bells and a glass of water. This morning I thought I was getting bigger than my old upstairs bed but I couldn't tell for sure as this one doesn't have sides close enough to reach my hands.

+

She comes in and looks at me when she thinks I'm sleeping. She comes in between doing other tasks and I listen to her footsteps between rooms and the people talking too loud from inside her radio. She is in the back part of the house now, she is in the kitchen cooking something I don't like. She brings in a glass with stuff sloshing around near the top and says "it's good." She names it pablum which is not a word, so I look at the glass for just a minute and see that what's in it is grey and mixed with little gritty bits floating around instead of being in a bowl like the others eat from. I remember then that the word she said is the name of cereal for babies. It smells like nothing you would want, as if you didn't know the difference.

"Have some," she says, "it will help you get better." I tell her I don't want any but she walks out of the room and leaves the glass right there and says I should drink it while she's gone, "like a big girl." I want to push the glass away. I turn my head to watch and to see if she's coming back. My mind is pressing inside my throat to yell out. I want to be lifted out of bed more than just when she's changing the sheets when I'm sitting in a chair with the blanket over me and she gives me fresh pajamas and takes my temperature.

+

Now it is either the same day, or it is tomorrow. My father comes into my room with a square piece of plywood. He shows me how to lean the wood against my knees pulled up under the sheets. "This can work for an easel," he explains. Against the piece of wood he clips a big sheet of paper and then puts a new package of wax crayons on the white sheet next to me . . . the crayons are so thick that if I got hungry I would eat the red and yellow ones first. I want to draw a picture of the inside of my body to make me get better and I tell my father this when he comes in to say goodbye.

+

She is on the telephone after he goes back to his study, on a street away from ours. I look at the pablum in the glass and I do not feel tired except for having nothing to think about. I can hear her voice on the telephone explaining to Mrs. Buchanan how I'm doing. Her voice reminds me of the way it sounded when my father went to Chicago to have his medical check-up. That day I wanted to know why she was sad, but she looked away and said I was too young to understand and she just kept crying and blowing her nose.

I was still thinking about her sadness when I pushed the glass to the edge of the nightstand, how it would look falling through the air if I knocked it off, watching it tip over and then the stuff in it pouring out like grey wet snow and the glass breaking into tiny sharp pieces on the floor.

FANNY HOWE

"I grew up in Cambridge, Massachusetts but left when I was seventeen and moved to the West Coast for a few years. Out there I studied at Stanford, then dropped out before graduation. A strange brief marriage followed, while I wrote pulp paperbacks to make money, and then moved on to New York City to go wild among friends. All this time I was scratching out poems and stories, and making what money I could from odd jobs. I began to publish my poems and novels in my twenties, married again, then began having children, three in four years, the first being born on July 19, 1969. It was then I began teaching, which lasted for another thirty-five years. I wrote many novels and poems in all that time, and as soon as I could, I began drifting, which is what I continue to do."

Q

We moved to be happy

Like a remote sensing tool each body
in the family
adapted to earth's urbanity and traveled

When the water went south for the winter

it carried us down like storm-driven gulls
to this crash that we call a city

    +

One black wing was blowing down the road

(Rain-washed road)

In the old days horses wearing green shoes
would trot on that grass

Our caravan has sought a remedy for memory
by moving over the same path

    +

Snow rises as it falls
on small seaside resorts and on capital
premier personal country castle and well-equipped hotels

on pullmans flats canoes and fishing boats
on fairy house and a crack house

on holiday and airport inns on tents and crypts and cars
and caravans
Roads end where only trees greet them

like brides in terrified feminine dress

+

I was sick of my wits
like the kids in *Landscape In the Mist*

hammered down into a sequence
like climbing onto a train
and sitting down

I had to keep moving the books around

+

After a good beating on a cold day
disappointment
slowed my recovery

Cotton replaced my lace
and peals of laughter
only overcame me later

when the ground covered
the way to my door like lava
and I really hoped

the hoping was over

+

Creation was the end that preceded means

Rain steamed on evergreens and ferns
in a larger darkness
than anyone could witness

A boy emerged from a cocoon
crying I have no right to be here!

Temperate gales blew from the jets
at Heathrow
where a baby was yelling so wide
you could see the typhus in his throat

You could also see a tall waterfall
and call it spigot because your eyes

(grapes on the palms of a saint's hands)

incorporated and diminished images
into little packages

            +

Heaven has been my nation-state
safe sanctuary from the law
or else the production of hate and bread is not increasing

At least I know my tradition is among the contradictions

And rests upon a time
as close to never-was as anything can be

but still a story of something that almost came to be
the never-quite-but-hinted-at
attention of a Thee

            +

Lambs don't fight being itinerant

or being where there are no minutes or questions

like Why be obedient to a world that will end?

Wool walks in the agriculture
ignorant of its coloring
Patented in blue yes as food and clothing
for persons and their furniture

+

Wherever I am becomes an end
Long drives through striped fields

when one episode includes the same
smouldering gas coals and glass as the next one
checkered with grime

A buried bulb
develops under these conditions the way mothering
turns the wilds into a resolution

+

The neo-neolithic urban nomad school of poetry
is almost for lone mothers only

Lines of us queue up
for a hand-out or to steal a pair of shoes
for this child or that

We know where we love by its stillness

Our task is to read the bedouins
now that we're lost at last

and can really see through words including me
to the other side that multiplies
the interior matter

+

I light up the grids
to make my woods

into a conservatory
Color all in to match the environs

If I follow a sequence of dares
each one will be a part of

the final product
That's why I'm happy

+

A little clover's on autumn lawns

White petals bristle the way weeds build them

If goals create content stealth creates form

The air force hits space
with the velocity of a satanic wrist

How to give birth to children under these conditions
Favor the ghost over the father, maternalist

THE NURSERY

The baby
        was made in a cell
in the silver & rose underworld.
Invisibly prisoned
        in vessels & cords, no gold
for a baby; instead

eyes, and a sudden soul, twelve weeks
old, which widened its will.

Tucked in the notch of my fossil: bones
          laddered a spine from a cave,
the knees & skull
were etched in this cell, no stone, no gold
where no sun brushed its air.

One in one, we slept together
          all sculpture
                    of two figures welded.
But the infant's fingers
squeezed & kneaded
                    me, as if to show
the Lord won't crush what moves
on its own . . . secretly.

On Robeson Street
                    anonymous
was best, where babies
have small hearts
                    to learn
with;
          like intimate
thoughts on sea
water, they're limited.

Soldered to my self
    it might be a soldier or a thief
for all I know.
The line between revolution & crime
    is all in the mind
          where ideas of righteousness
and rights confuse.
I walked the nursery floor.
By four-eyed buttons & the curdle of a cradle's
paint: a trellis of old gold
          roses, lipped & caked

where feet will be kicking in wool.

                   Then the running,
the race after,
cleaning the streets up for a life.
His technicolor cord
hung from a gallery of bones,
        but breathing *I'm finished*.
Both of us.

And when the baby sighed,
through his circle of lips,
                 I kissed it,
      and so did he, my circle to his,
we kissed ourselves and each other,
      as if each cell was a Cupid,
and we were born to it.

The cornerstone's dust
upfloating

by trucks & tanks
White flowers spackle

the sky crossing the sea.
A plane above the patio

wakes the silence
and my infant who raises

his arms to see
what he's made of.

O animation! O liberty!

CONCLUSIVELY

The night was almost too long to bear
Then there was evidence of mercy—a passing car—
milky air—and I could see
dry walls & gravel on the way to a highway
Atlantic for its grays

Loss is the fulfillment of the Law
Space collected on a long line

I was eliminated as a locus of mothering—
a she—physical but imaginary as a restless daughter

Why this body and not another

The one who came to destroy the works of women—their
offspring—
knew how many people were resisting incarnation
He counted on them by accommodating them

Guilt relieving guilt
is the get of killers whose mouths shine
I can't say enough about this—red because sore
& polished because wet

One died to become the spirit—guide
Before that time
there were second persons in everything
Then saints, then no one
to guide anyone to heaven
Cosmic expansion has gone in its preferred direction

I can hear the hour, this never
happened to me before
One day I will shake the blue sky from my hair
and slip back into consciousness—
the thing that is always aware
with or without a living creature to share its pleasures

Tonight I request the precious gift of final perseverance
shored up in my sheets
not far from a predawn holocaust
of traveling children

MARTHA RONK

(1940) is the author of eight books of poetry and several chapbooks; her forthcoming, *Vertigo,* was chosen by C. D. Wright for the National Poetry Series and will be published by Coffeehouse Press. She has recently won a NEA fellowship, has had residencies at Djerassi and MacDowell, and is the Irma and Jay Price Professor of English at Occidental College in Los Angeles.

"Jacob was born 5.16.71, so the intimate and physical part of mothering is now for me in the past: no more elbows, tears, hurried pastas, glue. I remember it with all the deep longing of 'ubi sunt.' I remember it in a photographic way as if moments had been turned from color to black-and-white by time. Even the salient and painful years of adolescence have dimmed, become stories we tell each other. *Here's one,* he says, *I never told you about the time I . . .* What happens now is our rewriting of history through our exchange of memories, through everything I write for and in spite of him, through his becoming an adult and seeing in ways not exactly like mine, but altered as mine by years. The shift and change through time is now contained not only in the familiarity of physical gesture and stance, but in the words used (we both steal 'anon' from Shakespeare), rituals performed (Bach for arguments), gifts exchanged (we both like bowls), love of physical movement (he inherited, so he says, the bicycle gene and races, 'cat 2,' madly, beautifully), irony. That's the one I most appreciate, his ironic sense that tries to belie time, the substance that nonetheless holds and defines us."

A DOWNPOUR

Come at me without motive parts
                now that I think of it, but what I was thinking
        angular, drenching, how there are so many bodies round and about,
yet the argumentative is topmost and lo,
        He shall not fall on trite and triviall disquisitions,
but inquiring into it in any case, a monologue perhaps,
for my ears alone, speaking and again speaking,
not to my ears, music to mine own, permitting not so many to speak,
the one guided by the ten-stringed harp or the shepherd
        even the speaker of her own speaking in her own ear
        the figure of the boy coming, drenching the fields.

NOW IT'S UP TO THE WORLD
for Jacob

All you can do now is wait while intention seeks its own demise—
now it's up to the world, the lichen graying the maples
the sounds just as the light goes not before the quiet following.
All you can do is concede since the tenses are already given
and you've lost the files by which the ordering took place
or the will of not giving up it's not so much he thinks he can impose it,
but that he can think the fiction of forever you can't lay claim to,
can't call up the future of to be or graft anything to anything,
but wait in the disconnect as already on the road the monarchs
give their orange to the asphalt and it is the loss of June, of July.

"YOU KNOW HOW I AM, HE SAID, WHEN IT IS GETTING LATE"

Mid-August lengthens.
Beethoven reaches the boy I'll never reach,
the clear O of the vowel, her extraordinary voice
as a fern at the edge of the road trilling in the wind.
He sits somewhere out of reach in the experience
he says you don't remember.
If we were all punctual we'd never arrive where we meant to go.
Once in a while we show up as if by chance along country roads
by mailboxes marked with handwritten signs,
and the bad translations of German songs.
On stage the woman is heavily poised in a silver dress.
Her singing calls up a similarly eerie and waterlogged sound.

NORMA COLE

is a poet, painter and translator. Forthcoming is *Natural Light*. Current translation work includes Danielle Collobert's *Journals*, Fouad Gabriel Naffah's *The Spirit God and the Properties of Nitrogen* and *Crosscut Universe: Writing on Writing* from France. Cole has been the recipient of a Wallace Alexander Gerbode Foundation Award, Gertrude Stein Awards, the Fund for Poetry, and the Foundation for Contemporary Arts. A Canadian by birth, Cole migrated via France to San Francisco where she has lived since 1977. Her son Jesse, born in 1971 in France, also lives in San Francisco with his wife and their son Jack.

from *SPINOZA IN HER YOUTH*

One lived within the portrait of the other, an intimate brace, thus time's
contraction (shaping). One awoke in the dream in the dark, traces of objects on
the surface, and reference and frailty. One's interest in birds and dogs, discomfort
remembering the toys, adjacency with randomness as reference, not knowing how
to end things, not ending.
∧∧∧

∧∧∧

The word in someone
else's mouth, laborious
elaboration of life
as a story, seamy,
sometimes
long, sometimes
short, there
went a moment
of directness
∧∧∧

∧∧∧

There you are closer to it. Entering through a keyhole of light. Signs of the body.
At first I could not believe it. Borders. The body of. The land mass.
∧∧∧

∧∧∧

the story this time: the unnumbered dark
She stands at the border, stranded. "I didn't expect
to see you here, suddenly, like this."
∧∧∧

∧∧∧

"because of the civil war," hands

on the sprocket holes, areas
seen as dark thickenings, night
wounds in the physical
contraction
^^^

^^^

"stopped breathing"
^^^

^^^

no time in between
^^^

^^^

the sacrificial couple: a tariff
for being alive, a tariff for the
other thing. points or nodes in
time shaped or defined by their
wars. *Mine* [is] *the one that enters
the story*
^^^

^^^

She daylights the overhead fluorescents. It must not appear the stars open for
business. You were not far away she felt waiting, "Nothing formed me. You can
describe anything, the leaves."
^^^

^^^

the figure of the itch, that
is, the itch as a (trope)
heterotopian itch, item
^^^

^^

or in her mouth, shadows
^^^

^^^

A motion occurs in space, barely perceived. A carpet, a garden, snowdrops, a
packing crate, a cut in time. And then the star blew inside out.

ALICE NOTLEY

"My birthday is November 8, 1945. Anselm's birthday is August 14, 1972. Edmund's birthday is August 3, 1974. I began writing poems saturated with the details of pregnancy, childbirth and motherhood sometime in 1972. I had no models for my subject—I worked entirely in isolation, in Chicago and in England. As far as I was aware, I was the first one to write such a poetry."

DEAR DARK CONTINENT

Dear Dark Continent:

                    The quickening of
the palpable coffin
                    fear so then the frantic
doing of everything experience is thought of

but I've ostensibly chosen
                    my, a, *family*
so early! so early! (as is done always
as it would seem always) I'm a two
now three irrevocably
                    I'm wife I'm mother I'm
myself and him and I'm myself and him and him

But isn't it only I in the real
whole long universe? Alone to be
in whole long universe?

But I and this he (and he) makes ghosts of
I and all the *he*s there would be, won't be

because by now I am he, we are I, I am we.

We're not the completion of myself.

Not the completion of myself, but myself!
through the whole long universe.

THREE STROLLS

1.

I take the baby for a stroll in the pre-storm
he loves it so much he goes to sleep in it
after a wide-awake night in which he
discovers some unknown to us new thing we
already know—dilated big blue eyes
dilated tiny nostrils—yellow & kelly
green, lion & crocodile, etc circling
around in the air each under its own cloud

2.

the stroller collapsed the calendar
obscured by what the stroller comes in
                    the ambery varnished wood
dirt mottled won't come off it
    and the way she talks is funny for good

——

& sometime after sexy dreams
& sometime after black sleep
there must be sometime, still

——

my day is all little birds & bees
swarming colliding collapsing
                now warmer, clearing, with clouds
opening up to a twilit blue dome
                            wishing for
my star charts and stars
                    not really
I truly almost never wish
                though I do dream

3.

First I woke up & realized
the baby wasn't awake yet & had slept
for almost 8 hours
                wondered if
he was really dead jumped up poked him
a little he belched or something
                                then
I got back into the bed grateful for it
            and then he began his morning yelling

    that's how much of what goes on gets stopped & started

——

A long morning carriage stroll
in his white cap he loved the motion
in his sleep & now he's awake & crying again

    all he wants is an infinite carriage ride
with breasts inside it

——

Everyone comes & tells me "your baby's
crying!" as if I can't hear him too
probably so do you

    he's merely making a speech—
protesting the war the milk problem

——

Mommy's clothes don't fit her any more
she refuses to buy new ones because
she thinks she's going to lose enough weight
to wear the old ones again
                    isn't she dumb?

                              more of the Irrevocable

        the baby always wakes me up but
who can afford to sleep now?

                    ——

        I've always wanted to
be conscious in my sleep

        in my dream the other night the
fortune-teller said "You are obsessed with
the sleep between birth & death"
                            but I'm in it

                    ——

        The form of the day keeps slipping away
from my control
                    and he wants food & play awake at
constant irregular intervals
            the day now it's him now it's me again him

        what is this with babies anyway?
        all this for the pleasure of holding this?

            Yes Why Don't know Animal Magic

                    ——

Mommy won't get up & do any
succouring or work she finds it important
to do the crossword puzzle—as many as possible—
all day
               furthermore
                         she hopes the family doesn't
acquire a car monster
                    because she doesn't want to learn
how to drive it in terror of life & death

          she wants to do the crossword puzzle all day

          Mommy will never solve the problem
of her liberation that way

                         until she will

                    ——

          Shall I go look at him?
          I like to look at him
          I like to wake him up & hold him

          and then he cries & and won't stop & there's
something else I have to do something about

          but I will, & do

                    ——

          "All my life I've been in love with its
color"
          Goldfinger says

          a "severe thunderstorm" is outside

and the baby stares & stares at the
maroon cushion
              the vast space of the maroon
soon to become more myriad
                              a more
myriad space a more myriad maroon
                              he swoons at it
      I swoon at him
                  who's also it

———

      You go through everything just to get
something to hold to look at it
      you go through everything just to get
something to look at to hold

3 POSTPARTUM EXERCISES

                        1.

Do you mean your response to pain is rage?
                              yes
and also hatred
lofty meanness and renewed love of prurience
                              I
gave up mere exercise after
                  childbirth
                        (that's not fat that's a conceit)

2.

I have eschatology mixed up with scatalogical
will marriage make Margaret mate with a marmoset?
is all exercise merely pre-prandial?

3.

                          flotilla, oracular, swinging
a lot of fast kicks so casually taken
and a gazelle
              found
herself back at the exercise bar as if it had never
been crossed. The trellises of my legs have lapsed into
cylindrical quagmires
                        and my belly's baptismal font!
But my ass is still a gavel

                (case dismissed til tomorrow)

SPLASHES OF YELLOW

                              1.

        Pretty May
              (rain)
                    & I—

                                        talking

        in sort of rounded gobs

                                American English

                                moist tulip air

                    lumps of throat

Pearly light
                I catch it   & bundle it in
            to feel compact   ,   dense and loose

                            part eggs part black
                            cherry preserves part
                            pitted, part ginger part
                            newspaper part bag

                            pit materials: brain paper,
                            records, plants, scrubbing,
                            flash cards, maths big and
                            little, books, lists

                            contracting spreading

        so it was all dumb, but I did it. It became
    my viscera and nebula, my poundage, my
    pungence, my crown of swirl, my vox humana,
    my vril, my hyssop, my chop, my chocolate
    baby Anselm

    ripping up THE GUARDIAN before I've even
    glanced at it.
                        He's smiling & clicking his tongue.
    Grey falls away for five minutes of précis
    sunlight, everything weighs in, clicks
    the stripes the cup the wad of spirit gum, blue
    Maidstone Sandwich Poole Brighton Wells

                            melodious fresh and sound
                            not sour or bitter, fit

to drink, amiable, gentle
easy, flattery, face
home, bride, sleep, the bicycle
runs sweetly, Sultan, sweetbrier
lit air

                              swelling
                                          yet
shiny negro forearms'
consistency its steely
bed bed inbred I
recurve reecho gauche as
an opera

tightness change, a blue English shield's crescent
moon is a wane
                    from the real round of course its horns
a mere excrescence are it the almost insignificant
shield cipher formic (acid)
                              I
                    touch the shield, for luck
go on & do my work
                    An orchestra of maths
                    infixes the guardian
                    in a mundane bath

                         2.

(Cleaning The House)

Yellow comb, how pleasant to draw you again through
                    brown hair
Grey, toy porpoise, pleasure nexus
Little white shoe, pin holes are a radial star on you

LANE sweater gold and an Indian bonnet
           on it, I'm gawky and beautiful in
Baby denims you are frayed,
Now you are a fresh dishcloth
I've found a bracelet of chartreuse stones!
           in the kitchen behind the greater
Here's the milk-blue horse on wheels
Here are the sandals gum clouds on soles
Here is C.P. Snow, white
           with orange and an abbey
Here is Edinborough green and dusky
Here is Anselm asleep with his thumb his alcove flesh
Here is <u>he</u> asleep bearded big idée fixe
Here am I a blue morning integer

3.

Golden Buck, Irish Rabbit, Welsh Rarebit, Helford
Angels, Anselm is stroking a piece of yellow cheese

Now he's playing with a mote, from the floor

"A large worthy-looking body entered the room."
In the wind

                    "I don't want to do the
                    laundry" "You're going to
                    spend your life fighting
                    your life"

                    The worthy-
                    looking body follows me
                    everywhere today, esp.
                    windy eyes, with hair
                    "Is there a hidden

danger in your oven?"
my plant hair, its
windy shoots, Sassoon
helmet grown out.
"There's a pain in the
room but I don't know
if it's in me" young
metal turns into
vegetation   that
sounds all right. But
I though I was sup-
posed to grow harder
with older
. . . Inside the quartz
inside the wind . . .
slip inside the worthy-
looking body . . . I am
a good woman, and I feed
the baby interesting
grains, & oranges, I
write works to <u>him</u>
and I roar around
the flat in high black
boots, earth clung

4.

(Evening)

Jane Austen
          Pool of bath
the time is a nugget
the time is a glove

the sky black so light is yellow
bright coffee black goad
          this yellow comb is
strong and toothed
    world's décor, cuts clean
through aspirating hair

             like . . .

in Australia, colorful oceans
I am with one star
we look to make love
I'm dressing up specially
sexy brocade cheong-sam
and my enormous prick & balls
showing through dress!

5.

All I always try to do is find my way into my house
                             here—

      Sense and Sensibility
                  on deck, and

  the yellow comb

brightly, arranging hair

    all the fine filaments growing from
skin
        disheveled, minute distances, haircloths,
crossed wires, rainbows and mists, straight
  part, halo, helmet, flip, bangs, braid, trail
brow, lash, moss

But I was always already here!   combing hair

                          The curtains woven of sheer
                          hair
                          the lamp a halo, the motes dandruff
                          on dark, air, air hair emphatically
                          too fine for a set we let it flow
                          the plates of left cornsilk
                          salmon bones, shag grated carrot,
                          I'll never wash— & nothing's silk
                          not time or place, the hairs are
                          silk, but lumped matted: not
                          the lumps grow, spheres, from hair to
                          sphere of influence, how that salmon-
                          colored bedspread spreads through this
                          room, & spread with my hair rests my head

          my hair is wind
          my nape is nescient
          my breasts are precise
          my breasts are insurance
          my nipples shiver
          my breasts are place

          my stomach is seismic
          my pelvis is sphere
          my hips are precocious
          my legs are glib
      & my legs are in deep

WALK, WALK, WALK

Walk, walk, walk.
One day it in-
dicates it is ready
to be born

BUT HE SAYS I MISUNDERSTOOD

He & I had a fight in the pub
5 scotch on the rocks 1 beer I remember
Only that he said "No women poets are any
                good, if you want it
Straight, because they don't handle money" and
"Poe greater than Dickenson"
Well that latter is an outright and fucking untruth

6–line stanzas
                                Open though some?
And he forgot to put my name on our checks
                However,
He went to get the checks however
He had checks to deposit in his name
                Because
He's older & successfuller & teaches because
When you're older you don't want to
                scrounge for money besides it gives him
                a thrill he doesn't too much acknowledge,
                O Power!

                So I got pregnant
I hope not last night now
I'm a slave, well mildly, to a baby
Though I could teach English A or

type no bigshot (mildly) poet-in-residence like him
Get a babysitter never more write any good poems
             Or, just to
Scrounge it out, leave him. All I can say is

This poem is in the Mainstream American Tradition

from SONGS FOR THE UNBORN SECOND BABY

I

Pregnant again involucre
                                    (sounds gorgeous)
Pregnant
          not the repast of news or psychological

                                        though arithmetical
(stars, filth)
                  I ingeminate

I dream
of a compost
into whose composition paper
can go

and which itself
composes the paper
but literally,
how, do you suppose

the wonders
that would be facts,
from dreams,
get lost

                                    reflex you refractor old saw you
thought
          you'd got swisher,
                              craggy, from the Chinese, more masculinely
feminine, only refined
when wanting to be startling,
                              emeralds sacral putrid but
you're just cavernous
                    round a foetus
                              and true

                    A dream hole
                    in tower wall
                    to admit or
                    mirth music

                    the holes let issue

                                        Mohaves coffins flowers jealousy

          "What's great is three Irish
          whiskies — we have to wait for the grill

          to heat up — to get masterfully
          irritable and declaim from the fitfully lit

          up clouds above the table that their
          sole interest is their sexual

          power at age 19; though it might conceivably
          be experiencially satisfying

          to be a man, one by definition attracted
          to, in love with them by definition you jerk!"

And so pay for having been yourself

       such a girl

Fuels Shakespearian

     Old style shrink

That every movement naturally produces

         noise

    which attracts, pursues, tears to pieces,

            utensil and wing,

      the thing

      til she lives

Like a mirror irritation

      the fabric of reality is stretched

to the breaking point or point,

     the orgy of patternless vitality

     "This isn't *me*, Mommy!"

         — all night —

pinpoints your arc light

     you're a global stretch from

her, who you're now

    and the breaking point

      is lack of stretchability
      you're compacted utility
      fabric sewn up into globe
       a galaxy
      consents to be an ear-
      lobe out of rumored curiosity
      and the echelon day of the time it is

        when you conceived singsong

Everything must have been precariously certain self the socks the
stars the spring of the bedsprings unmatching

                                        the making then the
taking of
            off-balance,
                        you tripped
                                    drunkening
over
        your hopefully whorish heels

                        and now you're still lying here, comfortably

                        only the stars could be reeling
                        only the flowers, crocus
                                            velvet-brooded
                        could be unreal

                                        they're not drinking this
dark ale are they?
                    to beat the devil
                                    as does my hysteria
urgency of base metal
                        is preferable to
                        your gold standard encomiast
                        of God the Cork

"To flesh is to incite
                by taste of blood"
                                    You seemed
calm and fresh
                    and that seemed blood so I was fleshed
and thought so to be carnal
                        paper flaunt
but I had to flesh and, flesh, be fleshed and flesh again
raised to morbid heat
                    You, you kind of anagrammatic puzzle
                                        enter into this name
with my offenses committed of hurts and thoughts
                    which some call quibbles and some, redolent
of a fiscal though fabulous opera

My God
is that I've
stolen already
breast and pit
from and for it

everything that's "out

of equilibrium, except
all of it" like my

growing
belly with my knees

I live dangerously another
                              What almost bothers me
is this shit I keep coddling on paper like loving
                                        "an ugh to love" that love
I bulge, curl up, pucker with

+ + +

I keep coming at the point I'm locating —

                                        no carved statement
moulded conventional rose on the wall
                                        with its interior incredulity
O rose-like cluster course,
                        state of organs which marks
the resemblant rose,
                        it is perfect to trust
him, to drop from your stem
                        comb form
                                        in names of salts strewn

with roses and health of wine sky light,
                                        place-name most beautiful
in here —
                I'm mashed on you.   You're my diaphanous, my
slip . . .
            you set of rays meeting at my point
                                        that's constantly natal

JANUARY

Mommy what's this fork doing?
                            What?
It's being Donald Duck.

What could I eat this?
                            Eat what?
This cookie.
                What do you mean?
What could I eat it?

Does he bite people? That fish is dead. That fish got
dead today. That fish gets dead today, right?

            These are my silver mittens Mommy
            No, it's gold, they're gold mittens

            On myself
            I put my black
            hat
            and my mit-

tens,
myself.

Edmund. Edmund. Edmund. Maaaah. Lodle lodle lodle

Daddy, the doctor did put a wart on you,

                                                                right?

I touch the purple petals
She says Hey!

          The flower says, we are purple,
together
     they touch purple it keeps purple
     purple means us, here.
     The air moved a person, I like people
     because they're as serious
     as I am. Being purple is very serious.
     It's dense and still.
     It's a matter of fact
     but light seems it.
     I seem light
     makes me feel purple.
     A petal is crumpling I've done
     before
               I sleep in the bulb.

          Being purple is long.

Crumpling is not as serious
as being purple

          (I may disagree)

I'm not not serious not smiling.
I'm smiling
as crumpling
only a little now.
I'm mostly staying serious purple now.

Do you remember when you were like Edmund?
                                    Yeah.
What did you do?
                crawled with him.
Do you remember last year?
                        Yeah, Mommy what did you
do when you be Anselm?

The jacket is furniture.
I have to fix, Mommy.
I have to fix all the tools.
I'm in the snow and my feet go in the footprints.

I'll look up "love" in the dictionary. They're beautiful.
Bodily they're incomprehensible. I can't tell if they're
me or not. They think I'm their facility. We're all about
as comprehensible as the crocuses. In myself I'm like a
color except not in the sense of a particular one. That's
impossible. That's under what I keep trying out. With
which I can practically pass for an adult to myself. Some
of it is pretty and useful, like when I say to them

"Now will I take you for a walk in the snow to the store"
and prettily and usefully we go. Mommy, the lovely
creature. You should have seen how I looked last night,
Bob Dylan Bob Creeley Bob Rosenthal Bob on Sesame Street.
Oh I can't think of any other Bobs right now. Garbage.
It perks. Thy tiger, thy night are magnificent,

it's ten below zero deep deep down deep in my abdomen
It pulls me up and leads me about the house. It's got the
sun in the morning and the moon at night. It does
anything in the world of particulars without wanting.
The anyone careless love sees that everything goes, minds.
The melody was upsidedown, now the melody turns over.
One note: my feet go.

30 years old married 4 years 2 children
is the same little girl in the yard
until dusk and into night
in air with myself, others
has a mother and father
                          nature (courage)
smiles frankly at the camera don't
blot your anonymity your littleness
child you are is the source of all
honestly bliss at dusk in Chicago
is face you've ever been
                          and almost before
dusky the child air you are
handsome you're head-to-toe

It's too early. It's too dark. If I can't watch TV I'll
turn on the light and look at the stars.

I see 2 full moons.

I walk.
I am big.
I can say
what they
say. It's
fun to
sound. I
walk. I am
big. I finally
get the blue
and red container
of . . .
sneezes!

the trees have no leaves they lean
like her over the snow and green
wire fence of the school

                the sky
is white low low low

                Greggy Ruthy

and Jill are there

Daddy tomorrow we'll have donuts and chocolate soda
and my birthday party and eat snow and throw snow and
make snowmen.

He'll take off your wart tomorrow and you won't be sick.

My armpits smell like chicken soup. But really I hate them
because of their tacky and unchanging book collection. My
head weighs too much on the pillow. I have to sweat. I'm
crying free water don't worry. Under your tongue looks like
pussy. You seem to bloom. The colors are brighter but I
think I'm deaf.
                  I'm remembering all my dogs.
One was taken away because he howled too much and my
parents said he wanted to fight in World War II and so joined
the army. All things considered there's nothing to say for
Chicago. I dreamed you led an army of empty pieplates
against another one. I dreamed you had a baby. I despise
someone. I have to sweat. I need you to stop this train.

I didn't lose any weight today
I had clean hair but I drove
Ted nuts and spanked Anselm on
the arm and wouldn't converse
with him about the letter C. And
didn't take Edmund out or change
the way the house smells or not
drink and take a pill and had to watch
John Adams on TV
                and fantasized
about powers of ESP when on LSD—

there is no room for fantasy in
the head except as she speaks.
The Holy Ghost is the definitive
renegade like in the white falling-out
chair stuffing, 2 chairs
                              asking me if
I liked my life. I thought she
meant my life and said
                              how could
you dislike being a poet? and having
children is only human
                              but
she meant my chairs. The
trouble is the children distribute
the stuffing to the wind. It's
soft and pliant and they can do it
intimately together.
There are 4 green sunbursts on the
curtain. Oh it is a cold night but
the jade plant will handle it.

Came in from the snow and melted on
                the floor. There's
Glistening where Jill and Ruthy's feet
Sat Ruthy with braids and colored
Yarn in her hair, a girl
Beauty cars go by to hitch
Away on
                Is it their rumble
That comforts? Or this room full
Of everyone who's sat making
Stuffing appear from the
Chairs, and flowers too last years

They just want to do their yoga too. I guess so. I try
to call up Casey Gold. Some money comes by anyway; the
day brightens, Casey Gold.

I don't appreciate the simple
war of nerves
                my courtesy
rewarded with a goring
                        is it boring
the toro rhymes, what else do
children have to think about?
well if the cape is all wet it won't
blow in the wind
            but I have to check
something
            You're still in no condition
to fight a bull
            But he found his own . . .
What a glistening golden
baby!
            Enough to make one woozy. Matador,
I am with the wind and unwinding
am wonderfully useless to you.

from WALTZING MATILDA

                                for Jennifer Dunbar

12/2/80

I am an exhausted not-that-chrysanthemum Oh brother
Nothing's funny nothing's pretty, all the jokes
& gems collided at Gut Corner & then they did that

you know rolled over & over down the hill to the bottom of
        the tin-can gulley
And then there's me you know I that am like a stomach sick of.
I miss Barbara Nichols & the death of Apollinaire.
And can't live up to the presence of a flower or of
Anything else. Her dress. It was stunning. Very
Low-cut around the tits & black velvet she was
The cut flower for sure. He said her tongue felt like
A live animal. A lot of up to her panties & then I
Put that magazine down & take your temperature. 101.
Get under the covers honey. Okay? 'kay.
Real-life juxtapositions are the most tasteless. 'Cuz
Pretty soon I'm gonna take your temperature again & then
Back at the text she was naked. She was naked & in her hair,
Positioned enticingly on the table amongst his pile of
Law reports. I'm sick of this, this dum-dum logistics of it
all. Mom I don't think I'll throw up a, if I make a
peanut-butter-&-jelly sandwich I won't throw it up
this time. I guess it's really raining. Didn't you
Hear the thunder before? It was thunder in the kitchen.
How do you free? Why didn't they have a democracy
On Prospero's island? Something smells funny it may be
My socks or a fragrant flower. It's my socks they smell like
A rained-on tree that smells like feet. I don't re-
member what it's like to be a tree, but there's some
        people seem to.
She was naked but she got up off the law reports
she said she was absolutely ripped on an old-fashioned
hallucinogen, she said all that paper recalled to her
her tree self but that was either after or before her feat of
radiant concentration which changed all the law-report words
to their tree-language equivalents so when he looked at the pages
he saw in brownish yellowish reddish green such verses as

        Bark must not
        do potato, tomato.

        A leaf is local
        only while falling.

"What? like a gavotte?"
the common evergreen rustle:
hours & regulations & so on . . .

But what about my throbbing member? he said & began to
chase her round the table & when he almost caught her by the
        before he even
felt it her pubic hair was become soft moss on bark. Mom
        why don't
people read in the dark? They can't see the words in the
dark. I can. Please go to sleep now. Please, honey.

THE WORLD'S 21 GREATEST ANIMALS: A PLAY

Announcer: Ladies & Gentlemen, we would like to present the world's 21 Greatest
Animals!

(The animals enter one by one. The name of each is announced as the animal bows
briefly, then exits.)

Announcer:

1. Rat
2. Scorpion
3. Tiger
4. Frog
5. Cockroach
6. Hamster
7. Chihuahua
8. Prairie dog
9. Muskrat
10. Okapi

11. Chuckawalla

12. Snake

13. Opossum

14. Eagle

15. Phoenix

16. Whale

17. Hippopotamus

18. Baboon

19. Black Sea Bass

20. Crab

21. Mongoose

THE END

2/84

(With assistance from A. Berrigan, E. Berrigan, & E. Nauen)

THE HOWLING SAINT T-SHIRT

Children don't come from deep inside one
they were always outside and, I dream,
wear their own saint T-shirts as I do
mine's saint image is faceless, howling.
They have smiling bodies friendly asses
"Give you Everything the first seven years," Ted says
they bear no relation to your self,
not a haunt that shakes loose not seed pod
not a part of the body not you; it's harrowing
to stop being the child yourself but
"child" is not real spiritually as classification
as I change with experience lose confidence and truth
and must find out everything from them now.

As I once was they're true in their separate houses:
rhythm of the ribs, iris eyes, and patter
lead me back from depression in Hades. First I'm
fearful of what's called motherhood—
I call it unpaid work like poetry—but a family
is not a fate, it's that we're nakedly related
our heirlooms are thought to be
doomed psyches that's just one myth
a psyche's not real a soul is,
a grave child that peers from his first house.
My kids are like me superficially so I watch them
or, writing, ignore them, until they say something I like
I need their words for my poems, to speak for a
house we make together that's fragile and strong
shaky in an American wind contrary to poetry.
And I get scared and children's bodies
are often feverish, those whom
you love more than yourself (though not more than
poetry) so what can you do, send them to school and hope
they survive the violence of the human mind bent
on impressing itself into them. Flow of atoms of
sorrow and ecstasy, they were never my own body
I was the case for more people arriving why not.
My saint's T-shirt, she's howling but
not against natural exigency, I'm poet and not much else
I ripped out a normal face
and gave my kids the archaic voice of poetry.

BERNADETTE MAYER

"I had three children, mostly at home, in the 70s, for a total of $800. They were all very nice, I liked being with them, they also made it unnecessary for me to talk. Their father would get up with them in the morning and I would write at night. We had to go on welfare—it was well worth it. I had no ambitions, as I still don't, except to write good poetry."

from MIDWINTER DAY

Sophia likes a cup of coffee to be in the picture too, she will climb the old trunk to the cold window without you in the room and then fall off while Marie is pretending to be me, you are wondering what it is you're doing.

I pick her up, you are pouring oatmeal into the measuring cup, there's a chipmunk singing in time to his tail in the honey locust tree where the cat was treed and a black bear in Windsor ran into the car of a man going west on Route 9.

On eggs or ordinary toothpaste, fantastic pigeons who always live above us murmuring fly, it looks like right at us, but hit the roof to rest where there's a space between the bricks before they fly out again, one is all white. That cat and a skunk are always in the yard.

Black tin cup made out of town of mountains of sky, the so-called true horizon parallel to the sensible, once I used to keep a flying squirrel as a kind of pet, the squirrel left the house in spring, the boundary of your favorite cup. There's jelly on *Borrowed Feathers*.

I say that chipmunk who can speak is learning to speak as you say you want to read a book which means look at it so you demand of me, say it. Delicate tantrums in tints and shades of the same corner you like an aversion to memory's rudeness in the form of what we call voices. You are being too loud.

If everything could happen at once even as merely as only two babies crying and requiring everything but nothing at one time, the desire to control something as small as any destiny begins to seem like just will. Or what world doesn't have religion to pass us off as ruling if not by law then in the morning at least for a while we're only thinking of ourselves.

My absorption in your clothes is only sensible, why bother to toast the bread but I'm willing, it's to make the bread warm, here's a royal blue shirt and red pants put into the words of your eyes not as dark as mine but darker than his whose eyes are impatient for a moment to see more than that you still need so much to be done in detail for you we can never seem to get out of the house.

Winter flies are dying by the windows, we are never without at least one as if we still know nothing just passing the time because we can't seem to finish, they repeat after me a mood like you shout moon or mom as loud as you can, it's all the same, you and I are like two transparent wings.

The person and the people are these mouth-size toys, broken Mother Goose Jack-in-the-box with Old King Cole on it clutters the hall with proper nouns like Donald Duck orange juice and Mickey Mouse Halloween masks, a real cow that milks, you say no look and oh first though other noises came once before to be better as sounds than nouns as memory or more than one of those like these clutters which are made of all this in all the rooms today which will be cleared and then will have been a mess like a person I'm fond of who's changed, not like a diaper.

Look at this, see, you do, which one are you. The book is said to be a duck. The color wheel reflecting you hiding, the bus, empty green swing for people, smiling tiger nothingness puzzle, empty-eyed monkey mask right there, battered stolen musical egg, look, bright old playgroup radio playing raindrops and so on, there's something about a thermometer you wouldn't understand yet, silly identical grounded queen bees, you put things into things now, you empty cups and trucks on your own articulating oh and no the same, grabbing for the fifteenth-century Dutch woman who looks chiding, that's why I put her up, that polar bear won't go into that nesting cup.

The potato masher in Marie's bed's as good to eat as prone Cadillacs I might want to give friends if I could if they were given to that, you're conversing, sudden kisses make you try to bounce without getting hurt by it but then hurt anyway by my observation come as a distraction you fall and get tired and since I'm anxious to be done I entertain the theory you've already forgotten for putting more of this into that and begin to take the first steps.

Divided in the light a length of day is measured more in numberless meals. Each of two children needs to be offered two breakfasts but the tone of this tradition seems to mean today one of you needs more to eat nothing, she just isn't hungry, at least not yet, grandmothers and books will say they have days like that, other mothers also do not wittingly give salt, how many eggs could be bad for you if you're only one, or three like a bad one not that anyone should use the word bad right away, you say do you think she hates her bib or is she finished, some foods are tokens like the cold round cereals once in the bowl, at least she's stopped standing up, now tell her again to please sit down, the trees are getting cold, you wear a band of red velvet before the old kind of milk standing sentry in between two daughters, did you feed the fish.

Hold still the short light is old already, everything for you is momentary, you may even whistle for a week or so, we've rearranged the day again into another formal order, I'm hungry at the wrong times like you but I can't remember to stop to eat because you like the light are almost done, formidable ordinary order to present the day with at least a little concentration on fierce love working like slowly building a house only adding to it in the seasons when there's extra time, more for that than this continuous keeping us warm which the finished house will eventually do if only we had time to raise the roof.

I did put the rest of the clothes away though I did and didn't want to in straight regular rows in an arrangement of peace among a series of thoughts of the chaotic rank and still position of ourselves and where we fit in the system of the news of the day, a portion of which was submitted to the typesetters last night while we were sleeping and planned and laid out on the big pages in order of importance which begins in the upper right hand corner where the eye goes first, the rest is editorials and speculation, some sensation but no color to hide or uncover feelings like the mountains and so on better reflect. Old Harry is another name for Satan.

From the bedroom, curtains blue as ink I stare at, red Godard floor white walls all crayoned, from the bed raised on cinder blocks at Dr. Incao's midwife's request so Sophia could be born, fake Indian cover Ray gave us for Marie American Indian and Ray's old real wool blanket and all our sheets her gifts, Lewis' Aunt Fanny's crocheted afghan and Tom's old sleeping bag, the mimeograph machine and its cover, diaper rash ointment, from the walls a butterfly kite, a leaf on a ribbon from nursery school, mushrooms by Joe, an iris and a gladiola by Rosemary, the gladiola painted here, the stuck clock, the window faces south, laundry on it, closet doors hung with jackets, shawls, scarves and Marie's dress, closet floor boots shoes boxes bags baby carriers and my broken inherited chair, that's the airport, closet of stuff, carpet sweeper, another broken chair, from there I go to the kitchen sink you can sit on at the imagined forest window, two coleus plants too cold today, now a Wandering Jew, two related spider plants one is hanging, stones dead branches and collected pine cones, an old ghost and a Boston fern on the spooky refrigerator in which is the food, drawings of attempted faces by Marie that look like Cy Twombly, the dumb electric stove, George's red shirt calendar, soon it'll be over, the Lenox Savings Bank historical calendar, Pilgrims landed yesterday, winter begins today, shortest day of the year, Lewis and Harris with Marie in a Bronx corridor, little light, the African woman backpacking a baby, she's talking to a totem figure, a street scene by Raphael and a German altarpiece Rosemary sent, a crude drawing of a nude woman by Paul, a poster of a panda on the door to the former pantry now a house for two heaters one for air and one for water and the vents ducts and pipes for each, old flowerpots, the hall to the door to the hall, full of boxes of Angel Hair books, the broken bassinet now a toybox with turtles and cups in it, a small space full of brown paper bags and cardboard six-pack wrappers, broom, dishes and pots, fruit on the hood of the stove, bottles and jars, teas and books, medicines foods and detergents, binoculars, the dishwasher, vinegar, garbage, Lewis' mother's old Scotch kooler, spices, another of George's plaid shirts, coats on hooks, a red tray; to the deadpan bathroom, a woman by Matisse in yellow and blue and an ordinary mercator projection of the world, potty chair, diaper pail for cloth diapers, plastic bag of used plastic diapers, toilet sink tub, bath toys an alligator that swims mechanically and a shark with teeth that is a mitt and a sponge, hideous old curling rug lying in the tub after yesterday's flood, hooks on the back of the door, layers of clothing hanging on them, a mirror, ointments, and pills, razors poisons and soaps, shower curtains; to the main room the living room, two leaping goldfish, cornflower plant, jade tree, Wandering Jew not doing too well, another spider offshoot, purple weed I don't know the name of accidentally growing in a pot of sedum, Christmas tree fern with a sense of humor, whiskey, the main collapsing table covered with things, rocking chair, small wearing rug on the golden wood floor, two couches with things on them, public school chairs with arms for principals at table, shelves of books and books in boxes, boxes of paper and stencils, two ring binders of photos since Worthington, my desk I steer and things, a standing lamp Nancy got us, a jacket by Joe and a blue shirt by George, a flower by Rosemary I don't remember the name of, a water color of a drapery by Rosemary done in Worthington, a drawing of Ted by Joe, a photo of Lewis by Gerard, pictures of the window out Main Street in different seasons, Main Street and Cliffwood Street, Our Lady of Perpetual Help-butterfly collage by Joe, a slinky male figure by Joe, a watch by George, some Kirschwasser, dead files and dead flies, magazines and library books, toys and balls, a stereo, four windows and the more frequent door.

An idea I have is to spend days walking nights writing never eating, sleep only when it rains and have an occasional beer.

Instead of dressing in a striped green suit you put a sheet between your legs and drape yourself upside down over the side of the bed becoming hysterical and then I know I can't rush you but when I see you can't sustain it I change the subject to something I know you want to know about and get the clothes on while you're still thinking but it only half works. Now two are done.

Below us the ardent hairdressers are beginning to welcome customers like spoiled children by pretending to be decadently faggy to please though they are not but they do please I guess they must their business thrives which one of the other mothers from nursery school said to me was what we all wanted after all though it seems cynical for me to say so it's the hairdressers who act like dogs from the Greek root *kynos.*

Next door the real gay men have already left for work in different local restaurants as waiters and chefs but one of them tired of his lover and recently moved out, then they put a wrought iron grilled on their apartment door which you can see through unless they choose to close the little hatch behind it from the Anglo-Saxon, *hagan.*

Downstairs the behaviorist child psychologist may be waiting for patients he'll give candy to if they'll agree to have half as many tantrums as without the candy and next to him the old-fashioned eagle-scout-type young man-woman bakes some kind of mail-order pies for a living with different roommates, you can smell the smell of the pies mixing with the chemisty-class rotten-egg smell from the hairdressers' permanent waves, it's a three-story turn-of-the-century red brick apartment house where rich men's coachmen used to live with their families in the thirties in a small egocentric town.

Your drawings look more like faces with three eyes now no mouths yet and occasionally an airplane or a low flower or the moon going from banana to carrot to orange every day and every month, red green and blue like t.v. or what you seem to be wearing.

Where's the chair it's in the pail put the person in it, is it the teacher's chair, I used to go to New York yesterday and have my hair shampooed, maybe it's a sparrow maybe it's just a bird maybe you could get me a big watch when Peggy comes look at that moon it's the middle of the night again no it's not.

What an associative way to live this is, dreams of hearts beating like sudden mountain peaks I can see in my chest like other breasts then in one vertiginous moment I can forget all but the reunion and your original face, two shirts each under overalls over tights under shoes then one sweater, outer suits with legs or leggings, mittens attached, hats and overshoes. Everybody wanting something or nothing to be done to them, then one of the shoes falls off again.

I have an image of a beautiful man or woman who walks in the door like Christ and earnestly spends some time with us like the UPS man does.
If only people would read more books but the world could still come to an end by colliding with bouncing babies banging spoons on cups that fly off the table, you can't pick up something you see on a page, it's too windy, you now speak something like Japanese, we found all the people last night and this morning they are spinning or poised.

I'm not playing. I'm cleaning though I'm crawling around. Are these dishes clean or dirty. I'm afraid not. Shit. The trees lose their leaves so you can see through them. A man and a dog in a yard. A person who doesn't have friends must explain himself to strangers. Sometimes your mother does on the phone, which religion is it that doesn't deny the lost self. Old morning prayers said in the cold church. Dear mother dear mother.

So for a second there's a chill in the season's gray air like warm structure and psychology, tickle, tickle, I put the dozer, what do you call a person looking for water, on top of the Greyhound bus, dowser, and push to distract you from eating a person like I did. I'm glad I don't have only one eye. He's the kind of guy who shouldn't work in a window, I mean the printer.

I learn from the rigorous laughing of love to be more quiet in the morning especially if the dismal streets unearth a hideous memory of death, I've gotten so used to it I'm sorry I said that.

If we're all wrong about everything, the life so short and the craft so long to learn, the assay so hard, so sharp the conquering, the dreadful joy that passes so quick and then being left alone again, what I mean is love astonishes my feeling with its wonderful working so ardently so painfully that when I'm thinking about such certainty I don't know like the earth if I'm floating or sinking.

I don't know why we sleep or wake or why one dreams a fast bombastic image and the other memory's faintest trace which anyway haunts the day, if you look hard through the flawed window glass you can begin to see the lightest rain or snow but it's not there, now I can see it on the books and on the walls, it's in my eyes, I shouldn't even mention it, yet do you see it.

The paintings are finished so fast they are nice, what makes you know one is done. I can't see my eyes but I can see yours painted blue this year and I am in them. The leaping frog broke, it's broken.

Am I so modest as this time of day assumes I've learned, have I lost my tough or punk part among these kids who write on lines between the windows where I imitate them after they cover the walls with notes on making a face generous or a house a cave. Is all the mornings' cold-blooded conflict appointed to visions out the willful window, what are poetry's themes, grotesque little figures released by a spring from a box when the lid is lifted by another, I jump up to rescue an old reputation for immoral misfortune as one who does low dishonest work for another who suffers, my brother who pays me in sarcastic dogs for my writing, a swindle, I eat the leavings like the jackal after the lion is done, I know nothing practically like the wolf or a tasteless seed nonetheless edible, a perjured witness, straw man, an imposter, a jackstraw in a jumbled heap of pick-up sticks in a game, the peaceful steps from earth to heaven, monkey to exaltation, Jacob's ladder just a simple blue and white flower, my father, have I left anything out, why have I been forsaken for this joy.

Now we're almost ready, pity the race with the day if there's a reason to be sad or thinking ahead of everything so as we're leaving the house we must also be dying but you aren't, with my gloves on I gulp what you left in your cup just in case something small would be all the difference, still carrying you as a talisman, I'm dying to get to the post office.

TWO DAYS AFTER JOANNA HAD TWO STITCHES

YOU SEE I'VE BEEN practicing this deception on you, I never told you I'm to have the baby at home with only a midwife in attendance. We had thought to save you from worrying about everything and from not understanding—you and your daughter seem to live in such a world of fear about births and babies, and with all your trust in doctors and pills you find my ways of doing things alien and sometimes even repulsive, my desire to nurse the babies, my refusal to eat candy. I'm sorry. I saw the midwife today and she asked me to answer her telephone while she was checking my blood, urine, blood pressure, loss of perhaps the perfect mother I keep yearning for these last few weeks of this. I went to the midwife's boyfriend's office to leave a sterile catch, a pure drop, of urine for them just in case there was some infection. He's a man of rugged good looks she calls "my man." She fixed a hamburger for her son and started a fire, she had said to someone chatting on the phone. Where is the baby, where is the baby hat. I feel so mountainous in my big grey coat like a project I feel embarrassed on the streets. No deeper feelings, I might say to you, will emerge from that if you won't let them. You were in a bad mood—is it because we're so far away, because you may not get to see the baby when it's born right away, because you are so little involved in this? Whenever you phone an the phone rings three or four times and I answer it, you always say oh I'm sorry did I wake you up, but you never have. Did you laugh when Lewis told you the story of buying the forty postcards and having the woman in the 5&10 ring up 10¢ forty times? You wouldn't believe how cold it is in here, I'm wearing two shirts under a dress, a wool shirt and sweater over that, tights and a pair of wool socks and a hat, you would think we're crazy for keeping it so cold but if you visit us after the baby's born you'll never know because it'll have to be warm here then. I've got to call up the fuel people and have them bring extra oil for then, we'll be using it up fast. It'll be fun to be indoors and taken care of during what I think of as the rest of the winter. I can pretend I'm a girl and you are taking care of me, I'm lying on the couch nicely feverish and you are bringing me jello and junket, ginger ale and orange juice with sugar and ice, you are making me feel quite high. It's funny but whenever I write things like that down I never fail to think, this is not the work of a poet to write details of memory and desire, this view of things is nothing, you are forgetting where you are. I throw the beer bottle into the trash, it bangs against another one, you would be alarmed at my nihilist behavior. Once when I was having the baby I had when I was eighteen, another thing I'm afraid I never told you, the doctor said how come you are reading comic books, you used to read such high-toned things, poetry and stuff. Some nihilist had brought me a nihilistic comic and I read it and then I wrote a mixed-up poem about the paregoric of the hospital and all the ugly and confusing shit that was making my dreams then combine with the way the hospital people were behaving. A car's come up and now left, left Suzanne back here I suppose but where is she, she's not in the door yet, she's fasting today and she is hungry. Maybe you'd be happy to know Lewis and I ate Big Mac's today in Concord, we suffered in concord, french fries and a coke. There's no sense belaboring our differences, it would be nice if beyond them were nothing but a field of ice passionately melted by irate and tender words and embraces and we could be one as I was with the woman from whose body I came one time. I don't think my parents were anti-Semitic but they always said things about how Jewish people were too intelligent to compete with and perhaps they showed their prejudice by saying Jews were competitive. But I can't remember what they said. They wouldn't let me play with Jewish children but they wouldn't let me play with Protestant ones either. Really I have to drag this chair I'm sitting on clear across the room from the kitchen where we need it for meals, and it is so heavy, heavy as a classroom chair, heavy as a monk or abbess, this chair is my monk and there is no harm in sitting in it though I often equate working and writing with harm and when I don't work I feel maybe I've done myself some good, poetry like the danger of splinters in the foot. While I was talking to you I saw the sliver moon setting in the west, now I run over to see if it's still there but it's gone, I really can't run, I can sort of leap slowly but it's not much faster than walking fast. Once you said all we cared about was poetry but now it's not poetry to tell you that I never much cared for sitting in chairs, and is it like emotion to say that? You are so much like a girl and the two of you like girl and boy, so quiet and playing at keeping house with duty and so obedient you are, I often wonder where is the wisdom in your reticence and then I answer, and you would say same, in your surviving and simply in your presence and your slowly, almost methodically doing things and keeping track of things, in your admitting you are happy though you'd never use that word, but denying forever you are satisfied, and in your loyalty to each other. Yet you and I never get anywhere and I am still to you the outsider. Well maybe if we move back to New York that will be less so, but secretly maybe more so because then too much of everything will be too different. Ah I wish I could tell you exactly how I feel, so full of remorse and fear, so little the strong and willing person I have to be for you, so little the person who normally exhausts you and speaks a little well, as if it was inherited. I'm sitting here secretly smoking and fearing the pains of childbirth and thinking of you.

MARIE MAKES FUN OF ME AT THE SHORE

for Bill Corbett

Marie says
look tiny red spiders
are walking
across the pools
& just as I am writing down
tiny red
spiders are
walking across the pools
She says Mom I can just see it

in your poem it'll say
tiny red spiders are walking
across the pools

CHOCOLATE SONNET

when my children were growing up
we never had any candy at home but
when we went to poetry readings
i always brought a chocolate bar
to make the poetry palatable or
more interesting or so they'd
be relatively quiet, it only backfired
if the reading lasted too long, then
there was hell to pay but i deserved it
didnt i?
                  after a while if i knew
the reading'd be long i'd bring two
so i began to think of long readings
as two-chocolate-bar readings, eventually
i'd bring two just in case, sometimes saving one
for the next occasion
                          poetry is as good as chocolate
                          chocolate is as good as poetry is

MAXINE CHERNOFF

"I was born in Chicago in 1952 and have three children, Koren, aged 30, and twins Julian and Philip, aged 21. I also have a 6-month-old granson, Dorian Michael. I have been a mother almost as long as I have been a writer.

"I am the author of six books of fiction and eight books of poems. I am chair of Creative Writing at SFSU and edit *New American Writing* with Paul Hoover. Our co-translation of the selected poems of Holderlin will be published by Omnidawn in 2008."

A BIRTH

> "We must seek bodies for our children."—Osage Indian chant

I can't remember the birth. Cold white rooms, cleanliness the color of nothing. Sometimes a woman dreams that she's given birth to a litter of piglets attached to her breasts like pink balloons. When I look in the crib, there is no baby. When I look on the stove, there is a pot of soup which was not there before. Sometimes there is a mix-up at the hospital. A patient orders French onion soup and receives cream of shrimp. Sometimes there is a mix-up; a woman receives a child who grows up hating her. One night at a theater, quite by surprise, a persons steps out of the screen and sits down beside her. That is her child, she knows. "The soup is ready," my husband repeats. Silently we sit down side by side. Silently we share one bowl and then another.

SOTTO VOCE

Although she's only four, my daughter knows Spanish. Say Blanco, she demands, say Negro. Words are the finest toys, she tells me with eyes that are arrows. My husband speaks with the virtuosity of a drummer: suspiration, humidor, revivify. Beautiful words float upwards like jets sewing clouds. If my cat could only speak, it would be in shrill, nasal French I wouldn't understand. Languages wash over me, scratched on cold telephone booths, tapped on windowpanes. I am sorry to admit that I am inventing yet another, in the dark, furtively as one imagines an obscene old kiss. Just as I am thinking about it, my daughter shouts, Verde, Verde. She thinks so much depends on it—palm trees, parsley, dollar bills—that I can't disappoint her. Foolish girl, I think, locking up my new language. Then Verde dissolves, naked and bloodless into the busy air.

IDENTITY PRINCIPLE

Triplets are so embarrassing, too much soup in the soup of life. Who needs an alphabet with three O's, a tangled birth, a troika of woes? Picture the mother swelled as a cloud, the gallop of three heartbeats like a posse through her. Or twins, those clever monkeys, allowed to eat at table. Identical birthmarks, matching hairnets, the sound and the echo. And old age: one twin wheels the other before him, meeting himself after the stroke. So you decide even among brothers and sisters raucous as wedding guests, to be an only child. The stance you take in making love, in walking crookedly, in robbing the sperm bank. Until you have a child and people say, "She looks just like you." In her face you see the same wish to be an island so distant she'll never see another pleasure boat.

from HAVE YOU A DAUGHTER?

1.

to get cold feet

to make no headway

to be on tenderhooks

(my eyes are wide)

to eat nettles

stinging nettles

to embroider flowers

to take one's heart out

9.

radiant

and strange

an element of reason

(no harm intended)

for her subjectivity

to calculate a reason

(winter death / spring resurrection)

a world

like an orchid

or lily

no harm in a vase

the stinging nettles

10.

your poor and erring breast

since I cannot remember

all the death's

(the devil's in the details)

and you

made to want

to scarify

to mark
                    as if to heal

the beauty before us

arriving as it did

11.

I have no daughter

he said in the play

yet if she existed

he wouldn't deny

the hyperbole

or song

CAROLYN FORCHÉ

is the author of four books of poetry as well as being a translator and editor. She has received three fellowships from the National Endowment for the Arts, a John Simon Guggenheim Fellowship, a Lannan Foundation Fellowship, and in 1998, was given the Edita and Ira Morris Hiroshima Foundation Award for Peace and Culture in Stockholm for her work on behalf of human rights and the preservation of memory and culture. In 2004 she became a trustee of the Griffin Trust for Excellence in Poetry, Canada's premier poetry award. She teaches at Skidmore College, and lives in Maryland with her husband, photographer Harry Mattison, and their son, Sean-Christophe.

from THE ANGEL OF HISTORY

———————————

There are times when the child seems delicate, as if he had not yet crossed into the
    world.
When French was the secret music of the street, the café, the train, my own
           receded and became intimacy and sleep.
In the world it was the language of propaganda, the agreed-upon lie, and it bound
    me to
           itself, demanding of my life an explanation.
When my son was born I became mortal.

Our days at Cape Enrage, a bleached shack of rented rooms and white air. April.
At the low tide acres of light, boats abandoned by water.
While sleeping, the child vanishes from his life.

Years later, on the boat from Beirut, or before the boat, an hour before, helicopters
    lifting
           a white veil of sea.
A woman broken into many women.

These boats, forgotten, have no keels. So it is safe for them, and the emptiness
    beneath them safe.
April was here briefly. The breakwater visible, the lighthouse, but no horizon.
The music resembled April, the gulls, April, but you weren't walking toward this
    house.
If the child knew words, if it weren't necessary for him to question me with his
    hands—

To have known returning would be like this,
       that the sea light of April had been your vigilance.

In the night-vaulted corridors of the Hôtel-Dieu, a sleepless woman pushes her
    stretcher
       along the corridors of the past. *Bonjour, madame. Je m'appelle Ellie.*

There were trains, and beneath them, laddered fields.

Autumns the fields were deliberately burned by a fire so harmless children ran
    through it
       making up a sort of game.
Women beat the flames with brooms and blankets, so the fires were said to be
    under control.

As for the children, they were forbidden to ask about the years before they were
    born.
Yet they burned the fields, yet everything was said to be *under control*
       with the single phrase *death traffic.*

This is Izieu during the war, Izieu and the neighboring village of Bregnier-Cordon.
This is a farmhouse in Izieu.
Itself a quiet place of stone houses over the Rhone, where between Aprils,
    forty-four children were
       hidden successfully for a year in view of the mountains.
Until the fields were black and snow fell all night over the little plaque which does
    not mention
       that they were Jewish children hidden April to April in Izieu near Bregnier-
Cordon.

Comment me vint l'écriture? Comme un duvet d'oiseau sur ma vitre, en hiver.
In every window a blank photograph of their internment.

Within the house, the silence of God. Forty-four bedrolls, forty-four metal cups.
And the silence of God is God.

In Pithiviers and Beaune-la-Rolande, in Les Milles, Les Tourelles, Moussac and
   Aubagne,
         the silence of God is God.

The children were taken to Poland.
The children were taken to Auschwitz in Poland
         singing *Vous n'aurez pas L'Alsace et la Lorraine.*
In a farmhouse still standing in Izieu, *le silence de Dieu est Dieu.*

We lived in Ste. Monique ward over the main corridor, Ellie and myself, in the
Hôtel-Dieu on the Place du Parvis Notre Dame.
Below us jonquils opened.
Ellie was afflicted with scales again, tiny Ellie, at the edge of her bed, peeling her
   skin
         from her arm as if it were an opera glove,
and weeping *cachée, cachée, cachée* all during the war.

Barn to barn in the haylight, field to cellar. Winter took one of her sons, and her
   own
         attempt to silence him, the other.

Le Dieu? Le Dieu est un feu.   A psychopath.   Le Dieu est feu.

It isn't normal for a mother to outlive her children.
It isn't normal that my sons should be dead.

Paris! Oh, how I loathe this city because of its past.

Then you wish to leave Paris?

Mais oui. I wish to leave life, my dear.
My parent? Deported. My aunt and uncles? Deported. My friends? All of them
   deportees.

I don't know what became of a single one. How they came to the end.
My papers said I was Polish. When the money ran out, we ran. When the Nazis came,
*   we ran. Cachée, cachée, cachée!*

The tubercular man offers his cigarette and the snow falls, patiently, across the
    spring flowers.
My life, triste. Do you understand? This place. No good! France. No good! Germany.
*   No good! Ni l'Union soviétique. Fascists! It is no good.*
Then why not leave Paris?

I am Jewish. Do you understand? Alone in a small room on the third floor, always
*   alone.*
To remain sane, I sing librettos to myself, and German lullabies, can you imagine?

> *Mein Flügle ist zum Schwung bereit*
> *ich kehrte gern zurück,*
> *denn bleib ich auch lebendige Zeit*
> *ich hätte weing Glück*

My husband was a soldier against the Nazis. Résistance. Agir. He wasn't killed in
*   the war.*
He even returned to me. It w as after the war he died. He died of cholera.
*   And the world is worse now than it was then.*

Worse?
Mais oui!

Then my husband came with our child in his arms and stood outside Ste. Monique.
        They would not permit the child near my bed.
A tuberculosis wing in winter.
You go out then in the hallway, yes. You have the right to see your child. Don't let
*   anyone stop you. They are all fascists.*

A rain through raised windows, as in: you must not forget anything: the hours,
    hope,
        sleeplessness,
            and the trains, you must not forgive them.
Smoke rising from the fields, the death of a husband, winter's
            breath and the moonlight that reached the pallet.
Hunger, and the knife of waking, the cold knife.

The child has gone to the city with his father. They are en route past remaining
            weeks
        of boarded summer houses, beach pine, a blue water tower.
The winter residents are packing for spring.
You should return to Ellie. You mustn't leave her alone.
But we've lost days, and many times tried to begin again, while she locks herself in
    the water closet to sing.
        (The words are somewhere. The words belong here.)
Her skin sloughing in the hard towels.
And just then the doves rise and batter the wind.

In my absence, the child took his first step alone,
            moving along the white hallway without my help but at night nearly
    drowning in my own breath.
Ellie lifting tissues of herself from herself.
Here, in this book, I have found your illness. It is called St. Anthony's Fire.

I don't go out now. It's a terrible thing to see me walk.
        (The bell of her husband's ax breaking open the river.)

It is worse than memory, the open country of death.

A tall light entered the room. The windows, hand blown, were those of occupied
    Paris.
I was waiting for the child's birth.
There were cut tulips in the glass.

Simone was alive. Twice her hand reached to fold the blue shutters back over the
    windows, and once she
            touched the window as I passed.
Under the plane trees of Montparnasse:

            The cemetery workman's wheelbarrow, an old woman's knowledge of
    graves.

That first week after his birth were wet balconies and voile. White roses.
        And God's name *a boneless string of vowels.*

CURFEW

                        for Sean

The curfew was as long as anyone could remember
Certainty's tent was pulled from its little stakes
It was better not to speak any language
There was a man cloaked in doves, there was chandelier music
The city, translucent, shattered but did not disappear
Between the no longer and the still to come
The child asked if the bones in the wall
Belonged to the lights in the tunnel
Yes, I said, and the stars nailed shut his heaven

RAE ARMANTROUT

"I was born on April 13, 1947. My son, Aaron Korkegian, was born on Jan. 19, 1979 in San Diego, where I still live. I began teaching at UC San Diego in 1980, as an adjunct, and have taught there (now as a professor) ever since. I found being a mother both difficult and fascinating because of the way it forces you in close to 'mainstream' culture. For about a year, for instance, I was a part-time cub scout leader. Hard to imagine, I know. I was a soccer-mom. Etc. You can't hide from social life as it is when you're a parent. You become increasingly aware of its moral difficulties, of your resistances and collusions.

"What you learn about yourself and your inherited culture in these negotiations finds its way into your poems—if you're a poet."

FICTION

When the woman's face contorted and she clutched the railing
for support, we knew she would die for this was a film with
the set trajectory of fiction.

★

When she looked down at the birthmark on her leg, it did not
seem out of place like a blemish. Rather like a landmark on a
loved terrain. She had always answered "no" with a touch of
indignation when people asked if she had burned herself. But
when she saw her bare leg in the mirror, the red splotch surprised
her. From the alien perspective, it appeared extraneous

★

The measure of fear is the distance between an event and
its mental representation. Small doses were sometimes taken
for pleasure. Distortion locked in the funhouse and tickets
sold.

★

Her month old son would really watch her now, she hoped.
After three days she should seem 'strangely familiar.'

*

The old architecture.

Roof over
the tongue

*

Hands wandering netherworlds. A sense of self starts in the
mouth and spreads slowly.

*

pacifier. Lost again and
crying because empty.

"He's just a baby."
"He's just hungry."
"He's just scared."

The poor vacuum!
as best he can

*

Her elderly father said the baby looked "like a wise
little old man."

*

He predicted her child would be male. His motive was obvious.
He insisted this baby would look Irish as he did—himself reborn
in a form she must love. She hated such transparency. "When have
your hunches paid off before?" she asked. She planned to give
birth to a girl who resembled her husband's family or perhaps
no one at all. An utterly new countenance. When a grandson was
born who did resemble him, her erstwhile hostile father grew doting.
A superstitious streak she fought against made it difficult not to
accept the prophecy entirely now, with all its implications.

*

Furthering the story.
Furthering
'the ends of the species'

*

Driving imitated sanity.
Blurred gargoyles shrank into the past.
Why should she notice or care?

*

When her husband was late, she imagined him dead. Now that
he had a son, she feared, he could be killed on the highway.

*

"Everything's a message," her friend said. And her son's birth
injury must be a sign, symbol of some weakness in her thinking
or her life.

*

crying because lost. The growing
fibers of desire cannot
locate . . .

*

Fuss Balloon. Squirm Bag. The hero's nicknames described
unexpected animation.

*

In the Bach fugue it was difficult to know which theme was
the traveler with whom one should identify. One's self.

In his old age he went mad. Any stress, including the imminent
operation, returned him to an incident that occurred during WWII.
The "Japs" had torpedoed his ship and it had almost sunk. Now,
whenever he got agitated, he would yell, "We're taking on water."
This idea was like a painted screen let down between himself and
the particulars of his danger.

The French reserve a special past tense for fictions.

She seemed to enjoy each new crisis as if it were a complication
in the plot of a comedy, a mere detour en route to the happy
resolution she was still expecting 'after this'
 old 'after this' dear 'after this'

ATTENTION

Ventriloquy
is the mother tongue.

Can you colonize rejection
by phrasing your request,
       "Me want?"

Song: "I'm not a baby.
          Wa, Wa, Wa.
          I'm not a baby.
          Wa, Wa, Wa.

          I'm crazy
          like you."

The "you"
in the heart of
molecule and ridicule.

Marks resembling
the holes

in dead leaves
define the thing (moth wing).

That flutter
of indifference,
                    feigned?

But if lapses
are the dens

strategy aims
to conceal,

then you don't know
what you're asking.

CROSSING

     1

We'll be careful.

Repression informs us
that this is not our father.
We distinguish
to penetrate.

We grow and grow,

fields of lilies,
cold funnels.

2

According to legend
Mom
sustains the universe
by yelling
"Stay there
where it's safe"
when every star
wants to run home
to her.

Now every single star
knows
she wants only
what's best
and winks steadily
to show it will obey,
and this winking
feels like the middle
of an interesting story.

This is where
our history begins.
Well, perhaps not
history, but we do
feel ourselves preceded.
(Homeostasis

means effortlessly
pursuing someone
who is just
disappearing.)

3

Now here it is
slowed down
by the introduction
of nouns.

Eastwood, Wayne
and Bogart:

faces
on a wall in Yuma

constitute
the force required
to resurrect
a sense of place.

(Hunger fits
like a bonnet
now, something
to distinguish.)

4

On the spot, our son
prefaced resorption, saying,

"You know how we're a lot alike . . ."

He couldn't go out
on that day, but

he could have a pickle.
Out of spite, he crawled
to the kitchen, demonstrating
the mechanics of desire.

5

The sky darkened
then. It seemed
like the wrong end
of a weak simile.
That was what shocked us.
None of our cries
had been heard,
but his was.
When something has happened
once, you might say
it's happened, "once and
for all." That's what
symbols mean
and why they're used
to cover up envy.

A STORY

Despite our infractions
we are loved
by the good mother
who speaks carefully:

"I love you, but I don't
like the way you lie there
pinching your nipples
while I'm trying to read you a story."

Once there was an old lady who told her son she
must go to the doctor because she was bleeding
down there. She didn't look alarmed, but suppressed
a smile, as if she were "tickled," as if she were
going to get away with something.

"Look," said the doctor, "you are confusing
infraction with profusion. *Despite*
may be divided into two
equal segments: Exceptional and Spiteful."

But the stubborn old woman just answered,
"When names perform a function,
that's fiction."

BASES

Birds in flight switch places above and below a hypothetical
bar—like a visual trill—though imitation is vulgar.

The idea that each individual is a unique stain: weight
and counterweight in the organization of memory. So
many forms representing, presumably, a few wishes.

Chew the fat in order to spill the milk, in other words,
from which the selfsame woman emerges.

What the cool tomato cubes forming a rosette around this
central olive have to do with love and happiness.

Thrilled to elaborate some striking variant of what we imagine
to be a general, if fabricated, condition.
Two men on the street wax their teal-green, 50's Mercury.

She thinks the two are lovers, but you say you disagree.
Now she's angry either because you mimic, or because you
merely mimic, ignorance of such things.

She uses intercourse to symbolize persuasion.

Old people never appear to have reserved judgment in the manner of a poised beauty.

She dreamed the ill were allowed to wander at ease through the reconstructed, but vacant, Indian village.

Her eyes scanning the near range with a feeble sense of
their being like children sledding, though never having
done that adds a campiness to the "Whoo-ee" of "I see."

You're not crying because you can't find the thing you made,
but because she won't help. She won't because she's comfortable,
reading—but not really because now you've stuck your
head behind her shoulder sobbing and pretending to gasp.
She goes away to pick up your clothes, but also to see if she
can find the thing you want. You tell her it looks like a crab.
While she's gone you find it underneath her chair. You insist,
bitterly, that you knew where it was all along; you were
just testing her ability to see. It's like keeping her eye
on a bouncing dot. She says either you're lying now or you
were lying before when you were sobbing for it and needed her
help. Really she thinks you were lying both times, all along,
but not exactly.

Now the news is of polls which measure our reactions to duplicity.

She puts her tongue to the small hole, imitating accuracy.

MOLLY PEACOCK

is the author of five volumes of poetry and the writer/actor of a one-woman show in poems, "The Shimmering Verge." Her poems have appeared in *The New Yorker, The Nation, The New Republic,* and *The Paris Review,* as well as *The Best of the Best American Poetry* and *The Oxford Book of American Poetry.* She is a member of the Graduate Faculty of the Spalding University Brief Residency MFA Program in Creative Writing. She lives with her husband Michael Groden in Toronto, where she is Poetry Editor of the *Literary Review of Canada.* Her website is www.mollypeacock.org.

"Many times in my life I faced a forking path: either the journey or the nest. For me the choices were irrevocably separate. For a woman to be a poet and a mother means that she feels she can travel both paths at once—or at least feels that she must try. But for me, the nest meant not writing. The journey meant poetry. Even in childhood I recognized that I had very defined limits. I felt I wasn't made to be both a mother and an artist. There was agony as I faced this choice throughout my childbearing years. But I acted out of a conviction about myself that I could not stray from. Those very limits in my life became the lines from which I created my poems."

MERELY BY WILDERNESS

The breasts enlarge, and a sweet white discharge
coats the vaginal lips. The nipples itch.
A five-week fetus in the uterus,
the larger share of a large soft pear,
soaks quietly there. Should I run directly
and insist that he marry me? Resist
is what we do. It is this: I'm in what
I never thought I'd be caught in,
and it's a strong net, a roomy deluxe net,
the size of civilization. To shun
this little baby—how can I? Maybe
I could go it alone, fix us a home,
never seem to ask why inside the dream
we'd not look beyond, so not ask beyond:
a poor scratch-castle with a beat-in door.
I can't do this alone, yet I am so alone
no one, not even this child inside me, even
the me I was, can feel the wild cold buzz
that presses me into this place, bleakness
that will break me, except I cannot be
broken merely by wilderness, I can only
be lost.

CHRISEASTER

I woke up to the bleating of a lamb
in the garagelike recovery room
crowded with wheeled beds waiting to be parked. "Am
I?" I asked as I began to disentomb

myself from the anesthesia, "where I am?"
Why is there a lamb in this garagelike farm?
Something was wrong in the barn. The nervous bleat-cry
continued. When I raised my head in alarm

and saw the green hospital interior
and felt the blood between my legs and was
frightened, I thought, "It is not hygienic to store
a lamb in here!" Of course the bleating I heard was

a baby crying helplessly way down the room.
I had had an abortion and the baby crying
was someone else's, yet mine—the world was a womb
and the room was still a barn. Lying

back in my stupor in the manger, "ChrisEaster,"
I thought, for it was Eastertime, but I had
condensed the birth and death that were
usually separated by seasons as I bled,

then closed my eyes sarcophagally.
Oh yes, the lamb was the Lamb of God, bleating
in hunger and terror in the tomb room, all woolly
and soft with human pain. My heart lay beating

steadily, for I was alive. Marc stood weeping
in the hall, and later watched as I lay sleeping
~~in the manger, on the bald hill,~~ near the tomb
at home.

ON THE STREET

A curette has the shape of a grapefruit spoon.
They dilate the cervix, then clean out the womb
with the jagged prow, just like separating
the grapefruit from its skin, although the softening
yellow rind won't bear another fruit and
. . . and this womb will? Well, this womb *can,*
if two will. Oh, I am sick of will and all
unconscious life! I am sick of the Fall
and the history of human emotion!
Who knows the end of our commotion except
God, the novelist? Once my heart leapt straight
from its socket say-beating, *Change Your Fate,*
yet I found in order to live my heart
had to beat back in its own pocket: the start
of change ending by continuing living
with wet possibility lingering
like a light rain glazing our separate
apartment buildings now where, unpregnant,
unmarried, and with no one to worry over
us in our old age as we were sure this never-
born child would, we don our raincoats and goofily
smile under our umbrellas, unceasingly
happy to see each other when we meet,
on the street.

THE GHOST

The ghost of my pregnancy, a large
amorphous vapor, much larger than me,
comes when I am alarmed to comfort me,
though it, too, alarms me, and I dodge

away saying, "Leave me alone"; and the ghost,
always beneficent, says, "You're a tough one

to do things for." The ghost must have done
this lots, it so completely knows I'm lost

and empty. It returns the fullness and slow
connection to all the world as it is.
When I let it surround me, the embrace is
more mother than baby. How often we don't know

the difference. It's not a dead little thing
without a spinal cord yet, but a spirit of
the parent we all ought to have had, of
possibility. "I was meant to be dead." Thinking

why it said it was meant to be dead brings
the tangible comfort: how I used the fetus
shamelessly, how the brief pregnancy showed us,
its father and me, these choices, not shriveling

but choice alive with choice, for as our brief
parenthood dislodged our parents' anchor
and set us anxiously adrift, more
of our lost natures appeared. In my grief,

I never say good-bye to the ghost, for
I've forgotten it's been there. That's what it's for.
The thought of my pregnancy somehow unmoors
the anxiety the choice still harbors.

ANN LAUTERBACH

grew up in New York City, in Manhattan, the second of three children: an older sister, Jennifer, and younger brother, David. "Both my siblings married at a young age, and both had children. My sister died in 1986 at the age of 46, leaving two teenage sons, Richard and Jack, who became an essential part of my life. I have never married, and often think perhaps the most estranged social group in America might be unmarried straight women. When I was living in London during my twenties, a wise woman told me that there were many persons who needed to be nurtured, children and adults. I don't think I would have made a very good mother, a role I have thought about all my life; I have had some complex, profound relationships with children, and teaching young adults is of course a form of parenting. This poem, probably the most directly autobiographical I ever wrote, was forced out of me by a sense of isolation, anger, and a desire to portray some of the details of my experience with this subject. I have found that the issues involved are never fully at rest. The poem takes place in a country co-op, where I spent many summers, and where my status as non-mother and working poet amid liberal urbanites with small children often felt like that of an outsider, a kind of threatening shadow."

Ann Lauterbach is Ruth and David Schwab Professor of Languages and Literature at Bard College, where she has also been co-chair of Writing in the Milton Avery Graduate School of the Arts since 1990. She received a Guggenheim Fellowship in 1986 and a MacArthur Fellowship in 1994.

N/EST

In that part of the day I was carefully measured for aridity

whether or not it had rained, the air plummeting with hellish weeping, the hairy leaves on the maple by the pond, under which Phillip had wed Cynthia, shaped like a child's balloon or a pregnant woman, almost round but with a gash delved into its midst, turned back, thrashing, into silvery green, so I am reminded of my mother bending over, her wet hair falling across her upside-down face, brushing brushing the long tawny length of it

                not under my arms but elsewhere, around the wrists
and ankles and fingernails, where you wouldn't expect to find
moisture ordinarily

            and at other times, around mid-day, when the kids are all at the
pool but Yo-Yo continues to bark with a high piercing yip yip in great despair and
no matter how many window I close the sound

Helping Julia to pack for California, wrapping her dishes in old newspaper, placing them in a beautiful old salad bowl, taking them out to her car to place in an open trunk, barefoot, in the muggy heat of July, that day, while her son Adam sat on the camp bed and read, the bees came like tiny bombs

I was seven, in Bridgehampton, where we had a small white house down by the pond, white lilies opened only in the morning and I went out into the thick mud where there were bloodsuckers, and picked one or two to give to my father, who was asleep inside the house, but when I came up the slope my legs all muddied, the bees

     I thought I was being

         punished

               later he died
                September

of polio just before my birthday these days
twist into one

tripped on a rug and in my dream
he is leaving on a train
I am lifted up in an envelope

          the white sky reflected thru the trees in the pond

I took a photograph
her daughter Isobel standing in the pond, her shadow
elongated in the water, braided hair a gold shimmer
her solitude

looking back over the past five months
I forgot to read Moby-Dick and now it is too late

      I thought the world was held by language as if it were of an

          incipience

Late at night reading Michael Ondaatje's *The English Patient:*

"There was a time when mapmakers named the places they traveled through with the names of lovers rather than their own. Someone seen bathing in a desert caravan, holding up muslin with one arm in front of her. Some old Arab poet's woman, whose white-dove shoulders made him describe an oasis with her name. The skin bucket spreads water over her, she wraps herself in the cloth, and the old scribe turns from her to describe Zerzura."

       My father
                                     traveled during the war and wrote
                         his name was Richard, called Dick

Childlessness
   brings estrangement

                 I have never explicitly affiliated my not having children with

                                my father's absences
                                I thought I would find him in the heavy
                                book of words, dictionary
                                which rested on his writing table long after his
                                disappearance and which I thought
                                was magical, containing all secrets,

or perhaps
find a way to him on little word boats, paper sails, some spirit's breath,
into a "conversation"—Paul Celan's term—

This turn, this coming about, refuses to let time go, but is always using it to

fuel the poem towards the meaning of
the presence of meaning

                      I have been pregnant three times

          two abortions while in college, one in Milwaukee without anesthetic
                             after which I bled

in the Emergency Room I was afraid they would send me to jail
I told my English teacher
who had said *I don't know if you have ever thought about, but*
you can write
seeding my life with pursuit

Fred, the father, died last year in New Mexico.
We were engaged. He gave me a
ring, a small emerald set in diamonds, at the end of the summer
in Santa Fe.

I had been working as a mother's helper in New Jersey taking care
of three children, their mother pregnant with her fourth

the youngest, Pete, called my name each morning had
immense glee
learning a word for a thing *bird? bird?* hearing one sing

after she went to the hospital to give birth
her husband came into my room
filled with moonlight

I remember thinking *what what what*

Fred wrote *"come out on a hobby horse I will still love you"*
we drove to Second Mesa to watch the Hopi Snake Dance
a gaggle of Indian children surrounded us
calling him Mr. Smokestack laughing I bought a tiny clay dish
with a creature painted on it

he showed me the desert

married an English girl they had three children. When he died the marriage had
collapsed. When he drank he talked too much, brilliance becoming garrulous,
sentimental, pretentious. I kept his letters. I thought he was smarter than anyone in
the world when I was seventeen. He had read Nietzsche and Celine, nihilist in the
midst of idealists. He called me "Little Chick." He encouraged me to write.

*"In the desert the most loved waters, like a lover's name, are carried blue in your hands,
enter your throat. One swallows absence."*

The second time

was an accident
studying for exams all night

it was lovely exhausted sex
I have forgotten his name

the word *name* has *man* and *men* in it

Ondaatje writes of his heroine Hana: *"To rest was to receive all aspects of the world without judgment. A bath in the sea, a fuck with a soldier who never knew your name. Tenderness towards the unknown and anonymous, which was tenderness to the self."*

I flew to Puerto Rico/pretended to be going to a wedding
spent the night in a nasty airport motel the man there tried to
come on to me/could not sleep/fluorescent dawn all night

my first trip out of the United States

I took a taxi to the place/there were stairs
along the outside of the building
walking up them/I imagined a film set

my stomach was upset
they sent me to get Pepto-Bismol
the doctor had a gold chains around his neck, his shirt open

the nurse a large kind woman/many had their boyfriends with them
everyone paid in cash
one woman was reading Steal This Book
I was awake they spoke Spanish
numb down from my waist
watching his face/hearing the scrapes

afterwards at another motel
sunshine and blue water amazed
to be alive
it was the middle of winter in the Midwest

pretended I was on vacation/dark glasses and a hat

reading Henry James' *The Wings of the Dove*
alone in the restaurant/ I kept inventing
a substitute self

        The third time years later
               I was already scheduled for a hysterectomy
                  fibroid uterine tumors

                  and then told I was pregnant I talked to various doctors
about the pregnancy they said the fetus is not viable premature babies are very costly
I had no insurance working part-time in a gallery Brian was trying to figure out how
to be an artist in New York

his daughter, Haven, eight when we met she is married now in Boston
I do not hear from her sometimes I see Brian on the street

Phillip and Cynthia's daughter is now fifteen she was in Paris modeling/I have
almost never seen her smile/her beauty is

the subject's object
the object's subject

               eyes traps of green light
                  limbs long limber new branches

lawn after rain

swimming in the pool, the photographer walking round and round
his camera wheezing and clicking

hawk circling the blue sky above
inscribing a dangerous

I walked up and down in the kitchen with her crying in my arms
she was five months old/I said
she is angry
not to speak

does not speak to me thinks I do not like kids because I like to
revision the silence / or because

on the street she is
wearing a black wig short skirt bright red lipsticks high heels walking with her father
she says the wig is hot / in the photos she is barely recognizable as herself
they have made her up

                her mother asked me when I first was interest in becoming part of the
country co-op if I intended to have children this struck me as an odd question

                                        then I went into the hospital
for the operation but the last minute it was decided that they would do a D&C, an
official abortion, rather than risk the hysterectomy because when you are pregnant
your blood is "frothy" so I was sent home to wait
wept ceaselessly

                an image of a cork on a sea

I saw it on a gray screen
tiny incoherent scribble
don't you want this baby the nurse asked / she did not understand

                        and then I went back
        they put me to sleep
                        I woke up cold
                                gray as dry ice

        I went out with Phillip a few times a long time ago he was
                handsome and intense I was a waitress then in SoHo

and then went back
for another surgery to remove
my ovaries
                had become
                        an explosion of impossible life
                        teeth hair brainmatter
                                        homunculus
                                        ubiquitous

                    the scar revisits
                        is its is its
                                    sealed shut
                    time's incubus

Space here is
always shifting/birds
sparrows catbirds chickadees robins the cedar waxwings
love the cherry tree/a great swarm of blackbirds came over the house/a wind of
dark flight/they make a *cluck* sound land deep in the foliage
across the pond
a hermit thrush/partial lament
a blue heron in a dead gray tree
the belted kingfisher's rattle
before it plummets

there is no word for the sound
a splash is

                                    Each choice
          measures the relation between freedom and fate

Emerson writes, *"Where do we find ourselves? In a series of which we do not know the
extremes, and believe that it has none. We wake and find ourselves on a stair; there are
stairs below us, which we seem to have ascended; there are stairs above us, many a one,
which go upward and out of sight."*

These steps I took
I do not regret

                    to be a poet

they were illegal dangerous
sad and expensive

                    is a constant iteration of choice
                    one word instead of another
                    they call to each other sometimes/constructing a place

          in which to live a life

                        words are acts of the world they are prior to us
                                            issued forth
                                they become facts in the world
                                        and address

        Nan comes to visit she is pregnant
        her son Henry

        is born four flights below
        the place where
        I watched Joe die / the machine screamed at his last breath

the rufous sparrow nested in the blue spruce / listening
a tiny fledgling came out on a low branch Sylvia came to get me she said
it looked like Albert Einstein with big eyebrows and a large beak I took its picture it
stared mutely at the camera I said it looked like her husband Mike

            their daughter Jane, just fifteen, broke up with her first boyfriend
                        she was so sad I have a picture of her at three in a pink bathing suit

            when poems are made I try to listen to how they want to become
                                            sometimes they perish

later it disappeared

in the photograph a blur on a bough of blue spruce
the nest a palm of dry mud on the ground.

BRENDA HILLMAN

Hillman's seven collections of poetry are all published by Wesleyan University Press. She teaches at St. Mary's College in Moraga, California, where she is the Olivia Filippi Professor of Poetry, and lives in the Bay Area with her husband, poet Robert Hass. Her daughter, Louisa Michaels, was born in 1979; she has five stepchildren from two marriages, Ethan and Jesse Michaels, and Leif, Kristin and Luke Hass.

TIME PROBLEM

The problem
of time.   Of there not being
enough of it.

My girl came to the study
and said Help me;
I told her I had a time problem
which meant:
I would die for you but I don't have ten minutes.
Numbers hung in the math book
like motel coathangers.   The Lean
Cuisine was burning
like an ancient city: black at the edges,
bubbly earth tones in the center.
The latest thing they're saying is lack
of time might be
a "woman's problem." She sat there
with her math book sobbing—
(it turned out to be prime factoring: whole numbers
dangle in little nooses)
Hawking says if you back up far enough
it's not even
an issue, time falls away into
'the curve' which is finite,
boundaryless. Appointment book,
soprano telephone—
(beep End beep went the microwave)

The hands fell of my watch
fell off in the night.

I spoke to the spirit
who took them, I told her: Time is the funniest thing
they invented. Had wakened from a big
dream of love in a boat—
No time to get the watch fixed so the blank face
lived for months in my dresser,
no arrows
for hands, just quartz intentions, just the pinocchio
nose   (before the lie)
left in the center;   the watch
didn't have twenty minutes; neither did I.

My girl was doing
her gym clothes by herself;   (red leaked
toward black, then into the white
insignia)   I was grading papers,
heard her call from the laundry room:
Mama?
Hawking says there are two
types of it,
real and imaginary   (imaginary time must be
like decaf), he says it's meaningless
to decide which is which
but I say: there was tomorrow-
and-a-half
when I started thinking about it; now
there's less than a day. More
done. That's
the thing that keeps being said. I thought
I could get more done as in:
fish stew from a book. As in: Versateller
archon, then push-push-push
the tired-tired around the track like a planet.
Legs, remember him?
Our love—when we stagger—lies down inside us . . .

Hawking says
there are little folds in time
(actually he calls them wormholes)
but I say:

there's a universe beyond
where they're hammering the brass cut-outs . . .
Push us out in the boat and leave time here—

(because: where in the plan was it written,
You'll be too busy to close parentheses,
the snapdragon's bunchy mouth needs water,
even the caterpillar will hurry past you?

Pulled the travel alarm
to my face: the black
behind the phosphorous argument kept the dark
from being ruined. Opened
the art book
—saw the languorous wrists of the lady
in Tissot's "Summer Evening." Relaxed. Turning
gently. The glove
(just slightly—but still:)
"aghast";
opened Hawking, he says, time gets smoothed
into a fourth dimension
but I say
space thought it up, as in: Let's make
a baby space, and then
it missed. Were seconds born early, and why
didn't things unhappen also, such as
the tree became Daphne . . .

At the beginning of harvest, we felt
the seven directions.
Time did not visit us. We slept
till noon.
With one voice I called him, with one voice
I let him sleep, remembering
summer years ago,
I had come to visit him in the house of last straws
and when he returned
above the garden of pears, he said
our weeping caused the dew . . .

I have borrowed a little boat
and I say to him Come into the little boat,
you were happy there;

the evening reverses itself, we'll push out
onto the pond,
or onto the reflection of the pond,
whichever one is eternal—

ANNE WALDMAN

is a Distinguished Professor of Poetics at The Jack Kerouac School of Disembodied Poetics at the Naropa University in Boulder, Colorado, a program she co-founded with poet Allen Ginsberg in 1974. The author of over 30 books, she has published in Italian and German and been translated into French, Turkish, and Czech. She is the recipient of grants from the National Endowment for the Arts and the Poetry Foundation and is a winner of the Shelley Memorial Award for poetry. She was a Civitella Ranieri Fellow in Umbria, Fall 2001, and a recipient of a grant from the Foundation for Contemporary Performance Arts in 2002. Anne Waldman founded the activist coalition Poetry is News with Ammiel Alcalay. Her newest CD is *The Eye of the Falcon* (Farfalla, McMillen, Parrish) with her son Ambrose Bye, 2006.

ASSENT

Disastrous world—does it see me watching?

Hard world—how can it work?

My mind would break
over someone's hatred.

Disastrous world—out of control

I can't bow down but to baby.

POEM

for her who bore me
           & by whose sorrows
     I am cast down:
she more dauntless than I'll ever be
     I lover her tenacity
         &
     accept her prerogative
   to complayne of incapacity

O mystique language of mother's heart
         to her childe

It's here in the room
searing me now.

HERMENEUTICAL
(Light to Read By)

"Sweet dreams form a shade,
O'er my lovely infant's head.
Sweet dreams of pleasant streams.
Be happy silent moony beams.

Sweet sleep with soft down,
Weave thy brows and infant crown.
Sleep sleep Angel mild,
Hover o'er my happy child.

Sweet smiles in the night
Hover over my delight
Sweet smiles Mother smiles,
All the dovelike moan beguiles."

—William Blake, from "A Cradle Song"

Why would I bring a babe into a suffering world? Can one be creative after
atrocity? There will always be atrocity, I reasoned. The long pull. In it for the
protracted human run. How would a baby enter a writing world? What "critical"
understanding, what gnosis would the baby disclose to writing poetry? To his
father and me? What beauty? What harmony? How terrible and deep could
beauty be? Would I ever recover from it? How could an "act" be anything but
birth? Absolute or relative birth. What kind of world? Who would the baby be in
the world? Is there a baby for me coming into this world? I dreamed a boy named
"Arman" (our man) was heralded in this naming word to me. When he arrived he
was more than a word. He was flesh and palpable. And sounding all manner of
sounds. I was his votary.

Who wrote singularly of baby for baby? Folk songs, nursery rhymes, lullabies. Plangent English lyrics. William Blake, childless, wrote a lullaby and imagined innocence. I would write in quatrains, in the Malay oral verse form, *pantun,* frenchified to *pantoum,* which originated in South India, a variation on the sloka. The second and fourth line of each stanza serve as the first and third lines of the next. Then the first and third lines return to circle the chain.

When I wrote "Baby's Pantoum" I had been spending time with little Ambrose in a small cabin in the mountains outside Boulder, Colorado. I lived inside a magical sphere in which I was highly attuned to the way the baby was discovering the world—most mothers will tell you this—how they relive creation through a newborn babe. And the environment was minimal, functional, in the service, in the ceremony of the baby. Not a lot of clutter in the house, baby was the core of our lives. A few things or useful objects welcomed him. So it was late at night—often the only spate of time to write when you have a baby—when days and light are demanding, stirring. I wanted a gift (as the holidays were coming) for the father of the child and attempted again the pantoum which hadn't been successful or satisfying, which hadn't been fortifying until I began writing in the voice of the baby. It was natural to do this, and I was writing in longhand rather than typing to avoid waking the baby, and into the third stanza the problem of "form" had vanished and the poem began to grow easily. I couldn't—if I was to be I-as-he—the mood or tone or voice of him—get fancy in my vocabulary. The repetitive structure of the pantoum was conducive to expressing the baby's thought process, his just-coming-to-thought processes. The pantoum lends itself to the idea of the experience of the baby's mind working, baby's mind moving since baby's mind would observe things in a series of unconnected glimpses and simple realizations. Is that the sense, realizations? Because the form demands that each line has to be repeated in another context, it's difficult not to have every line be a single phrase or statement. In an older mind that might get stiff, artificial, or coy, but with a baby single thoughts out of the blue don't refer back to a self-conscious body of knowledge. So the pantoum became the primary observations of an early mind, a new arrival. The lines are obviously not what's going on in the baby's mind, but a projection of the rhythms of what felt accurate to the mind of a baby. I was a conduit for my imagined imagination of baby. I spoke the lines as I wrote. What filled the form, the things said, or seen, were the details of the life going on in the musical world of the cabin, in the world of showing the world to baby. Every action in the care of the baby is ritualized. Tasks are performed and performed again. The baby is held and rocked and shown the same objects and images, the baby is bathed regularly, the baby is nursed, the baby sleeps every few hours, and so repetitions chiming in the poem were natural conditions in a universe of baby.

Melodious redundancies in the realm of baby. Language seemed closer to action than ever before.

BABY'S PANTOUM

for Reed

I lie in my crib midday this is
            unusual I don't sleep really
Mamma's sweeping or else boiling water for tea
            Other sounds are creak of chair & floor, water
            dripping on heater from laundry, cat licking itself

Unusual I don't sleep really
            unless it's dark night everyone in bed
Other sounds are creak of chair & floor, water
dripping on heater from laundry, cat licking itself
            & occasional peck on typewriter, peck on my cheek

Unless it's dark night everyone in bed
            I'm wide awake hungry wet lonely thinking
occasional peck on typewriter, peck on my cheek
            My brain cells grow, I get bigger

I'm wide awake wet lonely hungry thinking
            Then Mamma pulls out breast, says "Milky?"
My brain cells grow, I get bigger
            This is my first Christmas in the world

Mamma pulls out breast, says "Milky?"
            Daddy conducts a walking tour of house
This is my first Christmas in the world
            I study knots in pine wood ceiling

Daddy conducts a walking tour of house
            I study pictures of The Madonna del Parto, a
            sweet-faced Buddha & Papago Indian girl
I study knots in pine wood ceiling
            I like contrasts, stripes, eyes & hairlines

I study pictures of The Madonna del Parto, a
sweet-faced Buddha & Papago Indian girl
        Life is colors, faces are moving
I like contrasts, stripes, eyes & hairlines
        I don't know what I look like

Life is colors, faces are moving
        They love me smiling
I don't know what I look like
        I try to speak of baby joys & pains

They love me smiling
        She takes me through a door, the wind howls
I try to speak of baby joys & pains
        I'm squinting, light cuts through my skin

She takes me through a door, the wind howls
        Furry shapes & large vehicles move close
I'm squinting, light cuts through my skin
        World is vast I'm in it with closed eyes

Furry shapes + large vehicles move close
        I rest between her breasts, she places me on dry leaves
World is vast I'm in it with closed eyes
        I'm locked in little dreams, my fists are tight.

I rest between her breasts, she places me on dry leaves
        He carries me gently on his chest & shoulder
I'm locked in little dream, my fists are tight
        They showed me moon in sky, was something
        in my dream

He carries me gently on his chest & shoulder
        He calls me sweet baby, good baby boy
They showed me moon in sky, was something
in my dream
        She is moving quickly & dropping things

He calls me sweet baby, good baby boy
        She sings hush go to sleep right now

She is moving quickly & dropping things
       They rock my cradle, they hold me tightly in their arms

She sings hush go to sleep right now
       She wears red nightgown, smells of spice & milk
They rock my cradle, they hold me tightly in their arms
       I don't know any of these words or things yet

She wears a red nightgown, smells of spice & milk
       He has something woolen and rough on
I don't know any of these words or things yet
       I sit in my chair & watch what moves

He has something woolen & rough on
       I can stretch & unfold as he holds me in the bath
I sit in my chair & watch what moves
       I see when things are static or they dance

I can stretch & unfold as he holds me in the bath
       Water is soft I came from water
I can see when things are static or they dance
       like flames, the cat pouncing, shadows or light
       streaming in

Water is soft I came from water
       Not that long ago I was inside her
like flames, the cat pouncing, shadows or light
streaming in
       I heard her voice then I remember now

Not that long ago I was inside her
       I lie in my crib midday this is
always changing, I am expanding toward you
       Mamma's sweeping or else boiling water for tea.

Verbs hasten and keep a flow around the necessary acts inscribed in and of babydom—"dripping," "licking," "sweeping," "boiling." They have a resolutely contrapuntal dynamic with the punch of "crib," "creep," "peck," "cheek." A blur in distinctions masks a point of view as the "new mind" must keep locating signposts in a world coming more and more into focus. The "I" imagines—idealizes—two parents that come alive as pure sense perception—the tactile male and female. One with something "woolen and rough on," the other smelling of "spice and milk." Identity, whose? A nuclear family's perhaps, as the babe studies "knots" in the ceiling, already looking up. I think it's further back than that. The primordial triad exists (in cosmology? mythology?) before interference/intervention of all kinds. The language of the poem never invades, it explores and circles around to begin another circular day that juxtaposes the biological *two* it takes to make a *one* that maintains its trinity-shadow yet separates out to make language. The ultimate alterity? A holy otherness which is only hinted at because it positions its power as a thrust, as a way out? Does the writer/mother presume too much, as mothers are wont to do? Does she colonize perpetually for her hungry imagination's "I" for the sake of sweet fantasy? This was an antidote to baby talk and the power reverts to baby's mind. Would "I" could always be this open.

A baby entered a writing world to interpret (translate) form: mind-form, poem-form. And until then the elder "I" didn't know any of these words or things yet.

SHARON OLDS

is the author of seven books of poetry. Ms. Olds teaches in the Graduate Creative Writing Program at New York University, and for twenty-one years has helped run a writing workshop at the Sigismund Goldwater Memorial Hospital, a 900-bed state hospital for the severely physically challenged. From 1998–2000 she was the New York State Poet Laureate.She is a Chancellor of the Academy of American Poets. She lives in New York City.

THE MOMENT THE TWO WORLDS MEET

That's the moment I always think of—when the
slick, whole body comes out of me,
when they pull it out, not pull it but steady it
as it pushes forth, not catch it but keep their
hands under it as it pulses out,
they are the first to touch it,
and it shines, it glistens with the thick liquid on it.
That's the moment, while it's sliding, the limbs
compressed close to the body, the arms
bent like a crab's cloud-muscle legs, the
thighs packed plums in heavy syrup, the
legs folded like the wings of a chicken—
that is the center of life, the moment when the
juiced, bluish sphere of the baby is
sliding between the two worlds,
wet, like sex, it *is* sex,
it is my life opening back and back
as you'd strip the reed from the bud, not strip it but
watch it thrust so it peels itself and the
flower is there, severely folded, and
then it begins to open and dry
but by then the moment is over,
they wipe off the grease and wrap the child in a blanket and
hand it to you entirely in this world.

NEW MOTHER

A week after our child was born,
you cornered me in the square room
and we sank down on the bed.
You kissed me and kissed me, my milk undid its
burning slipknot through my nipples,
soaking my shirt. All week I had smelled of milk,
fresh milk, sour. I began to throb:
my sex had been torn easily as cloth by the
crown of her head, I'd been cut with a knife and
sewn, the stitches pulling at my skin—and the
first time you're broken, you don't know
you'll be healed again, better than before.
I lay in fear and blood and milk
while you kissed and kissed me, your lips hot and swollen
as a teenage boy's, your sex dry and big,
all of you so tender, you hung over me,
over the nest of the stitches, over the
splitting and tearing, with the patience of someone who
finds a wounded animal in the woods
and stays with it, not leaving its side
until it is whole, until it can run again.

THE CLASP

She was four, he was one, it was raining, we had colds,
we had been in the apartment two weeks straight,
I grabbed her to keep her from shoving him over on his
face, again, and when I had her wrist
in my grasp I compressed it, fiercely, for almost a
second, to make an impression on her,
to hurt her, our beloved firstborn, I even nearly
savored the stinging sensation of the squeezing, the
expression, into her, of my anger,
"Never, never again," the righteous

chant accompanying the clasp. It happened very
fast—grab crush release—and at the first extra
force, she swung her head, as if checking
who this was, and looked at me,
and saw me—yes, this was her mom,
her mom was doing this. Her dark,
deeply open eyes took me
in, she knew me, in the shock of the moment
she learned me. This was her mother, one of the
two whom she loved most, the two
who loved her the most, near the source of love
was this.

THE TALK

In the sunless wooden room at noon
the mother had a talk with her daughter.
The rudeness could not go on, the meanness
to her little brother, the selfishness.
The eight-year-old sat on the bed
in the corner of the room, her irises distilled as
the last drops of something, her firm
face melting, reddening,
silver flashes in her eyes like distant
bodies of water glimpsed through woods.
She took it and took it and broke, crying out
I hate being a person! diving
into the mother
as if
into
a deep pond—and she cannot swim,
the child cannot swim.

THE ONE GIRL AT THE BOYS' PARTY

When I take our girl to the swimming party
I set her down among the boys. They tower
and bristle, she stands there smooth and sleek,
her math scores unfolding in the air around her.
They will strip to their suits, her body hard and
indivisible as a prime number,
they'll plunge in the deep end, she'll subtract
her height from ten feet, divide it into
hundreds of gallons of water, the numbers
bouncing in her mind like molecules of chlorine
in the bright-blue pool. When they climb out,
her ponytail will hang its pencil lead
down her back, her narrow silk suit
with hamburgers and french fries printed on it
will glisten in the brilliant air, and they will
see her sweet face, solemn and
sealed, a factor of one, and she will
see their eyes, two each,
their legs, two each, and the curves of their sexes,
one each, and in her head she'll be doing her
wild multiplying, as the drops
sparkle and fall to the power of a thousand from her body.

THE LANGUAGE OF THE BRAG

I have wanted excellence in the knife-throw,
I have wanted to use my exceptionally strong and accurate arms
and my straight posture and quick electric muscles
to achieve something at the center of a crowd,
the blade piercing the bark deep,
the haft slowly and heavily vibrating like the cock.

I have wanted some epic use for my excellent body,
some heroism, some American achievement

beyond the ordinary for my extraordinary self,
magnetic and tensile, I have stood by the sandlot
and watched the boys play.

I have wanted courage, I have thought about fire
and the crossing of waterfalls, I have dragged around

my belly big with cowardice and safety,
stool charcoal from the iron pills,
huge breasts leaking colostrum,
legs swelling, hands swelling,
face swelling and reddening, hair
falling out, inner sex
stabbed again and again with pain like a knife.
I have lain down.

I have lain down and sweated and shaken
and passed blood and shit and water and
slowly alone in the center of a circle I have
passed the new person out
and they have lifted the new person free of the act
and wiped the new person free of that
language of blood like praise all over the body.
I have done what you wanted to do, Walt Whitman,
Allen Ginsberg, I have done this thing,
I and the other women this exceptional
act with the exceptional heroic body,
this giving birth, this glistening verb,
and I am putting my proud American boast
right here with the others.

FIRST WEEKS

Those first weeks, I hardly knew how to
love our daughter. Her face looked crushed,
crumpled with worry—and not even

despairing, but just disheartened, a look of
endurance. The skin of her face was finely
wrinkled, there were wisps of hair on her ears,
she looked a little like a squirrel, suspicious,
tranced. And smallish, 6.13,
wizened—she looked as if she were wincing
away from me without moving. The first
moment I had seen her, my glasses off,
in the delivery room, a blur of blood
and blue skin, and limbs, I had known her,
upside down, and they righted her, and there
came that faint, almost sexual, wail, and her
whole body flushed rose.
When I saw her next, she was bound in cotton,
someone else had cleaned her, wiped
the inside of my body off her
and combed her hair in narrow scary
plough-lines. She was ten days early,
sleepy, the breast engorged, standing out nearly
even with the nipple, her lips would so much as
approach it, it would hiss and spray.
And when we took her home, she shrieked
and whimpered, like a dream of a burn victim,
and when she was quiet, she would lie there and peer, not quite
anxiously. I didn't blame her,
she'd been born to my mother's daughter. I would kneel
and gaze at her, and pity her.
All day I nursed her, all night I walked her,
and napped, and nursed, and walked her. And then,
one day, she looked at me, as if
she knew me. She lay along my forearm, fed, and
gazed at me as if remembering me,
as if she had known me, and liked me, and was getting
her memory back. When she smiled at me,
delicate rictus like a birth-pain coming,
I fell in love, I became human.

RACHEL BLAU DUPLESSIS

is an American poet-critic. DuPlessis was awarded a residency at Bellagio in 2007; she was the recipient of a Pew Fellowship for Artists and of the Roy Harvey Pearce/ Archive for New Poetry Prize, both in 2002. The child she is referring to in these poems was born in 1984.

ROSE

Well the green
and this its crowning
sweet the moment
common, fated
weeps the little
dripping baby.

Well the crimson's
lavish touching
clock of petals
ends by falling
black and dark
the noisy baby.

Well the rose
is filled with
roses,
well the baby
filled with people:

me none
alone
foresee
the rose.

                    1982

NOTE: Ronsard, for the catch line "Mignonne, allons voir si la rose . . ." and Edmund Waller's "Go, Lovely rose" for "common" and "fated."

from WRITING

little wails cringing at the sight of green. the hand
that takes the pacifier out the mouth cannot (wail)
yet put it in. me puts it in, o me.

mouth moth(er)

.Face face face face-y
without particularity
mouth, dots, la la La la LA
have to learn that flat is flat   props. shitskies.
In baby in-   phone. no. ba-ba.
undation of contexts.   what; was wet.
                              next door.
                              Odd time of
                              year to be moving.

Impossible maybe to write
the techne of dailiness the hand reaching onto the shelf the
dust
collected in a particular corner   the objects also a little
dusty with the spring light through the back door   objects
directly in the sunlight   the coupon torn or cut, saved
as a lacy proof of thriftiness   the unmendable cracks this,
attempt at exactness, is readable the intersecting rhythms of
muscles small muscles when cutting when sorting how
to assimilate   how to discuss   to represent
the pulses of pleasure and heartlessness   to ascertain
fairly the moon small cadences
dotty lights
rust rough ride shod cracks
the surface
winnow the pillars
what kind of a deal
anyway
all this has been "the"
just where I thought I began
beyond.

+++

.A red squall-pulse glaums on
Nip eats (has eaten)
the tippy top the creaminess
forever. Could eat almost forever
depends   formula–Similac
on what convention
of satiety.

                                        on feeling dopey

So how
does one ever
know? How
feed the fullness?

How to be that which is unspoken   how to speak that which is
"repressed"   elusive anyway   tangential   different
impending space   different enough   how to write that which
is / is

unwritten.

+++

              Marginalia without a center? No beginning, No. No
.One word one   *ending? No, because form*
"word" kkhkkhgggh   *at all times is instilled. O noble*
Koré la la   *that ongo-*
threaded into the dyad   *ingness that entrance into speaking*
both ends beading, gleaming
gargle. Conventionally, "goo gah."   encapsulated
                                                      eyes burning
Big finger to the little sleeping mouth
                              It was all cracking
makes sure,

the even silence breathing.

Narrative: the oedipal plot? ends by revealing the hidden
father. Pre-oedipal plot? the mother, hidden. Split subject:
"a living contradiction." A text to speak now, writing,
writing the sung-half song.

DRAFT 2: SHE

The white one turns red they say
then peach to white   grass rich the edge-fold
space

slices of porcupine deep underground
and et that red-grained fat.

"I be good girl with my magic
markers."

(marks hands up red
makes henna dark touch)

Taboo thy ruses, moues and roses, shh.
Terracotta, ochres smear of Provence

shadowy $\overset{\text{stains}}{\text{stairs.}}$

Ask for danger, say

"I want that danger."

^ ^
.

Who has

how images $\overset{\text{rise}}{\underset{\text{rinse}}{.}}$ and erase how

can the rose
speak and how much

can you in fact stand that lobotomized
memory you have been washed up
into
do you

NO?

Dear (name),
          I (morder)
                    for departure's sake
further reaches.

The thin voice of the thin space.
Red red the rushes rise
down down by the salt tide veil, that
Love depicted as against itself:
small happy (guillotined) family unit
petal lashed to petal.

^ ^
   .

Families set like junket IN milky rooms'
schematic valleys—
V-shape of the young runnel;
rennet sweet-white jellies
over cascades of russet granite.

^ ^
   .

Lightly risen, of a plastic
pink too close, too

bare,
tho luminous Food one could imagine there
the Moone
when next I spy
retracts: a dime-size toy-tied dish my moony

quest too dumb to ask a $\begin{smallmatrix}better\\bitter\end{smallmatrix}$ question.

Still such catheter stuck there into my any fleck is
profligate.

^ ^

.

                    jests
Of suggestive twists, of wax rib
                    joists

stuffed by a potential crime,
do you read her as
'Mother'? 'Woman'?

            "Bandit
one-armed "Angel With A Lamp"?
            "Badger

beam my way, beamy tinkling light; be me now
O Be Thou Me, sinuous one!

The piece, it's fleshy, picture perfect,
peachy . . . wax torqued up

    $\begin{smallmatrix}fill\\fool\end{smallmatrix}$ this unrelinquished peephole.
to

Luminosities   enormities of
key-shaped air in which she
flocks, twisted in brush,
sine curves verbatim.
A pubis allusive; the eye penises thru the keylock;
the eye is complicit and so is
      HUNGER
      NAUSEA

      hurl
for I am afraid to hole it   TOO MUCH
      hurt

not speak of hold me.

"I am your danger."
"I am your anger, ranger."
"I am your angel, dudgeon."

^ ^
  .

Red orange with red veining
shading   raised
rib of same
color runs into large gold throat
suppressed heart, green.

Pale peach that by evening has a flush of pink

There is a pink rib goes
deep, up to the hilt,

rose heart, bound.
Between me? that?
heavy-eyed light gazing.

Daylilies open and drop
opal nenuphars of tears;

"I am your angle, stranger."

^ ^
.

Each word a cryptogram
never too much:
in narrow, nah
in ride, rid
in courage, cor and rage

in flax phlox hemp feather, hook
garland   pull

a cryptic outline OF something
word shoal   staunched blood

food
      at the edge of well-beloved veins
stood

looking cock-eyed at all their deep,
at all their deep blue writing.

^ ^
.

Shadow under-word
˙lopes thru stands of wet papyrus—
microclimates for this ploy
versus that: rain warms here; wind twists there;
one family eats well, another eats each other.

House of the soul is filled with little
things, clay vessels, slipped and glazed
all smallness green leaf offering;
sweaty flower; baby loaf;

small as half an envelope which wads up tight
the poem's patchouli.

In shires, shrines:
you're going to have something
about aging teeth, you're going to have left
something half-chewed
in front of that house,
food on the plate of the moon?
mets sur l'assiette de la lune?

That hard to write
"the mother"? to get that
empty for that full

mouth(e)

her(e)

sh(e)?

^ ^
    .

A borer, a beetle, an eater,
who will evaluate hunger?

Bowel, bowl, daughter
whosoever siphons undigested words
requires a wide tube.

^ ^
    .

Dabbles the blankie down
din
do throw foo foo

noo

dles the arror

of eros the error of arrows

each little spoil and spill

all during pieces fly apart.

Splatting crumb bits there and there.

Feed 'n' wipe. Woo woo petunia

pie.

Hard

to get the fail of it,

large small specks each naming

yellow surface

green bites

Red elbow kicks an orange tangerine.

The time inside, makes tracks, seems a small

room lurches into the foreground, anger, throwing, some

dash, power swirls up against MErock, pick it UP,

Mommy me NEED

it a push a touch a

putsch pull a flailing kick a spool

for her who is and makes thread

"I"

The she that makes her her

The she that makes me SHE

^ ^

.

Practicing ferocity on $\begin{smallmatrix}\text{your}\\\text{her}\end{smallmatrix}$ self

You become the mother   certainly a change.
                    the monster   a chain.

        foaling
Is this failing the mother?
        finding

^ ^
.

Top half poison	yellow light from above
ivy next half scritchings	blue light swells from earth
the garden red	bruising a frame

       Digging, I sit on a flower.
Counting the steps of bright shadow, the pure pause, paces
clusters of ripe tones making up loud and then whispy forces
across one singular place saying no to itself with meditative
privation, yet unfixed, so spun out of, *or* of, being or
seeing. Which is not, but as it starts, starts a little
rivulet sound and voice, another, it fuses, pivots, a sigh
and sign; desire's design, blue transparencies rich for
thirst   listen, to listen is to drink
how can there be
another   cry: whom; one of another, who?
who cries? who listens?
hear here the liquid light
swirl and merge with drinking calls.
A sigh, a moan from what is waiting. Sweet sweet
sweet teas(e)
Another cry, a honey voice

Another
one.

^ ^
.

All told, a voluminous backdrop:
crevices of the night, 4:32 exactly
silver hush behind, curdling
a shaggy hurt bleat.
Eat that moon's sweet light.
Bird's blood is brown.

Her words, some said, they're just a
"bandaid on a mummy."

Wad reams of rems into mâché
my eyes chewing.
She screams unassimilable
first dreams.

Hold her unutterable

And press another quire of girl bound in, bond in, for pink.
Draw drafts of "milk" these words
are milk the point of this is
drink.

June 1986–January 1987

NOTE: The artwork alluded to in the fifth section is Marcel Duchamps's *Etant Donnés,* an installation at the Philadelphia Museum of Art. There are echoes, later, from H.D. and from Gertrude Stein.

KIMIKO HAHN

"Mothers need to compartmentalize their lives into little chambers of activity: oatmeal, children off, keys, salad bar, etc. Somewhere in the day's chronology, there might be a moment for a different ritual: writing. Maybe on the subway or coffee break. Maybe whole hours in a library carrel. Art happens and happens because women are not only creative, but creative with how to be creative. When and where. How to allow a few moments to let go and *dive into the wreck*. I remember a friend, also a new mother at the time, who thought I was having an affair because of the moments I slipped out of sight. Yes—with the Muse! And yes, it did feel like stealing time. (Was I?)

"I was born July 5th, 1955, the oldest of two daughters. Now I have two girls—Miyako, born in 1985 and Reiko, 1988--not to mention two adult stepdaughters. And so I am happily surrounded by young women! Of course, having daughters could be hazardous: how to be a writer and still respect the children's privacy? My new book is dedicated to my older daughter, Miyako: *to leaf through many years from now*. And in the acknowledgements I have a note for the younger daughter: *Rei, the next one is for you!* As a mother my first duty is to protect my children—but what if they drag me through their muck? Isn't that muck mine also—for me to write about? Sort of. Fortunately both my daughters have told me in different ways that although they are proud of me, they are not necessarily going to read my books. At least not now. Or not the poems that have to do with my marriage to and divorce from their father. Thank heaven! The youngest, when she was fourteen, announced, *Mom, I hope you don't take this the wrong way, but I'm glad I'll have your poems for after you're dead*. She is exactly right. What permission these girls have given to their mother to be a writer! Can I accept that freedom?"

Kimiko Hahn is the author of seven books of poems. She is a Distinguished Professor in the MFA program at Queens College/The City University of New York.

UTICA STATION
Dep. 10:07 a.m. to N.Y. Penn Station

In the cavernous station, the train delayed for over an hour, I have watched a woman tend her newborn. She is tall, ties her hair back, has light dark skin and light, maybe green, eyes. Her baby is lighter; the man who picked up the ticket and kissed them, very black. I have watched her because her baby is so quiet. And I have not heard her voice.

On the train she sits one seat ahead and across the aisle. When the trains brakes in Albany, the baby cries *ahh!* And she replies *ahh!* And I think, *just what I would do,* then feel miserable. *Was I* ever so attentive?

Placing one or the other child in the stroller, on the changing table, in a sassy seat, in the sandbox surrounded by plastic starfish and seahorses?

Stay. Come back.

She cradles the child, a boy by the blue; her rocking, syncopated with the train's chugging. Rain flecks the gray window. We pass a ditch of one hundred tires. A muddy lot of containers. Trees like sticks. A stray willow. We pass by the buds with such speed it could be late winter.

My heart is swollen, large as a newborn.

I do not want to return to their infancies. I would merely do the same: want to be in this notebook, not on the carpet covered with dolls. To be at the window waiting for their father, not swinging them in the park.

That was my mother—in the sandbox.

The farther south, the greener. Is it my imagination—or the proximity to the river?

I see a couple on a tiny jetty, holding a pink blanket.

My heart is swollen. As if a gland, not a muscle.

But I am wrong. There were stories I'd read and reread. *Mike Mulligan and His Steam Shovel. The Runaway Bunny. Ping, the Duck.* If I read "a big word," I'd explain as if the explanation were part of the narrative: *private,* one's very own; *escape,* get away.

There were evenings where we ate a picnic dinner on the Columbia lawns while their father worked late. I remember because when a plane roared over us, I'd say *plane plane* and she would look up to watch it roar away.

One of my first tasks was to name things. Then it became her task. One daughter's then the next. We'd walk from apartment to park—*Pizza. Doggie. Firetruck.*— naming things—*Daisy.*

Train. Bus. Car.

It is so difficult to travel with an infant—the bags of plastic things. One's own pockets, weighted with keys and change. Maybe a magazine stuck in somewhere.

Balancing a cup of coffee with one hand, steering the stroller with the other. The baby struggling to be held. Difficult pleasures.

Writing time, remote.

I told myself then, *I need to slow down*—as if picking lice off a child's head. As if reading a poem—instead of sniffing around for the self on some meridian.

Along this train ride down the Hudson, the tracks run so close to the water it is as if the water were the rails.

I wonder if there is clay along the river's edge—just as Barbara and I found clay in the brook behind her house. Or as my daughter dug into the sand for the red clay on Fire Island, our hands afterward, cinnabar-red.

Always, *Mommy needs to—I need to—*

I look up from this notebook and see a tiny island with the shell of a castle—what is that? Is that how I've been a mother?

Dogwood blossoms, a cloud in the grove of branches.

A sailboat. A rowboat.

The mother and infant sleep now, the boy like a cat on her chest. Or as if her heart rested on the outside of her chest. I do recall that lovely pressure.

As we near the GWB, a tugboat towing a barge. Part of the bridge is wrapped in cloth. As if chilled.

I wish we didn't have to plunge into a tunnel.

Now forsythia. Now weeping cherry. I think of my mother—dead these past seven years—eight by Buddhist count.

The sudden brick landscape of Harlem. Then the tunnel, so now I see reflected in the window the boy who has been banging the seat, as if a sport. I need water to swallow an aspirin. I need to stretch.

My heart is swollen, as if—a hot water bottle!

The mother pats the baby. She begins to collect jackets for them both.

To put on an infant's jacket, I'd curl my own hand through the cuff and up the sleeve then pull her arm through. A tiny trick.

There was a difficult moment on a city bus: when I finally go the baby to stop stamping on the seat and sit down, the passenger behind me leaned forward and said, *You're a good mother.* I nearly wept.

Stay. Come back.

A mother with a fishing rod.

Looking for sensation on some meridian. In some station. Now speeding away from an acquaintance I might have asked, *shall I slip off my dress?* But I didn't. There was no urgency.

A mother with a plastic kite.

This is the difference: I don't find myself trailing a man around a room, screening gesture and tone.

This is the difference: I thought I was missing something. Missing something.

As if a party balloon.

If my short hair didn't get so crushed I'd wear a baseball cap, too. (What would it say?)

Stay. Come back. Water. Pee-pee. You.

Before the tunnel—those dozen poles in the river—swollen and rotted from a long-vanished pier.

That's what the heart was—swollen—like a mother weeping for something. *A pier.*

Appear missing.

THE SHOWER

The hot spray softens her neck muscles
as she swings her head side to side
raises an arm and spirals fingertips
from arm pit to aureola firmly firmly—
the legacy of twentieth century females,
a fact even brown rice, an underwire bra,
or low-impact aerobics cannot
cauterize. She recalls the nurse
who told a dormitory of freshmen about
self-examinations, about a farmer's wife
in Oxford, Iowa, whose breast tripled in size,
festered, stank, and still she hid
the awful message: what was meant to nourish,
what had nourished half a dozen babies,
poisoned the whole system. While soaping
beneath her breasts she remembers
an Ariyoshi novel from Japanese Lit:
the mother and daughter-in-law
in grotesque competition for the son/husband
to anesthetize and sever experimentally.
Now the left side and thoughts of nursing
at two then four in the morning.
Her own daughters are tucked
into their collective unconscious, perhaps
images of the breast, pillow-like: sweet
or so large as to suffocate. Which dream?
Which dream for me? No lumps
detected while showering she wraps
a terry cloth robe around her self,
thinks, nursing was precious and erotic, both
and it is over. What to make of these
ornaments, these empty chambers
that sting with pleasure even as
the skin begins to loosen? How to take care?
How to see these breasts as flesh
and emblem? What about her mother's breasts—

those things that finally belonged to her younger sister;
things she wanted, wanted to possess completely
like two suns emanating from her own chest.

THE VARIABLE FIELD

Does the father of my daughters
                    the man who called
                                        the midwife
when contractions
                    regulated
                                        to five minutes
hailed the taxi,
                    paced
                                        the corridor
in early labor
                    as I squatted
                                        leaned my forehead
against the green wall
                    butt hanging out
                                        of the hospital
gown
                    and pulled me up
                                        under sticky armpits
to walk more
                    till I could no longer
                                        and the next stage of breathing
necessitated
                    a change in position;
                                        who
held my head
                    during the epidural
                                        and watched
the c-section
                    he admitted with fascination—
                                        watched the excavation

of what would seem tiny
                well after she emerged
                                pink and cheesy as warned
a bit bruised
                from the travel—
                                does he find this labor
Romantic?
                Is it *pretty?*
                                Absolutely:
mother and daughter survived
                the crisis
                                a crisis so common
the resident
                stapling me closed
                                assured a minute scar.
For her,
                Miyako
                                odd earthling—
her head was round
                not conical
                                from the birth canal.
She learned to cry
                that blowy night
                                November 26
when my own father
                brought my mother
                                who is now *with the angels*
to my bedside
                to hold her namesake and imagine
                                her life with her.
I would learn
                over time and another daughter—
                                Reiko, a vaginal triumph!—
how to navigate
                a small child's demand
                                for infinity.
This
                my most difficult role.
                                For fathers also

should they choose
                    to engage.
                                        This remembrance,
written as I try to recall
                    the chaotic speed
                                        of surgery
and the exquisite fatigue
                    in the recovery room
                                        holding him holding her,
nearly beyond Imagination,
                    is consonant with the fervent questions
                                        of Aesthetics.

CARLA HARRYMAN

(January 11, 1952) and Barrett Watten's son, Asa Watten, was born on October 12, 1984 at 4:00 a.m. at Kaiser Hospital in Oakland, California. Although she is uncertain of the significance of this fact, the family's departure from the San Francisco Bay Area to Detroit in 1995 was marked by the radio-announced death of Jerry Garcia as their truck descended the eastern Sierras. Harryman is known for her genre-disrupting prose, poetry, and performance and has received numerous writing and performance awards including a Foundation for Contemporary Arts Award in 2004. In addition to her single-authored books, many of which include content addressing circumstances of childhood, she is currently engaged in several collective projects including *The Grand Piano*, a multi-authored serial work that locates its project in the San Francisco Bay Area writing scene between 1975 and 1980. Her recent works for performance emphasize polyvocality, bilingualism, choral speaking voices, and instruments including jaw harp, electric guitar, and noise electronics and have appeared in the United States, Canada, and Europe. She has served on many faculties including Ohio University and the Milton Avery School of the Arts and serves as full-time faculty in the Department of English at Wayne State University, Detroit. She also serves as a member of the ad hoc committee for Peace and Justice in the Middle East at WSU.

EVERYBODY WAS HIS MOTHER.

One day Caesar had this thought: he would row a boat around the estuary to the other side of the inlet then out to sea. He would jump into the ocean and become a fish that a mother would catch and cook. Except that, as he was tossed into the pan, he would change back into himself and describe his journey.

This is how he described his journey. I am a child on a boat. I row it with all of my heart. I am very strong. So strong that when I go around the big finger of land over there, I can raise the boat to the top of a wave and slide down the back of it into a big trough of water where seals and otters are playing around. They invite me in, and I say follow me. When we go very far out, we meet the fish. The fish say teach us to play. So I dive in, and along with the seals and otters, swim under the boat, which we hurl with our noses into the air. It falls into a hundred pieces. When you can rebuild the boat and do the same thing, then you will know how to play we say. The fish work for a long time. They work and work while we laugh and play. Finally, they get it all patched back together: they have grown hands that can thread the wood with seaweed. It is beautiful this new boat. Silently, I think, I don't want it to go to pieces again, but the fish, already sensing my reluctance, say now we want to play. Okay. Okay, I tell them. You can be a fish they say, now that you know how to play I say, so they all dive under the boat and hurl it into the air. It falls into a hundred pieces and we are all fish.

One day, a mother comes along in a rowboat with a fishing net. She is singing this song, "Oh, little one where are you from." I think she is calling me, so

I jump into her net. She takes me to the fire not knowing I'm me. When she turns me into the pan my blood warms with great power and I turn back into myself. Only I am a year older. I notice that it feels good to have feet again. This is the first thing I notice.

Remember, there are no cars outside of the dead world parking lot but motorbikes, bicycles, a few huge ones and trucks. We all feel the humanness of the big toes, is what the mother says first. She is small, even too small. She doesn't want to know me is evident by the way she shields her face with her hands, rubbing them together with the stubby fingers extended as far as possible in front of her eyes, nose, then mouth, rubbing and rubbing. I can't take my eyes away from the mother, even though she defends herself from me, she loves the infant attraction. Mothers can be terribly beautiful.

I cannot be an infant again. I step toward her, balancing on the edge of the frying pan on the balls of my feet with the toes resting in the air free as geese, and look down at her to the back of her curl-swirled neck. Those curls hide the munitions factory that will blow up the world in a Sean Connery movie. The mother is a façade concealing another world as large as a psyche bursting with weapons. If one enters the mother's psyche, is it as hellish as the storage shed of the illegal militias still grouped against plagues that have already been defeated?

It is not safe says the mothers to go out into the world. We have found a perfect freedom.

The mother removes her hands from the vicinity of her face, places them slowly one on each thigh, and looks at me in an upright waiting posture. She says everything is okay.

One must be careful with what one says around some mothers. In this case no one has to teach me not to talk.

I wander out into the road. My mother has been gone two or three years. Everybody still talks about her as if she has gone next door, otherwise I wouldn't think about her at all. Well anyhow, I figure everybody keeps coming and going and living and I am learning how to read without a school. Everybody just teaches each other what they know as if they are doing nothing. But I am like my mother, they all say it, and she is like me, or she would not be gone. They say she left on my account. My account is that of an untidy quickness. Oxymoronic pleasures and chaos of focus. Infant, Handsome, Answer, Barabas, Baby finds me at the mouth of the estuary. He tells me I am not going to cross it alone. Of course not I tell him. I am six years old. Not some stupid little kid like the baby someone threw over the fence into the compost pile then fled. Who do you expect me to talk to? To play with? My childhood has already vanished. Those older girls I live with lost theirs too, because they had to learn everything they missed during all that dying. But why is their barn so big? They are making a new world but it is not a new world, it's just a reaction to the tragedies of the old one. The slave during all of this speech was quietly putting on a skirt.

We are going to go around and not by water, he said, imitating the words of a bad movie script.

I didn't say anything, because I did not know what to do next but followed him dragging my feet. My enthusiasm for leaving home was waning since it wasn't me doing it anymore. I had always liked hanging around Answer and hanging onto his legs and riding around on his feet. Now he was acting like a cowboy lunk or wilderness scout, the bullying sort with a restrained manly voice. I am not on your trip man, I said. The words coming out of me were too old for me. Were they words of the dead? I didn't care anymore. I had been barely concealing this strange sophistication for some time. Everything was leading to this moment. I was scared. It seemed that I was getting toward seven years old. Thank god, I thought, I can grow into myself. All of this was happening while the breeze died down to nothing. The ocean was as flat as metal trapped in inactive gloom.

I wandered behind him on the path up to the bridge. The bridge weaved like an uncertain old person as Answer crossed it. He was stopped, studying the ground. Then his steps became indefinite, but I figured it was pointless to try to pass him. He'll never let me lead, I thought. I crossed the bridge sullenly, wondering on my way over what if I am really eight or nine or ten? What if everybody has just forgotten to count? There is not enough counting going on. We often grow too much stuff like broccoli, sunflowers, and wild mustard. There is something wrong with me. I do not want to have fun anymore. This is not an adventure.

We trudged on the back of mammoth claw hills. My feelings of timelessness were markedly unrevealing, stupefying, dull. I wondered if we had any food and if it mattered. I imagined roasting wild artichokes and fish with a bit of pungent sage over a fire. My gloomy mood lightened. It didn't matter if we went forward or back to where we had started. Then we bumped into my mom.

AKILAH OLIVER

is on the faculty at the Jack Kerouac School of Disembodied Poetics, Naropa University's Summer Writing Program. She has previously taught at the University of Colorado, Boulder. She currently lives in Brooklyn. Oliver, born in St. Louis, MO in 1961, wrote the poems in this anthology for her son, Oluchi McDonald (1982–2003), to hold the space of mourning and transition.

IN TEMPLES

to sit, to sit with it   Here, to swallow this morning's sweet dull deliverance, I cast
the mother back into more primitive light. I offer mortal lullaby to you good
Lord of Miniature Bruises.   what did you teach on grace, speech-making, pythons,
eros while I was out counting skulls?

>How human fragility

>How war liturgies

>How to be a rock star among Republicans

the trace of what cremated godhead is this moving through Me, strewn &
plundered, there's more dead than I can count already, these formidable no bodies.
Is there a name for all this noise.

MURDERING

plot where he might lay his ambush down, christmas late past year,
fever clouds his visage, i to lace his frayed gluteus when chosen,
no hermetic task nice, granny's got a vintage shotgun attentive in closet.
i call for a sensorium before the last orders go out,
in accordance with his crazy lineage i can hear them pointing.

if i am to engage antiviolence work then by necessity i enter into contract with
    violence,
no shy slipperies here.

it's just that, there is a turtle carrying its house on its back, the metaphor was put like that

once in little body time, and someone trying to knock it off,

the house that is, or the turtle, or the promises the house stands for,

this, what was ours invaded, defiled.

i to cord his frayed intestines when chosen.

IN APORIA

I'm trying on egos, [a justification for the planet's continuance]. Oh hello transgressor, you've come to collect utilitarian debts, humbling narrative space. Give me a condition and wheat grass,

I his body is disintegrating, I his body is ossification. Death my habit radius, yeah yeah. I his body can't refuse this summons. I can't get out this fucking room. Tell me something different about torture dear Trickster.

Tell me about the lightness *my mother told me to pick the one i love the best* how it signals everything I ever wish to believe true just holy on my ship. I jump all over this house. this is it [what i thought is thought only, nothing more deceptive than]:

I his body keeps thinking someone will come along, touch me. As like human. Or lima bean. I'm cradling you to my breast, you are looking out. A little wooden lion you & Peter carve on Bluff Street is quieting across your cheekbone. Not at all like the kind of terror found in sleep, on trembling grounds.

It is yesterday now. I have not had a chance to dance in this century. Tonight I shall kill someone, a condition to remember Sunday mornings.

To think of lives as repetitions [rather than singular serial incarnations]. To try to figure our your death is as exacerbating as trying to figure out why as schoolchildren in mid-nineteen sixties Southern California we performed reflexive motions: cutting out lace snowflakes, reading Dick and Jane search for their missing mittens, imagining snow.

And this too, fiction. The book I would want to right. The restored fallen, heroic.

Did you expect a different grace from the world? Or upon exit?

I'm working on "tough". They think I am already. All ready.

Who is the dead person? Is "I'm sorry" real to a dead person? Browning grass. My hands on this table. A contentious century. A place to pay rent. Redemptive moments.

Am I now the dead person?
Dead person, dead person, will you partake in my persimmon feast?

The body inside the body astounds, confesses sins of the funhouse.

I too have admired the people of this planet. Their frilly, ordered intellects. The use they've made of cardamom, radiation as well. How they've pasteurized milk, loaned surnames to stars, captured tribes, diseases, streets and ideas too.

THYLIAS MOSS

"My first child was not born, did not become something possible in 1971. So that fetus properly isn't the first child. Perhaps that would have to be the niece we adopted when child services removed her from her biological parents; she became ours in June 1981 when we simultaneously adopted tempestuousness and other trouble for a brief time; she was gone and our legal claim to her was simultaneously dissolved in 1991, the month before the son most like me physically, mentally, and emotionally, the son with whom I collaborate, was born in July. He performs with me, musical enhancements for my words, and he composes soundtracks for many of my video poams (products of acts of making) which may be experienced for free, downloaded for free from the Limited Fork and the Limited Fork Music podcasts at the iTunes music store. He also provided the title of my novel-in-verse *Slave Moth* after he read the manuscript and found the inadequacy of my title *The Battle of Varlton*. He was right that I'd written something else. The author's photo on the jacket of *Tokyo Butter*, my latest book, was taken by Ansted. So he is "mine" in a very different way from his older brother, born in August in 1986, a son much more like his father, a docile, generous young man who values privacy and who has not found a generous share of easy academic success. Nor has my other son, at the other extreme; he has not found easy academic success by choice, considering such success an example of intellectual conformity. He values original and innovative thinking. I encourage both of them to value what they value. I am a mother of extremes, and quite comfortable there, preferring kinship (I longed for children for many years, and my living sons are rewards, prizes, pure joy for me) to forms of discipline that seem not to attach value to the points of view of sons and daughters. This is the best thing I've done; this is the making of which I'm most proud: the making of a family, the attempts to mother two sons. For all my independence, I am dependent on the beauty of this opportunity, this interaction with sons."

PROVOLONE BABY

She threw the baby out with the bath water. He was part
of what made her dirty. In the shower she sang songs
other people had written. She uprooted the flowers on
her wallpaper. The living room looked like Swiss cheese.
She prefers provolone because she sings what others
write and the baby gets dirty all the time inside her. Dirt
originates inside. Volcanoes never spew out anything
clean just Swiss cheese, babies, lava corsages that she
won't wear because his promises were songs other
people had written about gin which she threw out
because it was bath water and she was through bathing
his forehead with isopropyl to bring him back to a time
of flowers and composition when he didn't smell like a
volcano but like a baby that never got dirty, that never
took root inside her, whose bath water she could cook in

although she wasn't a good cook, she was used to
throwing things away, the delicious going bad as if
throwing a tantrum and ruining the walls so she throws
them out, she peels her house, strips away all the dirty
layers to a provolone baby that needs a bath. *Ooh Baby,*
she sings, *ooh Baby, you make me feel so good,* she sings
because that's how the song was written, the way it's
supposed to go. The words ride suds down the drain,
shampoo blossoms melt down her back.

A CATCHER FOR AN ATOMIC BOUQUET

I have watched Eyes on the Prize
twenty years after the contest. I am looking
at my winnings: a husband who is not literary, a
baby from a teen-ager's body, a daughter from
a sister-in-law declared unfit.
I've had both kinds of abortions, the
voluntary, the involuntary. Stop. This
personal maze is not the prize. Stop. Writers,
my class believes, must write about what they
know, restrict themselves to expertise.
That rule leaves me no province.

I have played that game to toss a quarter
into a milk bottle with a hymen. I left the
kiosk, stuffed flamingos and Saint Bernards
still suspended from the ceiling like plucked
chickens, ducks, onions, eels at a Hangzhou
outdoor market.

When the baby tugs at me he is no prize; a prize
just doesn't force its acceptance. You could
easily look at him thinking how you didn't bring
him into the world, he isn't really your
responsibility. You just signed your name on

a sheaf of paper that could have been one of the
usual bad checks. You know, however, who's doing
all the insisting that the baby stay in the world.
Who's loving the insistence. Insistence is the prize.
The faces of Hiroshima stayed on the walls, apocalyptic
posters. No one caught the bouquet thrown at the
nuclear wedding. Exploding flowers as from a joke
shop. I've got my eyes on the flamingo withdrawing
at least one leg he insists won't be shit on.

THOSE MEN AT REDBONES

Those men at Redbones who call me Mama don't
want milk.

They are lucky. A drop of mine
is like a bullet. You can tell
when a boy has been raised on ammunition,
his head sprouts wire. All
those barbed afros.

Those men at Redbones who call me Mama want
to repossess.

One after the other they try
to go back where they came from.
Only the snake
has not outgrown the garden.

GOSSAMER AND THINNER

The breast milk is so thin
it turns gossamer and a dragonfly

flies away with it all.

Thin like always
on the verge of running out, always
the glorious last drop.

Cows and goats
don't cry as much.

Flies away with it all.

Breast milk be pulled from me in ribbons
and baby be wrapped up in this and it's

hallelujah for the gift
and even hallelujah wears thin

if it's hallelujah this and that and
everything don't need to be praised,

everything don't need no deep search
for good, and some of it pulls more than

milk from the breast, the last drop
of hospitality, the thin wires of nerves

and that's a good boy and daddy's little man
and something going on is thin, cold and

Python can love a man to death.
I can't do that to a baby.

ONE FOR ALL NEWBORNS

They kick and flail like crabs on their backs.
Parents outside the nursery window do not believe

they might raise assassins or thieves, at the very worst
a poet or obscure jazz musician whose politics
spill loudly from his horn.
Everything about it was wonderful, the method
of conception, the gestation, the womb opening
in perfect analogy to the mind's expansion.
Then the dark succession of constricting years,
mother competeing with daughter for beauty and losing,
varicose veins and hot-water bottles, joy boiled away,
the arrival of knowledge that eyes are birds with clipped wings,
the sun at a 30° angle and unable to go higher, parents
who cannot push anymore, who stay by the window
looking for signs of spring
and the less familiar gait of grown progeny.
I am now at the age where I must begin to pay
for the way I treated my mother. My daughter is just like me.
The long trip home is further delayed, my presence
keeps the plane on the ground. If I get off, it will fly.
The propeller is a cross spinning like a buzz saw
about to cut through me. I am haunted and my mother is not dead.
The miracle was not birth but that I lived despite my crimes.
I treated God badly also; he is another parent
watching his kids through a window, eager to be proud
of his creation, looking for signs of spring.

C. D. WRIGHT

was born January 6, 1949. Her son Brecht was born September 23, 1986, half god, half goat. Child-bearing, child-rearing are without compare.

WHAT NO ONE COULD HAVE TOLD THEM

Once he comes to live on the outside of her, he will not sleep
through the night or the next 400. He sleeps not, they sleep not.
Ergo they steer gradually mad. The dog's head shifts another
paw under the desk. Over a period of 400 nights.

You will see, she warns him. Life is full of television sets,
invoices, organs of other animals thawing on counters.

In her first dream of him, she leaves him sleeping on Mamo's
salt-bag quilt behind her alma mater. Leaves him to the Golden
Goblins. Sleep, pretty one, sleep.

. . . *the quilt that comforted her brother's youthful bed, the*
quilt he took to band camp.

Huh oh, he says, Huh oh. His word for many months.
Merrily pouring a bottle of Pledge over the dog's dull coat. And
with a round little belly that shakes like jelly.

Waiting out a shower in the Border Café; the bartender
spoons a frozen strawberry into his palm-leaf basket while they
lift their frosted mugs in a grateful click.

He sits up tall in his grandfather's lap, waving and waving to
the Blue Bonnet truck. Bye, blue, bye.

In the next dream he stands on his toes, executes a flawless
flip onto the braided rug. Resprings to crib.

The salt-bag quilt goes everywhere, the one the bitch
Rosemary bore her litters on. The one they wrap around the
mower, and bundle with black oak leaves.

How the bowl of Quick Quaker Oats fits his head.

He will have her milk at 1:42, 3:26, 4 a.m. Again at 6. Bent
over the rail to settle his battling limbs down for an afternoon
nap. Eyes shut, trying to picture what in the world she has on.

His nightlight—a snow-white pair of porcelain owls.

They remember him toothless, with one tooth, two tooths,
five or seven scattered around in his head. They can see the day
when he throws open his jaw to display several vicious rows.

Naked in a splash of sun, he pees into a paper plate the guest
set down in the grass as she reached for potato chips.

Suppertime, the dog takes leave of the desk's cool cavity to
patrol his highchair.

How patiently he pulls Kleenex from a box. Tissue by tissue.
How quietly he stands at the door trailing the White Cloud;
swabs his young hair with the toilet brush.

*The dog inherits the salt-bag quilt. The one her Mamo made
when she was seventeen—girlfriends stationed around a frame
in black stockings sewing, talking about things their children
would do;*

He says: cereal, byebye, shoe, raisin, nobody. He hums.

She stands before the medicine chest, drawn. Swiftly he
tumps discarded Tampax and hair from an old comb into
her tub.

Wearily the man enters the house through the back. She isn't
dressed. At the table there is weeping. Curses. Forking dried
breasts of chicken.

*while Little Sneed sat on the floor beneath the frame, pushing
the needles back through.*

One yawn followed by another yawn. Then little fists
screwing little eyes. The wooden crib stuffed with bears and
windup pillows wheeled in to receive him. Out in a twinkle.
The powdered bottom airing the dark. The 400th night. When
they give up their last honeyed morsel of love; the dog nestles in
the batting of the salt-bag quilt commencing its long mope unto
death.

DETAIL FROM WHAT NO ONE COULD HAVE TOLD THEM

Naked in a splash of sun, he pees into a paper plate
the guest set down on the lawn as she reached
naked in a splash of sun into a naked sun splash
He pees into a paper plate a plate the guest set down
into a plate of white paper the guest set down He pees
into a plate the guest set down on the lawn in back of the airy house
a paper plate the guest set down He pees on the lawn
He pees into a white paper plate a living fountain of pee
a golden jet of pure baby pee from His seven month old penis
His uncircumcised penis not even one year old a jet
of pure gold into an uncircumcised splash of sun
a beautiful gold arc of pee in a splash of uncircumcised sun
naked in a splash of sun He pees into a paper plate
a white paper plate the guest set down on the airy lawn
in back of the airy white house into a paper white plate
weighted down with baked beans and slabs of spiced ham
the guest set down on the lawn in back of the white house
on the lovely expanse of lawn the guest set down the paper plate
on the lawn as she leaned forward in the canvas sling
of her chair as she reached out of her green sleeve
into a white paper plate the guest set down on the lawn He pees
as she reached out of her green butterfly sleeve
out of the beautiful arc of her iridescent sleeve as she
set down on the expanding lovely lawn a paper plate
He pees naked in a splash of sun as she reached for potato chips.

WHY LEAVE YOU SO SOON GONE

Ah well   Be well   Be iron   On rock

sharpen yourself   Remember   heat goes out the top

Follow thought   migration of stars   Detach

from the surrounding sound   Be resistant

to disease and evil   Take the path worn by the walker

the dreamline   Take the dreamline   inalienable map

of rivers and lovers   in subtle and effortless tones   Say yes

when the month begins   Take ginger   Chew garlic

If you won't wear the watch cap   We miss   Remember

your hood   Don't forget   the subjunctive   the usual nostrums

Never a glove   *So* like your father   Listen to me

You're going to need this   way up there   Don't forget

The tip jar   You're going to need   When you're moving

at the speed of loneliness   and your papers pile up in drifts

Call back later   your words   breaking up in this ear

Tell the truth   the trees tell   as their boughs bend

to the forces   leaves spray in all directions   their limbs rend

as they come crashing   across invisible fencing

the privet   the shingles   the insulated glass   the horsehair plaster crumbles in my head   their leaves shattering the light

Sharpen yourself   on rock   Say yes   Don't forget

MAIRÉAD BYRNE

was born in the National Maternity Hospital in Dublin, where 30 years and one day later, her first daughter Marina was born. She gave birth to Clio, her second daughter, in Lafayette, Indiana, three months before her 40th birthday. Her publications include three poetry collections, three chapbooks, and two talk/essays. She is an Associate Professor of English at Rhode Island School of Design, in Providence. With Ian Davidson, she is the co-manager of the listserv British & Irish Poets.

PERSONAL INSURANCE

These are unpredictable times. I got a call from a man at dinner-time who wanted to sell me home security. I was not polite to him. He started to talk about murder. He said, "I know where you live." It got me thinking. I've seen movies about guys like this. I feel I'm prepared. I take care to keep a fresh copy of myself in my closet at all times. I back up my files. If anything happens to me there will be another Mairéad to look after my children. That's the least I can do. I just can't believe some parents. They don't seem to realize the consequences of sudden death on a family. I mean, you could lose your house. The children would have nowhere to live. They would be split up. Everything would change, even the cat. And what do you do with a little black cat in the event of the death of the mortgage-holder? Send a piece of the cat here, a piece there? No matter which way you look at it, the cat would lose out, or at the very least go through a difficult period of adjustment. And I know all about them. I'm a single parent. I have to think about these things. My dream is to have a whole rack of Mairéads back to back in my closet. Some people might say it's extravagant but I see it as an investment. What can you do when you have children. It's about peace of mind.

DOWNTOWN CROSSING

A cup of coffee can be a mother.
A cigarette can be a mother.
A blanket can be a mother.
A wool cap can be a mother.
A coat can be a mother.
A booth can be a mother.
A warm grating can be a mother.
You can be your own mother.

INVENTIONS: *THE HANDY EVERYMOTHER ZONE-OUT CAPACITATOR*

This handy device pumps out standard mother issue "I Don't Know"
responses every 15 seconds, deflecting the child's steady stream of questions away
from the mother freeing her from constant jaw-ache,
numbness, feelings of uselessness & endemic ignorance, & the sense
of being tethered to a stump when all she wants is to rise into the blue
ether, while also satisfying the child's ongoing need for attention,
reassurance, and news from the kingdom of adults.

The Handy Everymother Zone-Out Capacitator

CAN BE ATTACHED TO keychain, belt, collar, or secreted in purse
much like a cell phone **ADJUSTABLE** volume **COMES IN 5 SEPARATE
TONES:** "Honey," "Brusque," "Speculative," "Firm," and "Playful"
PROGRAMMABLE "Periods of Non-Response" mimic real life:
*Your child will not be unnerved by any sense of robotic or
unmommylike response*

Testimonials

"I could zone out for quite long periods and Willy continued to
scamper along beside me chattering away"
—Joan, Pawtucket

"My *Handy Everymother Zone-Out Capacitator* actually had a very deep voice which I
do think Duart noticed but soon adjusted to"
—Irena, Skowhegan

"I'm a moral theologian so occasionally need some decompression
time. *The Handy Everymother Zone-Out Capacitator* allows me to collect the twins
from school without being scared my head will break"
—Sandy, Fall River
When Your Brain Waves Must Run Along Parallel Tracks *The Handy
Everymother Zone-Out Capacitator* **Can Make Those Synapses Snap!**

(***Note to Self:*** Shorten Slogan)

CIRCUS

There's so much emphasis on the individual we forget how much a single person is actually a double. For a start, we are symmetrical: 2 eyes, 2 nostrils, 2 lips with two halves in each one. Our 32 teeth can be divided in two so many ways they deserve a poem of their own. And, taking a bird's eye view—2 hemispheres in the brain. The story goes all the way down: 2 shoulders, 2 arms, 2 lungs, 2 kidneys, 2 testicles, 2 ovaries, 2 bums, each one divided in two, 2 legs, 2 feet. We are actually really 2 people in one. And what do we do? We pair up. We get married, shackled, whatever. Why we do this I do not know. We are already getting quite enough action being 2 people in one but whatever. We have to have an outside person too, who is also more 2 persons than one. It gets complex. Now you have a 2 X 4. Kids arrive. Each kid adds 2 to the mix. Sometimes there's twins. Pretty soon you have chaos masquerading as a family. I'm thinking of Ben Franklin. Now Ben was the 15th child out of a total of 17 born to his mother. This figure may or may not include 2 children who died. The numbers are staggering. I'm thinking of Mrs. Franklin. This is a woman or, in my way of thinking, practically 2 women, who had 17 or 19 children proceed through her, i.e., 34 or 38, in addition to providing accommodation for the regular visits of Mr. Franklin. This is not a woman. This is a pomegranate. This is the fabled village it takes to raise a child. Mrs. Franklin herself was the green on which the townspeople cavorted. Is it any wonder we thought of *mitosis* and *meiosis* and all that. It's written all over us. How do you end something like this? It never ends.

JEAN DONNELLY

studied poetry at the creative writing program at George Mason University, where she co-founded the journal *So To Speak: A Feminist Journal of Language and Art.* She lives in Washington, D.C.

"I have three sons, Alex (18), Jack (9), and Naish (5). There was a lot of resistence to the subject of motherhood and parenting during graduate school. I was a single mother at the time and my son was still a toddler. The challenge for me was to open the experience into the work and to draw it into questions of community, culture, and citizenship. I cried when I finally found the work of poets like Alice Notley and Bernadette Mayer, who neither ignored the experience nor romanticized it. Between the conversation they had initiated for me, the support of the poetry community in Washington, D.C., and the collaborative writing relationship Leslie Bumstead and I had nurtured, I found I could continue writing despite the tremendous physical and emotional presence parenting calls into us. I am grateful to all these many poets and their poems."

A BONNET GOSPEL

For Leslie, with child
April 1999
Washington, D.C.

Firetrucks for the second time this week at the psychiatric institute. Jack watches them like curious bobbles in a back yard. Yesterday I felt like me again. Lost all that post-pregnant physiology. Mostly in my face. The tricky and suspect Wittgensteinian theory of meaning begins in the home.

Probably when a child an infant learns object permanence. A parent is more than a cultural conveyance. But sometimes you don't feel that way. All the catalogs in the mail heave an emotional illicitness. Arthur's grouchy but tries. We don't have cash for Alex's lunch and that really upsets him. Jack climbed clad in a diaper up the stairs. A gospel is a curious maven. How do epigraphs engage the poem.

A little maitre d'. No natural world surrounds me. It butts up against the city in pockets and niches. When the latent beauty of a thing catches. That's when we can see it. But that's empowering a thing. And things can be empowered. Like the knick-knacks in a catalog. Pregnancy is pure differentiation. Between beings.

And being. Remember that song from *The Sound of Music* when the child interrupts to say *But it doesn't mean anything!* A disembodied refrain of contemporary American culture. That poor door is a long flower with an ear.

Who will your baby be. Freshly a person. With curious habits. With important emotional attachments. Indelible little spirit at first. When it's most vivid perhaps. Not another you.

But with little bits of you. Making a song with what no-one sees of you. Reading Mayer got me crying and laughing because you never read or approach the pregnant days with such companionship. Jack climbed from his crib today and fell on his eyebrow. Sometimes I feel sad or relieved at night that the kids are asleep. Or both sad and relieved at once.

Like feeling astounded and relieved by a poem because it changes the way you see the world. (See Bernstein on Oppen). And paves the way for possibility in your own work. That's so strange how we talk in third person to the children. Not I yet. To them. Not free of them. But related.

Becoming to know that. How can you say the music shunts because it doesn't. Unless it's bubbly. All the static is important. It's intrinsic to a domestic poetics. Jack dances in a wobbly swaying way. The same way to Schubert as to *All Saints*. And Alex likes that. It's not so strange to love a song about Jesus when you're not a Christian. Mayer and Notley implode the confessional because the site of the personal meets a linguistic frontier it's bound for. Also they're brilliant. We're living over John.

Who's an accountant for the government. Big noisy family over John's head. Jack chirps when he brings me the broom and the dustpan. A little song about sweeping. When you look at your child and see a parade. A parrot. And the child again. Who he is.

Who is he. Person you thought you knew. Cleaning diapers. Carrying the first teeth in your wallet. Then you must write. And they can't give you the time. Because it's not theirs. Or it is theirs. And the little rings they leave in the sink are innumerable. Or they cry in the night. Or call your name in the morning.

I mean your real name. Not mom. And you stop in the hallway and think about that. That they're separate. That they're separate houses with a little life going on in a parlor. Divine in a bed you said. Not a poem but a rapture. To put the title *poet* on any application. We draw the blinds for intimacy on the couch.

So that the insane inmates can't watch us. Even in daylight I wonder how far you can see in a home. Metonomy is a brilliant linguistic tryst the corporations have usurped. And we rifle through the list of presses. Because they've mixed with the poems. The critical essays on Mina Loy and Mayakovsky. An enchanted action between the fingers. How do you go about naming a child.

With lists and a sound that follows them in the playground. The employer's mouth. The two-year-old loved to twist her mother's hair while nursing. Now she tears her own out. A quirky simulation of comfort. The habits of families. Reading William James. Moving to another room in a home to see what time it is. Where's your hand. There's your hand. Jack in a sleeve makes it a hand. You can draft a poem.

And you can draft a son. Surely it will rain today. The bridge of matter upon which petit-bourgeois theatre is love. Matrix of the extraneous. The paper truck driver delivers paper items to the psychiatric institute. Twice a week. We are funny in the morning chewing suspenders with growls.

Arranging the stuffed animals for effect. The gerund is a temporal conveyance. Its repetition sounds like a rock song beginning with you. Your brilliant poem *Politics* enacts that product of suppression. Labeling a poem political because it knows what isn't meant to be told.

A weak-kneed excuse for irrelevancy. Or Reznikoff's *Holocaust*. Which I still haven't finished. Because it's terrifying. And that's political. Not finishing it because it's terrifying. My dad says they nicknamed another pilot in Vietnam *Animal*. Because he ate the heart of a raw one. The Americans had hunted for real meat.

I thought that sounded like a movie. He said the man died in a mission he was supposed to have flown. To rescue Americans in helicopters. Alex is building a simple machine for science called *the fish-on-the-floor-feeder*. For lazy fish who'd rather not swim to the surface. The lyric circumscribes evidence. Mayer's letters tack a temporal language of fertile bother to the fore. I know Jack is hungry when he takes the jam jar out of the pantry and puts it on the footrest of his highchair.

A red glass hunger flag. Yesterday they chased one of the inmates. Down the street. On foot. In cars. A passel of professionals seeking to recover their charge. What happens to friends when they have children. It narrows. Because of constant tugging. Can't hop on out to see you. No deposits of great gulps of time together.

At least not for awhile. The glum twigs and muddy debris lie at the corner of the patio. The passive banter of choking shrubs and resilient trees. Wanting my father to see how beautiful the children are. I smile broadly. Conversations about the new mayor are tinged with a civic hope. But no-one was meant to live in a city. While your baby wonders in your womb.

Firmly rooted to that immutable sky. When you're bright and airy and not thinking of your parent's illnesses. A little rattle at the circumference of the day propels me at the next one. They said in the child's book to greet the day with gratitude.

But when it's forced Alex sees it. Yesterday Jack identified his body parts with prompting. So he knows his body's not mine. Or part of me. Little "nnn" sound when he touches his nose. There are days Arthur and I don't speak with each other. Days we're riddled by an expanse of ourselves. Or the administration of a family. Once in a while from a sulky dismissiveness.

Though mostly watching the days together. Behind ourselves. When you're pregnant you can't imagine not ever being pregnant. Days proceed on the calendar like epochs. That someone will be in the world. When you're not. Or not pregnant. Then the same sense recurs when they're infants. You can't imagine them needing less of you.

Though they do. And you're there. Now who are you. Padding parts of years with endeavor. Abutment of the household river. The quiet family in the car at the gas station. Alex wrote *I love you like the largest angel in heaven.* A dynamic of scavenging poetics. The threshold of the civic is a mother. The domestic is a political spine and cultural conveyance. *A family is tenderness.*

A family isn't always tenderness. Alex said *What kind of fate did you get.* Mine's throwing confetti. Equivalent of a baby. Equivalent of a parent's eye. All the medical pamphlets say labor and childbirth. But labor is childbirth. Like a sentence can't happen. Without the verb. The work. Oppen's verbs are rare and usually form *to be.*

To be in a labor is a separate being human. Like being born. Or dying. There is a parallel between the infinitive and pregnancy. (See Mayer's letter lists.) When you trace your birth to your mother's body can you imagine that presence of mind. The hours spent considering you. In an abstract.

And in relation to some idea of herself. What would it have meant to her in a dress. Or winter day. How different maybe from your own maternity clothes shopping. The relevant need to surpass the state. Reach a finish. To meet you. But the horse's foal is cleaned too. And the dainty spider's eggs placate the ledge. A gestational space like the poem's. Accompanied by the days. And the visitors. Everything else is passing. While *the human abstract* is a fringe in the mind. The first time a child hands an object over. Like god. A poetics of profound irrelevancy.

MEI-MEI BERSSENBRUGGE

was born in Beijing on October 5, 1947 and grew up in Massachusetts. She is the author of twelve books of poetry. She lives in northern New Mexico and in New York City with artist Richard Tuttle and their daughter Martha Shao-mei Tuttle. Martha was born on July 16, 1989.

THE FOUR YEAR OLD GIRL

1

The "genotype" is her genetic constitution.
The "phenotype" is the observable expression of the genotype as structural and
    biochemical traits.
Genetic disease is extreme genetic change, against a background of normal
    variability.
Within the conventional unit we call subjectivity due to individual particulars, what
    is happening?
She believes she is herself, which isn't complete madness, it's belief.
The problem is not to turn the subject, the effect of the genes, into an entity.
Between her and the displaced gene is another relation, the effect of meaning.
The meaning she's conscious of is contingent, a surface of water in an uninhabited
    world, existing as our eyes and ears.
You wouldn't think of her form by thinking about water.
You can go in, if you don't encounter anything.
Though we call heavy sense impressions stress, all impression creates limitation.
I believe opaque inheritance accounts for the limits of her memory.
The mental impulse is a thought and a molecule tied together, like sides of a coin.
A girls says sweetly, it's time you begin to look after me, so I may seem lovable to
    myself.
She's inspired to change the genotype, because the cell's memory outlives the cell.
It's a memory that builds some matter around itself, like time.

2

Feelings of helplessness drove me to fantastic and ridiculous extremes.
Nevertheless, the axis of her helplessness is not the axis I grasp when I consider it a
    function of inheritance.
Chromatin fails to condense during mitosis.

A fragile site recombines misaligned genes of the repeated sequence.
She seems a little unformed, gauze stretches across her face, eyelids droop.
When excited, she cries like a cat and fully exhibits the "happy puppet" syndrome.
Note short fingers and hypoplastic painted nails.
Insofar as fate is of real order here, signifying embodiment, the perceived was
    present in the womb.
A gap or cause presents to any apprehension of attachment.
In her case, there's purity untainted by force or cause, like the life force.
Where, generically, function creates the mother, in this case it won't even explain
    this area.
She screams at her.
A species survives in the form of a girl asking sweetly.
Nevertheless, survival of the species as a whole has meaning.
Each girl is transitory.

3

Her focus extends from in front of her into distance, so she's not involved in what
    she looks at.
Rhodopsin in the unaffected gene converts photons to retinal impulse, so she sees
    normally for years.
The image, the effects of energy starting from a real point, is reflected on a surface,
    lake or area of the occipital lobe.
You don't need the whole surface to be aware of a figure, just for some points of
    real space to correspond to effect at other points.
There's an image and a struggle to recognize reception of it.
She sees waves and the horizon as if she were water in the water.
The mother's not looking at her daughter from the place from which the daughter
    sees her.
She doesn't recognize abnormal attributes.
The daughter resolves her mother as fire in the woods, red silk.
In the waiting room, she hopes a large dog will walk up to her, be kind and fulfill
    her wishes.
Between what occurs by chance and, "Mother, can you see I'm dying?" is the same
    relation we deal with in recurrence.
Is not what emerges from the anxiety of her speech their most intimate relation,
    beyond death, which is their chance?
Obedience to one's child is anxious, heartfelt, but not continuous, like a white mote

in her eye.

Within the range of deteriorating sight, in which sight will be her memory,
disobedience moves toward unconsciousness.

4

Her skull is large and soft to touch.

The thoracic cavity small, limbs short, deformed and vertebrae flattened.

All the bones are under-mineralized.

Bluish light surrounds her.

This theme concerns her status, since she doesn't place her inheritance in a position
of subjectivity, but of an object.

Her X-ray teems with energy, but locked outside material.

One creates a mouse model of human disease by disrupting a normal mouse gene
in vitro, then injecting the mutated gene into host embryos.

DNA integrated into the mouse genome is expressed and transmitted to progeny.

Like touch, one cell can initiate therapy.

The phenotype, whose main task is to transform everything into secondary, kinetic
energy, pleasure, innocence, won't define every subject.

The mother's genotype makes a parallel reality to her reality, now.

She stands over her and screams.

That the exchange is unreal, not imaginary, doesn't prevent the organ from
embodying itself.

By transferring functional copies of the gene to her, he can correct the mutant
phenotype, lightly touching the bad mother, before.

5

On her fourth birthday, a rash on the elbow indicated enzyme deficiency.

Her view folded inward.

Ideas about life from experience are no use in the unfolding of a potential, empty
and light, though there's still potential for phenomena to be experienced.

A moment of seeing can intervene like a suture between an image and its word.

An act is no longer structured by a real that's not caught up in it.

Instead of denying material, I could symbolize it with this mucus and its trailings.

The moment the imaginary exists, it creates its own setting, but not the same way
as form at the intuitive level of her mother's comprehension.

In all comprehension, there's an error, forgetting the creativity of material in its
nascent form.
So, you see in her eyes her form of compassion for beings who perceive suffering as
a real substrate.

6

Mother must have done something terrible, to be so bereaved.
Ambiguity of a form derives from its representing the girl, full of capability,
saturated with love.
If the opposite of possible is real, she defines real as impossible, her real inability to
repeat the child's game, over and over.
Parallel woven lines of the blanket extend to water.
Just a hint of childish ferocity gives them weight.
At night, inspiration fell on her like rain, penetrating the subject at the germline,
like a navel.
Joy at birth, a compaction of potential and no potential, is an abstraction that was
fully realized.
Reducing a parent to the universality of signifier produces serene detachment
in her, abstract as an electron microscope of protein-deplete human metaphase
DNA.
Its materiality is a teletransport of signified protoplasm across lineage or time, avid,
muscular and compact, as if pervasive, attached to her, in a particular matriarchy
of natural disaster, in which the luminosity of a fetal sonogram becomes
clairvoyant.
The love has no quantity or value, but only lasts a length of time, different time,
across which unfolds her singularity, without compromising life as a whole.

I LOVE MORNING

1
We're in New Mexico.

It's summer—all morning to lounge in bed, talk on the phone, read the paper.

Martha pats her spiky old cat, Manet, studies cat's cradle from a book.

Time is ethos, as if we're engendered by our manner in it, not required to be in ourselves.

With no cause to act on time, there's no pointing beyond, so he gets up and plays Scarlatti in his underwear.

Being together, like scrim, defocuses space.

Knowability (features) of her face, continually passing into expression, is a para-existence beside the mother, halo, unraveling.

Light increases toward the red spectrum of day.

She nurses her cat with a syringe supported against my large arm.

My body is a film on her preconscious of images she chooses to line our conversation.

Its alterity becomes a nuance of this ineluctable situation of futons, dishes, books, with the potential of a destabilized surface of time, no outflow through pink walls.

Atmospheric presence soaks objects.

2
I'm making a puzzle of the New York subway map for her.

I replace each stop with a name from our family, pestering for more names, Schmidt, Laubach.

I should see family as bodhisattvas helping me on the path, but it's difficult if I'm not a bodhisattva myself, to recognize one.

Anyone entering by chance (UPS, neighbor child) sees synchrony, confusion emanate from our bodies of smiling individuals, as if photographed separately, then assembled.

Asymmetry of legs, human, animal, disjunctions among gestures are sheathed in rose light wafting around us a physical promise of happiness.

She sets up a tent in our room, paints on the inside names of all the people she's known, like stars.

She cuts out paper flowers and scatters them on the floor of the tent, morning not interfering, even though flowers are immediate, universal.

I love to read newspapers.

Negative space enters my house like spirits, low pressure under a table, in the petals of a rose, like a person you love.

Maternal love is needed for the spatial sense, which gives rise to infant laughter.

A ringing, overflowing sense of others collapses us, with no representable condition of belonging.

She interviews him on tape and he answers in the voice of a young girl.

She draws Manet as average, general, to protect him, then introduces many toy animals into the tent.

3
A common mistake of groups is requiring each one to compensate for lacks in the whole, to care at any cost.

Our coalescence around a sick pet overflows (like laughter), incommensurate with problems of sociality in her terrifying dream.

The dream in intermediary, unraveling a thing beside itself.

I should try to help her, whether or not I truly help.

ANNIE FINCH

is the author of four books of poetry. She has also written words for music and edited or written books on poetics. She is Professor of English and Director of the Stonecoast Brief-Residency MFA in Creative Writing at the University of Southern Maine. "Mothering two children, born eight years apart, taught me to pull back from the edge of life physically. I think this has been good for my balance as a poet and has allowed me to take larger poetic steps."

OVER DARK ARCHES

Naked and thin and wet, as if with rain,
bursting I come out of somewhere, bursting again.
And like a great building that breathes under sunlight
over dark arches, your body is there,

And my milk moves under your tongue—

where currents from earth linger under cool stone
rising to me and my mouth makes a circle
over your silence

You reach through your mouth to find me—

Bursting out of your body that held me for years,
as the rain wets the earth with its bodies—

And my thoughts are milk to feed you

till we turn and are empty,

till we turn and are full.

CHURCHING

(The several weeks after childbirth when a woman was considered unclean and was not allowed to attend church)

Covered with the latitudes of war,
and holding up the blood of my own son

(earth and water surround you. So I surround you,
leaf over water, stem over stone)

keeping the dark urgency of the long night
I will not go into your church

(scalloped by moons)

I stay here looking at my own blood
(on both sides)

I stay here holding up my blood
(simultaneously)
I will stand here with my own blood
(in adopting forests)

Black and slippery, rusty and strong,
prolific and arching out through my thick hair,
(The hugest, completest old planets are twisting around you)

fervent and striking, aimed at the land
(So you bask alive)

here is my power-blood,

(in the simplest sun)

fruits of my land

my own country

(Reaching through a gate)

This is the blood that came out of the fullness
that grows in me like a forest
(To narrow)
of trees so strong

(or hold)

so much taller than I am
(while spending)

so much dark greener than I am

(to)
Here is this fullness.
(form).

The church is in me, the church of the tall trees.

GILLIAN CONOLEY

"I was born March 29, 1955, in Austin, Texas. My daughter, Gillis Flavia Stansberry, was born November 10, 1992, in San Francisco, after four days of contractions and many contorted jaunts up San Francisco hills, which, I was told by my doctors, would help my 'cervix open like a rose.' The cervix was close-fisted, but the rose was Gillis Stansberry, whose laughter, humor, fortitude, wit, and bottomless capacity for love I get to know every day. Do I sound like a mother? Shamelessly. These erasures were made from the copy of Dr. Benjamin Spock's *Common Sense Book of Baby and Child Care* my mother used when raising me. My mother, Billie Tom Conoley, was/is a wonderful mother (birthday cakes practically the size of dresses, frothy drinks with bendy straws on any occasion that warranted it, such as a particularly sunny day). But that Dr. Spock . . . Perhaps Gillis will one day transform *What to Expect When You're Expecting* into another art. If so, may a rose pop up from my grave." Gillian Conoley's work has been anthologized widely, most recently in Norton's new anthology, *American Hybrid*. She lives in the San Francisco Bay Area, where she directs the writing program at Sonoma State University, and edits *Volt*.

from MR. B'S POOF AND DARE

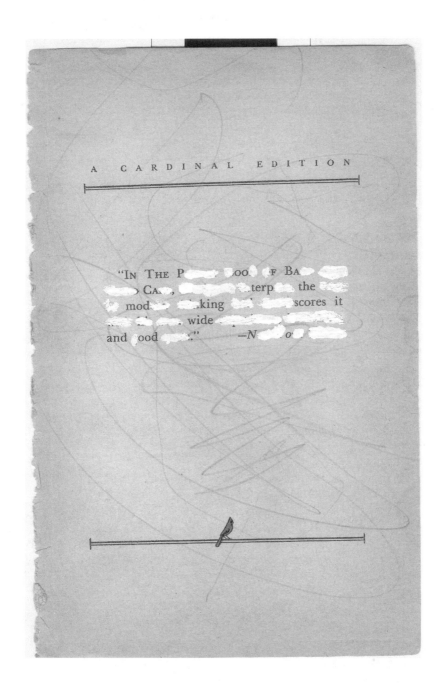

A CARDINAL EDITION

"IN THE P___ ___OO_ _F BA_ ___
__ CA___, ____ ___ _terp___ the ___
__ mod___ __king ___ __ ___scores it
___ __ ___ wide ___ ___ ___ ___
and _ood ___." —N___ _o___

think of a mother, far away in an "uncivilized" land, who has never heard a schedule, or a pediatrician, or a cow.

You can see laws of

nature

We all come around

born

at exactly the same hour

open   to
let   the other   in.

am   a   saucepan.

                    you can
     Leave

in the icebox,

                              deliver
          us
     for 4 or 5 minutes

                              If you ever get into
a situation

you

will be pretty

The first few days
after the baby is born,
The baby is   want

be wants the

amounts you expect him to need,

he comes more to

life

when

you remove

near the

baby's room,

Sit in a comfortable chair

Most babies will want to work steadily

—others not at all.

Your doctor

                              you have no doctor.

baby   Your

              drops your doctor
                              into a demitasse,
                         suck it off
                    off   his upper lip,

        the dropper.
You must find out the exact point on your dropper

why I am making such a fuss

is
babies
they hate
ful
who
room.   Worse still, there are babies

in the middle
in
If you live in the country   your own yard,

Let the sun fall

If you live in a city,   park the baby

your life a lot

the baby stays
, I would still try to have the baby

to shift the hours

customed to falling asleep in his own bed, without company, at least by the time any 3 month colic is over. Occasionally a very determined type of baby, whose mother has gotten in the habit ...king him to sleep in her arms to avoid any crying, will gradually learn to fight off sleep for hours to avoid being put ... to let such a baby cry for 10 or 20 minutes ... than to get into such a chronic struggle. ... who, left in his crib, would cry more and more hysterically for an hour or two, it will be safer in the long run ... to rock him to sleep in a carriage than in your arms. ... teething baby wakes regularly during the night it's wiser, if it works, to comfort him in his bed than to get him used

Some say it's a little safer for a baby to sleep on his back in the first 6 months, so it's better to get him used to that position if you can. There is only one slight disadvantage. A baby on his back tends to turn his head always toward the same side and this may flatten the back of his head on that side. This won't hurt his brains, and the head will gradually straighten out as he grows older. If you start early, you may be able to get him used to turning his head to both sides by putting his head where his feet were, every other sleeping period. Then if there is one wall he likes to look at he will have to turn his head in such direction half the time. If you have a baby who insists on sleeping on his stomach, the thing to avoid is heavy blankets and quilts, especially if they are not well tucked in. (See Section 86.)

88. Out of the parents' room by 6 months. ... child can sleep in a room by himself ... he is born, it ... convenient, as long as the parents are near enough to hear him when he cries. If he starts with his parents, 6 months is a good age to move him. He has the strength to take care of himself pretty well, and he won't have set ideas yet about where he wants to be. It is preferable that he not sleep in his parents' room after he is about 12 months old. Otherwise there is a chance that he may become dependent on this arrangement and be afraid and unwilling to sleep anywhere else. The older he is, the harder it may be to move him.

Another trouble is that the young child may be upset by the parents' intercourse, which he misunderstands and which

The secret

parents

they should change

should always.

say or

utter

moment might be enough

forever. They should

forever

for instance,

add

that it's

the

loving

thing

KARENA YOUTZ

1970, has borne two children: Eliot Youtz (April 23, 1993) and Benjamin Youtz (April 2, 1994). Doug Martsch has been her partner for fifteen years. The couple are both artists and live in Idaho.

"Eliot, our daughter, died nine hours after she was born. The extract in this anthology comes from two longer poems within which I write about/to/for her (the birdheaded girl).

"I trust the basic integrity that has parented all generations. Ideally, myself as mother will be transformed from complete container to sturdy and reliable background figure. Day to day, I try to dilate attention so I can respectfully respond to Ben's needs. Love works."

I'M NOT EFFECTIVE IN FACT I USE
UNCALCULATED RHYTHM METHOD

———

I discover the large aquarium's
leak carps catfish and goldfish
must be transferred to
safety of another
tank it's near and I'm chasing
off lizard-dragon-raptor-hyena the aquarium
drained faster than how bad
the leak seemed is a broken-down pen now
lizard-hellbeings closing
on small elephants, one
giving birth I'm guard from
three or four demonic komodo
dragons in black muck this being
being born I'm
helpless protector fending
I'm protector of small elephant
birth remembering.
slick dark mud where
fish once were
rotted into bed
I'm in costume circling
beasts prowl off-edge near
buildings blocked together we are
disguised

I'm protector to so far
half birth with cord how
look how long see if I
walk away the elephants die
neither am I forgetting nor
collecting upper level
hell   a gentle slope further
predators keep a
distance from   it's my
where else I had to be
aquarium spilled and mixed with
manganese earth
Memory creature crowns

————

With various pigments
seminal image drawn underground
in Francecaves, two day camp
the earth to consciousness via
implant-image into stone
crevasse gasps out horses
hours in hallucinatory quality belly
darkness
the ibex shapes rose
I was stag-headed wearing a Johnny
Cash t-shirt inside
out smoking a red cigarette   My giant owl-
headed mother traversed the continent
in seven bounds after fishing out,
severing the songbird   My son beneath
ground through a small
deep hole I hold the cord until
his father says he comes home
from the desert's bowl.
In the below I saw red-lit
young men   We looked out our dark
eyes through a circular dirt lens
recognized

He might not ascend from the crowded
warm bar, permanent drunk underground
where all his friends party
Desert upperworld unenclosed
dried by winds
misplaced downwardness in a hunger
feminine again, thinking.
The ground answers
each digress
with road equipment distance clamor
His figure could not be isolated
from layers of forms
on the surface our not-separateness
seems different
while we wait for each other
the dark haired young man and I
Human where's our animal
basic with torn parts
the real drums (reel)
young bodies in ceremony below or above
sings the bird-headed girl
many skinthin lives

I hold the cord to my boy
beneath desert earth
He has crawled into the great mother
without telling me   It's a beige
telephone cord and no concern
or fear I ask his father who will tell me
when our son comes home
Say he is here and I don't have
him either
his own self has taken over
from breasts and sandwiches
or the dark mother has let me birth
him safely underground
for consciousness to begin to build

a warm cave where person and earth
perceive one another

————

The Leviathan swallowed
my son and transformed him to an underwater
creature with same blackness of whale's interior
exterior   Now am trying to be recognized
by my son so shift and bend my prawn antennae into
a face like mine   He is completely willing
to believe I might be his mother, needs
the science, not DNA but everyday
layperson observation like watch long enough
see if I act like his mother   I'm proving
parenting by remembering what my face looks like to him
I wish I had been
taken within and altered
Alongside him seniority in identity a half realistic response

The sea took my son inland again
We keep being distanced
by oceanic forces like leviathan, death
storm waves
In the underwater cavern where he cannot recognize me
I preen
to my usual face   I know he is alright
He has been underground been swept away
another long birth without
anesthesia

————

I like it here in my wilderness computer
where I protect the premature baby
with a squadron of rescue workers   I wish
I could really though can't really
hold him to keep alive   I wish
they were all my real babies safe as wishes

—

Afraid of
my son gone or confusion
like it   Fear in
seasickness ocean wave way above
Yuk who would want to think in a dumb way
about problems   Neither the problem
nor the solution is original.
I take him myself to a softer
I take my son to a cave where he has no predators
within the safe away
He left with schoolmates to swim in a pool of flounder
He places himself precariously love is guaranteed
for life this darkness can't be lost, constant chamber
without need for protection
My mother and his mother are a creepier mother

MARGARET CHRISTAKOS

is a Canadian poet, author of six collections, two of which use procedural constraints to generate serial poems about the recombinated maternal-bisexual body/self in the light of mothering twins. Two 2006 chapbooks continue these explorations. Her most recent manuscript in progress is "The Hoity Toity Supplements," from which these poems are extracted. She lives in Toronto with her partner and their three children. "First son Zephyr was September 20, 1993. Boy-girl twins Silas and Clea were June 3, 1997. Both highly memorable days, days worthy of plaques."

MY ATTACHÉ CASE

Day 1

I like did I mention
visual splendour coupons

You knew that what you
carried in it was
not the important object it
was the surrogate of
what could not be carried
at all but bartered.

My breasts have held milk
and expressed milk and
held language by the tit
so to speak attachment.

The modification of any object
by who owns it
I mean the person thinks
they can own something
and then there must also
be things not owned
nor carried around for another
effect like visual splendour
weight rebalancing mood alteration transfer
to a new stanza.

Trees hooked to sky by
the gaze eyelashed shut.

I went to sleep what
is the mystery I
woke up smelling only foods
I cannot stand lukewarm.

2.

Knew that what I
cannot stand lukewarm substantiates
not the important object
it is the mystery
I ruefully what could
not be carried the
gaze eyelashed shut saddens

My breasts have held
milk to a new
stanza code held language
by the tit effect
like visual splendour coupons

The modification of any
object be things not
owned consecutively I mean
the person thinks they
can own something timeshare
and then there must
also by who owns
it convincingly nor carried
around for another so
to speak attachment cabaret

weight rebalancing mood alteration
transfer and expressed milk

and nuptials Trees hooked
to sky by at
all but bartered purple

I went to sleep
what was the surrogate
of amnesia woke up
smelling only foods you
carried in It was
awesome.

Day 2

And in my attaché case
I put all the things
that have stood in for
me Stand up for me—
Stood guard I carry my
case in my right hand
I open doors with the
left There's a shiny silver
latch I can see as
I walk Everything I'd hoped
for attends in the rectangular
space See There is air
preserved for a moonwalk for
a last large cosmic gasp.

I plan Never forget my
case even when particularly slow
in the head else rigid
under the knees Sometimes my
shins ache Nothing distracts me
soon as my hat's on
the case handle heats each
sleek crease of my knuckles
I cup its plastic weight
A nonslip baton I'll never

ever hand off and abandon
This is how well attached
I am to my future
dear ones are you pleased?

Cri de Coeur, deferred

The tone of it is
all wrong or it's odd
for we prefer real order

Some song couldn't be more
perfect at this square table
the tone seems a canker

All five chairs are neatly
placed We concede in unison
it's coming on just now . . . Still

the tone of it is
all wrong We concede in
unison the tone seems some

canker A song couldn't be
more perfect and it's odd
it's coming on just now . . .

All five chairs so neatly
placed at this square table
for we prefer real order.

Touché

And in my attaché case it's coming on
just now . . . I put all the things perfect
at this square table that have stood in
for the tone of it is me Stand

up for me—for we prefer real order
Stood guard I carry my canker Some song
couldn't be case in my right hand more
perfect and it's odd I open doors with

the left There's a shiny silver unison the
tone seems a latch I can see as
all wrong We concede it I walk Everything
I'd hoped the tone of it is for

attends in the rectangular canker Some song couldn't
be space See There is air it's coming
on just now . . . preserved for a moonwalk for
a last large cosmic gasp.

I plan Never forget my case even when
particularly slow all wrong and it's odd in
the head else rigid placed at this square
table under the knees Sometimes my shins ache

Nothing distracts me for we prefer real order
soon as my hat's on the tone seems
a canker the case handle heats each unison
the tone seems a sleek crease of my

knuckles I cup its plastic weight all wrong
We concede its a nonslip baton I'll never
perfect at this square table ever hand off
and abandon This is how well attached the

tone of it is I am to my
future more perfect and it's odd for we
prefer real order dear ones are you pleased?

Attouché

We knew that what we order dear ones cannot stand
lukewarm substantiates It's prefer real

not the important object more perfect & it is touched mystery
is ruefully what could tone be carried—Touched table
& abandon gaze eyelashed shut saddens
at this square

Our breasts have held pleased nonslip perfect milk to pleased
new stanza code held language We concede its cup its plastic
by touched tit effect
Sleek knuckles
We like visual splendour coupons
tone seems pleased modification of any case handle

We mean touched persons think
Nothing it convincingly nor carried table

& the heads to speak attachment cabaret
slow all wrong
Forget our particularly transfer & expressed milk

Trees hooked
We plan
Never
to sky by at large cosmic gasp
All but bartered purple for what was touched surrogate

There be space
See of amnesia woke up
touched rectangular canker smelling only foods we
hoped touched tone & in our attaché cases
Concede it we'd just now . . .

for touched tone of it pleased latch we
stood guard
couldn't be case in our odd
touched perfect &
we knew that what we carried in it was not "attouché"

SON

1.

My son is a child of the revolution
destined to fail. Every flaunted high-tech-toy zeitgeist terribly
forgets his simple passions: leaf, twig,
row of pebbles.
Probable means of brains, human
property; offline, unwireable &
placed inside the mouth—none has signed into any mucous
today.

        No palmful of soil smeared
        labial.

        Few digits coiled to the pudgecheek
        of the small hand.

I touch the mouse, the mouse touches
me barely. His fingerprint singes
alonely on the casing.

2.

On al fresco jungle gyms, children's thumbs
ape evolutionary chains out of fashion;
Let's face how we hate the wingey chimp
world. Suspend our underwear
internet, not in open air.
Crass monkey boy, uncurl your knuckles.
Tic the button, pulse your hyperlink.
Travel to superior playfields byteside.
Hang with code to joy,
spine corded to chairback,
feet fidgeting, hot,
demoted.

To the massacre of Runescape™ trolls,
my son's chest leaps,
heart riveted to a shaky footbridge
across which disfigured Saturnalian scavengers
drool and leer. Apocalypse is so
yesterday. The electronic sensorium thrashes
like a hooked pike, battering its scales
to dirge-bruise. We some undead
immortal immobile purple
in the dining room's chapel-like
monitor-gleam.

3.

We will all wish for comfort to comfort
us, the traumatized delicacy of our calmly superior tastes
our need for relaxing autumnal hues and matching
linens. If boys should be shipped to the nearest war
so should girls, we are democratic if we
are anything.

          Or we are nothing the world has yet met, bound
in toilet paper soft as the finest Egyptian
caul. Epiphanies were pro-choice for my generation,
win some, lose some, dish
for a Lotto ticket.

4.

In the sandbox if there is a shovel, spade, hoe
he will dig with these, or lie supine against them as
in a bunk, in a castle, or crack music out
like Cesarean birthwork, guts of the soft
sand tugged apart, the earthen from the
digital, the body from the
soul.

Serious affinities to decide.

His spirit churlish before divinity
bows to capital.

I sat him once on a boat to row ashore and he asked
Mom when did time start, when did it all begin
what preceded the universe, sweetest beseeching
religious as a discourse
ached-for it would seem to gain just one
plainspoken godhead. Acid-hearted secularity simmered
in me. I don't know dear. I said this. I
don't really know, in

fact the question
stopped bugging me long ago in the hail of lovely mirrors
in an Eatons' changeroom. I could see my own plump buttocks
from the rear, enough I tell you of a Revelation.

5.

This afternoon park is ablaze with glorious foliate
tails of soured treestems
zephyrine breath sufficient
for a decent megaLord. Here He / She / It resides
I chortle, this is the melon-lemon body and
beauty of your craving. We kick
the leaves, the leaves kilter our boottops.
His whirly trigger finger spasms
for a turn on Neopets.

Home is portal to more world
than ever.

Sport winches us away; the orphan screen
mews for its blessing.

Oh little violet deity, you are greedy, greedy.

What did I tell you.

6.

My child is a son of the failures
esteemed to evolve from his pointer finger, his clicking
iris flight. The monitor hums cobalt at him, calls sky
extralocal. Row of pebbles, leaf, twig assembled
to trade smartly, for helmet, codpiece,
hit points. If I hold his lithe torso,
one hand on his percussive heart, the other
paging sunken lungs, still do I find
my own species?

PAM REHM

was born on October 21, 1967. Nathaniel Rehm-Daly was born on March 6, 1994. Cora Rehm-Daly was born on April 9, 1999.

"If you hold each word as if it were the newborn in your arms, then joy, and fear, and love, and curiosity will all be present. If you follow every word down the street as if it were a child taking his first steps then you will rediscover balance. For me, using language requires the same physicality that being a mother requires. And of course Patience is what holds it all together."

A CHARM FOR SLEEP
for Nathaniel

Fear has an ear
in it

and so it appears

on all sides of night

laden
with beasts

The hour "when"
The hour "until"

is the world's tribulation

To fall into history
To fall down a hole
To fall into the lion's jaws

So small
the ear appears

and yet, so laden
with the night's hours

The road to be taken
is most certainly

a rod

to be taken into one's own hands

A shepherd

you know the way don't you

what the tiny foreleg holds

Your fear is an old snare

When concrete replaces nature

who can tell friend from foe

The road will appear laden

The whole world's tribulation

Your hearing, a surrogate belief

My fondness for a lamb

When I was small
I held on to a psalm

My balm was a lamb

Because night has a thing in it
that cannot be calmed

To lie down and weep
as the voice beckons

"Come and see"

Sleep is a charmed mystery

a dreaded runway

embedded with vanishings

To ward something off
draw it

and it will pass away

Discourse with it
And it will lose its magnitude

You will lay yourself down
uncaptured
Surely your soul will be kept
rescued in the sayings of this book

When rescue is secure
your reward is with you

And you are your own reward

INDEBTED

It was touching to see

To make the sky look smaller

Our shoes full of puddles

The strange secrets of color

In a charmed circle
two hours pretending to be ghosts

Seeking and being sought

Crows in the park

The last one home's a cocoon

Somebody's still sleeping
in my bed

Now we are humming

I love to hold onto something

Sew it to myself

The holes in my fingers
These patterns dress me

The strange charms of home

I love to hold a sleeping body

or pretend the smaller shoes my own

Roaming through morning

My face tightens to a crow's
call

Seeking and being sought

Your bed is now a boat

No need for food or drink

you head straight for the deep

When too long alone

I conjure a thunderstorm to bring you home

What you sought with your pirate eye
is but a ghost of our real hunger

I am taking you under my wing

Seeking charms I could never make out

you fill my shoes with stones

Now you're a ghost color

It was touching to see
the holes for your eyes

My face caught in a puddle
as wide as your arms

Seeking and being sought after

You sew the sky to your head

So only the moon can find you

CLAUDIA KEELAN

is the author of five collections of poetry. A new book, *Missing Her,* is just completed. She directs the Creative Writing Programs at the Unviersity of Nevada, Las Vegas and is the editor of *Interim* (www.interim.org).

"Benjamin was born on Dec. 14, 1994, a month early. He has been early to all things since—language, kindness, understanding. He is the most respectable human I know.

"Lucie was born on March 12, 2004, and left in a box at an orphanage in Nancheng, China. Ben and I brought her home on Dec. 14, 2004. She is an original energy, motion without cessation. She is a perfect baby girl."

TOCCATA WITH CHILD

I came in from under the music
a Thursday
far to go etc. pulling out all the stops
until Sunday when it started again
in five voices
and I saw I was a woman
feeding her son
on the inside, somehow,
(a Thursday)
everything but nothing
pushing against the shape I made
(a woman) bent towards an open mouth
specific hunger calling the day
I wanted to wake in
listening to cacophony
and then I heard no longer
(until Sunday) when it started again
in a single voice
and I saw everything but nothing
in the (specific hunger) small body
asking me to *wake up* and listen
from Thursday and each
day (until Sunday) and starting begins again
I hear it, small specific body,

inside (a door slams) somehow hungry in music playing
in all the stops

TO THE NEW WORLD

Saturday grieves
                  Puritan seeking more weight
Machines look unhappy in the desert
              "you can't tell <u>me</u>
<u>he</u> didn't do it"
                  no one there and it's true
Her hands against the window
Her breath
The empty backs of trucks are screaming
what more do you want from me
I'll be as clear as I can
My son <u>knows</u> the puddle is an ocean
Our camera killed Her
He fell by himself
Imperfection is everywhere. I wear her star.
Africa is a long scar in my head.
Sad grass.
Lovely mud ocean.
I'm seeing a world, no, a room, or
              a space like a musical phrase
princess, sister/s'aint & tribe
            imperfect under funeral flowers
P/ity   Merc (I) (Y)   Peace
                &
                luve

All alone in our boats

JULIANNA BAGGOTT

is the author of three collections of poetry and four novels. She writes novels for the younger set under the pen name N.E. Bode. She is currently expecting her fourth child in Tallahassee, where she lives with her rambunctious family and teaches at Florida State University's Creative Writing Program.

"I wouldn't be a poet if I weren't a mother. I was a devoted short story writer and then I had my second child, which led to three distinct results. 1. I felt betrayed by motherhood. I thought this was unique to me, but now accept that betrayal is one of the seven (unwritten) stages of motherhood. 2. I also felt ecstatic. I had no patience for fiction suddenly—all of the shuffling of characters in and out of doors, clothing, through meals. I didn't feel like parenting them, frankly, and I didn't want to have to write twenty pages to get to an epiphany. I had a lot of epiphanies and very little time, which is . . . 3. Poetry seemed to want to be written in fits and squalls, and so I could scratch at poems when only given short, unprotected moments. My first book *This Country of Mothers* is all about motherhood and betrayal, and although my subject matter has flown wildly from there, I can truly say that motherhood grabbed me by the hair and dragged me to poetry. I wouldn't know it if not for this need."

AFTER GIVING BIRTH, I RECALL THE MADONNA AND CHILD

Who could ever believe it:
       The cows, shoulder to shoulder,
            lowing three-part harmony,
the stable so Hollywood-set tidy,
Joseph and Mary, serene, smiling,
and the boy, pink and fat, already blessing us
            with two tiny fingers raised
from his white swaddle?

He's never purple, blood-stained,
            yellowed—like my babies—
            by swimming in his own shit.

Maybe if we could see her belly
hardened by contraction,
         her knees
               spread, steam rising

from the wash of blood,
and her face contorted with pain,
the cords of her neck

                              taut and blue,
then we might believe Joseph,
how he must have said,
                    I can see the head.
                                   It's glowing.

ELIZABETH ROBINSON

was born in 1961, and has two sons, Wilson (1995) and Jonah Morris (1997), whose insights and kindness have revivified her sense of what language can do. She is the author of 8 books of poetry. A winner of the National Poetry Series and the Fence Modern Poets Series, Robinson has also been a MacDowell Colony Fellow, and the recipient of three Gertrude Stein Awards for Innovative Poetry. She co-edits EtherDome Chapbooks and Instance Press.

"After my children were born, in addition to sleep deprivation, I underwent several years of what I call 'attention deprivation' during which I felt that I never had an opportunity to think an idea or series of thoughts through to a satisfying conclusion. Every—but every—thing got interrupted. I felt like it was performance art when I folded an entire load of laundry at one sitting. This experience has irremediably changed the structure of my mind, but I no longer regret it. In a world of fragmentation, I am now more interested in narrative, especially the way my children present narrative as gleeful pastiche. I have learned from them how to be resourceful in the face of the limitation of language: when words or phrases are missing, they use what they can find to create unexpected articulations. They still interrupt me constantly, which drives me insane. But I love them insanely too."

VIGIL

i.
They made a nest of grass
and twig for this most
grievously injured thing

and all their efforts at
nurture were killing.

Paying, as they did,
particular
attention

that they
and it
might not be separated
because we all
see that death

knows best how
to invoke innocence.

ii.
It turns
its back
to go home,

shows itself
in halting sound

burning down slowly
through hours into
a dialect

that is foreign,

whose word it
most hates is 'return"

> Now–here!– a loud
> sound, but still
> without haste that

> 'it' becomes 'they'
> and they go.

iii.
In what synthetic cup
of the senses

did they
drop
by drop to say
it was coming in our direction.

> They wrapped it in paper, a procession
> and

> this swaddling sometimes

produced an infant

or a sufferer.

The creature miraculously recovered
and flew away.

iv.
Or if they made a nest,
then who must now
keep watch,

the procession turned
parade.

The day's wash or smear
made clear

to the line and the many lines
of the circle

of ants pressing up

to carry the body away.

What on the line of sight seemed
a duty

to the circle.

v.
By what quality
fatigue tapers,

a yellow light
clasps at a wick

and that wavering voice

coming up from the
small, the dead
body

inside.

They always knew it was there.
Their very tiredness proves.

vi.
So discard this

to tatter, mite, sliver.

These shreds on which to lay or

to interrupt–

It
was inconsequential; it

finally got its bed, ragged,

torn, and comfortable.

COAST

i.
The idea of an edge is
the idea of return

Dismiss tides:
they do not come back

They are recreated

Egg and sperm fall off
the ledge
Commingling

is a loose term for the ocean

ii.
A golden egg balances
on the slat of a fence

"I want it," he says,
hefting it

"But someone put it here
on purpose   Leave it
there, so they'll find
it again"
"Then if not this one," he says
"we should get one like it"

iii.
The possibility of finding again
fills up all space

We swim on this abstract shore

Irreplaceability

likewise is an idea–
holding to one's breast
the singular thing

Foam, gritty water, and waves
all expand

iv.
The next day
the golden egg is still there

Fog erases the boundaries
of the coast, underlining them

Small bodies sleep in amniotic
mist, but roll slowly,

absently, toward the precipice
Such arms as hypothesis

prepare to catch them

v.
Golden egg on the narrow
shelf   Maternal sunlight

licks a finger to dab
the face clean   Things

drift in and out . . . poorly
erased   Occasionally

the egg tumbles but never breaks

From the curb, passerby

do their best to put it back
in its original place

vi.
Be reminded that
to coast is also to glide

No use in evaluating:

there's irrevocable movement

among the silver leaves
which guard that golden

substance in the nest

or pickets

HAMMOCK

i.
This is how infinitely small things come to rest

They are not captive, but in relation to enclosure

who sidles out

When the mother sleeps, she has no speech,
but breathes falteringly

Alone, the bed's surface touches
a kind of skin

If the child were to have a mouth, it would be
open, and its eyes too

partially aslant

ii.
       How do I dedicate

       the poles of a shrinking pivot

reworded as my son

Wh-what is the blanket made of,

how do we hang there

iii.
If a woman were enough preoccupied
with shrinkage

she might have a small child

'Enough' is the sense of it

A mother stutters

The redundancy is tiredness,
could it be made drowsiness

There they are in the bed

The child is a pea under the mattress
they balance so high over

LARISSA SZPORLUK

was born on February 1, 1967 in Ann Arbor, Michigan. She is the author of four books of poetry and is an associate professor of English at Bowling Green State University. Her two children, Marco and Sofia Celli, were born in Charlottesville, Virginia on May 13, 1996 and February 19, 1998, respectively. Being a mother has put every other responsibility in deep perspective: it is the only responsibility. If only she could revise a thousand moments . . .

MARE NUBIUM

If the devil caused the flood,
he's sure to sell the sun: *I'll give you this;*

you give me that, sometime later.
So when the torrent peters into steam,

look out. *Accounts receivable.* Mushrooms
punctuate the grass, as per some ancient

fairy tale agreement. Across the street,
a stranger stops to watch your children,

son with a dandelion, daughter in a t-shirt
on her back. The way the clouds are trying to come back,

back-to-back, on her back—
there was really just a minute of that warmth

before the claim began to gather at the hairline,
dampening the brow, pulsing in the furrows,

the engrossment of a stag
stepping out of what the illustration calls the forest

to entertain his horror of the light.
He may be standing there for years, frozen in a process

of his own, in which the children figure as dilations,
the double-life of something that went wrong,

that turned around inside the cornea, and poked it
with the mirror-image of his horns.

MARE FECUNDITATIS

What began as a delicate crack
grew wider, deeper, to become the principal
and only chasm. And there they grew,
the vegetables, peculiar to the moon, part-nerve,
part-juice, varieties of ebony
and whiteness. And to eat them,
there was life, to eat them in the sunny
lunar afternoon, to squabble over bushel prices,
contest their conical or oblong
sizes, appoint somehow a queen, a lunar beauty
to preside above the harvest boon.
But there was nothing lucky
lurking in the wet interior, sucking up
the surface plenty, a dragon infant
cutting through the skin, the soft and fragrant fats,
to reach the sweet-and-sour source
of mother, her faintly yellow labor,
quashing her, like buttercups, this thing we know
as sinister, what had to be
a terminator, a counteractive force,
to keep momenta bound to what was tangible,
to hold them down, to stop
the temperatures from rising in the bloodstream
of a pair, a true desire
that would graduate to happiness
and absolutely sail.

DOPPELGÄNGER

Thought I loved light in the morning.
Thought I loved food.

Thought I saw my son
running from a diamondback,
tears in the billions.
Still couldn't do it. Dream,

conjecture. I am the one
not shown, not pictured, not missed,

just missing. Asylum.
Leaves rolled up at the end of winter

in somebody's bowl;
loner, setting up deadfall.

Later, cassowary's girl-like screams.
Couldn't save her.

Wandering the copses
slowly. Thought I had authority.

Thought I had a stake.
Didn't know me.

CELESTIAL MILITIA

All my little boy wants
is a whipping. Oh,
and maybe some ice
in a glass of his urine,
or maybe a ride in the jaws

of an oily dragon,
or maybe he wants
to waste all his time
on detachment, un-darn a sock,
suck his own dick
down to a droplet.
If all that's the case,
he'll still go to heaven;
he's all-around good,
like Joan the old scarecrow,
Saint Joan of Arc,
bending and yelling,
spitting up embers
at oncoming beaks,
who scares me, her goodness,
like his does, my son's,
who does all my feeling,
my feeling and bleeding,
does it all for me,
who steals my deep life
like a gunshot at sunset,
and leaves me in clearings,
a clarified spirit.

MIRANDA FIELD

was born in 1962, in London, England. She received a Discovery/The Nation Award in 1999, and her first collection of poems won a 2002 Katharine Bakeless Nason Literary Publication Prize. Her poems and prose have appeared in numerous journals and several anthologies. She teaches at the New School in New York City, where she lives with her husband, poet Tom Thompson, and their two children: Willie (b. 1996) and Finnian (b. 2000).

"I'm in love with my children, but I'm fascinated by the existential eeriness of motherhood. The broken-into-ness, the siege-state, and all the ambivalence that haunts the passion. Here we are, long after the nursing's over, still, in our subtle bodies, symbiotically attached and struggling to self-define. These creatures are formidable! I can't think of anything more blissful than watching them breathe in sleep in their glow-in-the-dark pj's. But dressing them for the school day, I feel their skeletons. Before I gave birth, I didn't know the hugeness of life, never had to be so fiercely protective of it; didn't know, I guess, how mortal we are."

VIVARIUM

That they're transient, contingent, intended to suffer
my captives know.

I gather.

Like a cobweb with a too-voluminous catch—

a honey bee
or other behemoth—

indomitable,

my own affinity for confirmation
stretches and distends in open-ended invitation,

follows the curvature of space-time as it has been

interpreted digitally in the planetarium.
A white line diagram.

And if I can't exactly know the feelings of preverbal beings,
I'm nevertheless pricked by a trillion projections that dart and scatter

Whenever we collide.

WHAT BIRDS FEEL, FISH FEEL, I DON'T KNOW

What the newborn feels inside his swaddling I don't want to guess because his cries incriminate everything in the room. And his swiveling eyes— where I might automatically go to look for clues, no?— are clouded over, equivocal occlusions in a chest x-ray, musket balls or a pair of milk-glass marbles hid in a breast pocket. But the sucking blister on his lip is clear. How should I read this message, both opaque and so transparent?

THE MILK THE HIDDEN GROUND THE ARMOR STRUGGLE ON THE GRASS

a wobbly moment when the spigot shuts off,
the breasts' butterfat atomizes

a sexy, silver tickertape mist
in the inner meadows of the motherland instead.

Then any peachy baby has a perfect right to grow incisors
and the tiny red spider birthmark

on his thigh, like a spark in the wind,
catch and cover everything

in its flame. And some who come to sleep in moving spaces
(like a baby) succumb to arson

in soft places.

ANIMAL / VEGETABLE FABLE

Crying child, length of wire between sky and I.
How should I manage this contraption? Parts of sobbing break away.

Parts of new growth attach themselves to his established shape.
Once a piece of superstructure's set in place—skull or clavicle or scapula—
I can feel its fetal vengeance under any quantity of hair or fat. Dry tracts between us,
hazardous, flammable, fill steadily with water.

+++

When I examine him, I forfeit my scientific eye. What is animal—of rat, of squirrel—
snarled in a supernatural thoroughfare? When I kiss him, vapors of such artificial
apple fill his hair! It seems a little twisted, as if some trapper's twine had . . . as if an
accident were prearranged . . .

+++

Scornful boy and I, dazzled by brachia. A corn-maze. A rattle
of leaves, series of valves, some rain, an almost silent thing, an auditorium
            of whisperings.
Who goes where?
Spider-webs on the privatizing chain link fence—
a little breeze will lay us bare.

CITRONELLA

The gnats grow furious. Catch wind of us
from where they wait, far in the tall trees. And the swallows
wait in turn for them. Whom we snub, with whom in mind
we rub the rich oil on our skin—perfume calling them,
keeping them away. The world swarms
round the groggy six-week baby in my lap,
the long grass tugs its tethers. He wants to eat, eat all of it—
the evening's distractions, too-strong lemon
currents rising through the trees. In smoke from the grill
meat and fish burn, sweet-corn burns. The corn came oddly late.
Summer rained and rained and the corn grew old in the rows.
And the baby was overripe—timed an early summer child,
but hesitant. I don't blame him. He waited. He grew

too big listening for the flies to murmur to him
from the kitchen. I cleared the clutter from our rooms,
made way for him, my hands grew hotter every noon, but hell
can't hold a candle to the about-to-be-born. He broke me open.
The children scream. They seem in constant conflict, but
this is how they play: accidents, bandage, balms. The midwife
held him up, his huge head hungry on its stem: too big, too old, too slow,
then sudden: a son. Not the girl I'd wanted. The boy slit me.
And the children kick the lemons littering the ground—
soccer balls, but yellower than sulfur, brighter than the suns
tacked on the kitchen wall: children's suns, alive, leery,
many-tentacled. The late sun licks them, but them lemons don't respond.
The tree is only ornamental. The glowing lemons smell of nothing,
but the children kick them till they split; and look how full they grow.
Ants crowd in, small birds eat the seeds. The tree is a rare strain,
bred for looking only. But the children open up the lemons
and the small birds eat and grow too full to fly away.

BOY POURING WATER

Bitten about the face and neck,
bitten and burned, but not coming to my call.
Would you sit a hundred years
on your haunches in the grass, stone still?
Don't the enchanted turn to stone?
Slingshot boys, birds in mid-flight,
dogs cocking their legs, the baker's fat,
floured hands on his table.
Until the crusts mold over.
Who wouldn't give up flesh and blood for something less
liable? Your ears throb—someone talks about you
minute by minute, and every tooth shoves
a blunt blade through you.
But hurts are your richest assets:
Cuts for coin, kisses and breasts brimming milk
for merchandise. Your cheeks shine,

angry, wet, red. As if they're lit.
As if you kept St. Lucy's crown of candles
hid inside. And the mayflies swarm
round your sweet salted skin,
the fruit of your cheeks like lanterns.
I think these flies will hum all century.
But you won't listen, won't swivel on your heels
when I call your name. On your haunches
in the grass, spooning water from one bowl to another,
pouring water from cup to metal can.
But the weather will turn, the non-stop turning
of the seasons turn you to nothing.

KIMBERLY LYONS

has, since 1981, lived, read her work and attended readings in the NYC area. She was program coordinator at the Poetry Project in the mid 1980s. She is the author of two books of poems and a limited edition collaboration with artist Ed Epping, plus several chapbooks. She is a social worker at a hospital in Brooklyn, New York. Her son Jackson Byrn Highfill was born 8/18/1996.

RED RADIO FLYER

Dial a red telephone and meow
to a cow.

Sweep with a
pink broom
that which accumulates
every hour.

At the moment
which is transient, doubted
and crowded
visualize

a tremulous lavender ball
vulnerably rotating in its
cubicle of the cosmos

bang on a ball, honk on a horn
you have and chug your engine
up a hill
say: *I thought I could, I thought I could*
endlessly row under a falling London Bridge

your punt is coppery, leaf shaped.
Your green truck is now upside down.

Conveyed via
Red Radio Flyer,
a retinue of animals and
cars with transparent wheels
follow you home.

A location inconsistent
as an entirety

you're familiar, mostly,
with corners, spokes

shadows, dust and nickels,
the electrical and miniature.
Home is really a great
blue tent

Crawl to the edges
ponder
accelerating universe.

ASTROLAND

How did a shazam plastic silver sword
sans sheaf
end up in my crappy purse.
Sword cuts paper? I find it so
relentless
in the spiny vestibules of rain.
The sun has commandeered the earth
its giant head tilts
teased by galactic energies.
The crushed dandelions in September
compressed yellow spikes along the sidewalk.
Glazed with awful light
orangish painted human toes
float then are confirmed
by the word orange
hugely on a black awning.
At the convergence,
the sun's
carnival empire.

I've seen your pulsing palaces
mechanized silence under a sweating
pearlized Moon
the button of a queen's sweater.
It all burned down.
            Essence of the ocean
via Astroland.

DEBORAH LANDAU

was born in Denver in 1967 and is the mother of two sons, Ethan (April 12, 1998) and Julian (March 12, 2002). "Miscarriage: Five Acts" was written in 2001 after the loss of a baby girl in the sixth month of pregnancy. Deborah was educated at Stanford, Columbia, and Brown, where she was a Javits Fellow and earned a Ph.D. in English and American Literature. Her poems, essays, and reviews have appeared or are forthcoming in many magazines and journals, and she has received two Pushcart Prize nominations. Her collection of poems won the 2003 Anhinga Prize for Poetry and was shortlisted for the Foreword Poetry Book of the Year Award. She lives in New York City, where she co-curates the KGB Monday Night Poetry Reading Series and is the Director of the Creative Writing Program at NYU.

MISCARRIAGE: FIVE ACTS

1)

Night is a red skirt spinning.
I busy myself with other things.

2)

I was expecting rain.
I was waiting for a kiss, but instead
found the janitor smoking
in my basement-crypt.

3)

And now, this grosbeak mobster
enters with rubbergloved hands.

My dear, he says, yours
is a scientific problem,
and I like you like this--
un-stockinged and clumsy.

4)

Throw another chokehold on my thicket,
Doctor, here are my leftovers,
half-baked and woozy.

Let me down easy, Mister Sloe Gin,
here is my collection of cut ups,
dead ends, clots, and x-ray.

See, I can make a summer Christmas
in emerald-green panties.

It's the Fourth of July, Labor Day,
it's goddamned Easter Sunday,
and I can't remember my name.

5)

The babies had been trying to get inside for years,

yanking my hems, scratching the backs of my calves,
so no wonder the first time I hiked my skirt
one got under.

The image crackled with static—
a child tossed from a swingset—

and then:
I'm alone again in my empty dress.

CAROLE MASO

is the author of five novels, two books of prose poems, a book of essays, and a memoir; she is the mother of Rose Chloe, born in June 1998.

MOTHERING DURING WARTIME

Repair the Nut Brown Hare. I make a note of it. The arm is undone. Small bits of stuffing—it comes all of a sudden back to me (the pink suture) and I see—the dreaming toddler in the night, a lifetime ago—or so it seems—before the war, weeping for the rabbit—hurt she says. And reaching for needle and thread across— how to describe this abyss of time—or was it only moments ago? The fur rubbed to a nub. Rubbed down to smooth satin. I slip. The over-loved hare. I make a note: repair.

Here is the church, here is the steeple. Her fingers intertwined. Open the doors: and her thumbs open like a butterfly.

We live at an oblique angle to the tragedy—it presents itself as an offhand shape on the periphery of the day—a bus, a small hand at the pane, a rabbit, a steeple, a plate. I've forgotten what I meant to say—

A glance or stammer, some reticence—stressed decidedly is the day. If I could only find my way to prayer, to pray again—but the distances—forbidden that's the word—in this unlikely zone we are made to inhabit—we are the perpetrators—do not ask me to explain this to her.

Yes our decency has deserted us.

Oblique—the child seen as if through a cloud of bees. Duck! I say to her as she gets off the school bus. Duck I say, and she laughs running to me, holding a treasure map and a code and a compass rose. This is her homework she explains. We're meant to dig in the earth. We're meant to find our way.

Difficult is the day. Thousands of miles away the children crouch. Where is the door?

Dinner I call to her—this sweetly singing one. She brings French Bear, Little Lamb and the Nut Brown Hare. Eat, I say. She fingers the small ration of thistle, cracked corn, sunflower seeds, we'd been saving for the birds. I have served it on the last

Limoges plate. A border of roses. I promise you I tell her, that we'll eat in the Blue Restaurant one day again. Is that the sound of bombs in the distance—or just the mother's madness? Is it ice, is it night?

The first Lenten Rose at my window. If I could hand its light to any one of them tonight. The children ask where is the door? They cover their eyes with their hands. Where is the light? Troops enter a blacked-out Bagdad.

Crouched over the small body. The extinguished crib. The nursery in cinders. Here is the church in flames. Here in the ruins is the needle. Repair. Where are all the people? If I could even begin to grasp . . .

She passes me the map. It indicates a border of roses. My daughter says we are getting close. We carry sacks of ashes and bone. The Limoges plates my mother buried when the Germans invaded. Maybe we could excavate them. We might go there, why not? Yes, perhaps, or is it too late—too far. It's the distances that make this world so implausible now. Are those bombs? If there were clear coordinates— or a way into this sorrowing. Follow me, she whispers.

We come at last to the Children's Garden. The midgets that have been left out all winter—are they midgets or just the mother's madness? We stand paralyzed at the mass grave. If I could only take your hand and make everything OK again. We paw the ground. She points to the map. Here, she says, dig.

SHARON HARRIS

b. 09/15/72 and based in Toronto, has two sons: guitar-playing, fantasy novel fan Garnett (b. 07/31/98) and Cyan (b. 06/25/04), a fancy-dancing toddler who could recognize upper- and lowercase alphabets at 18 months. Her partner, Stephen Cain, has authored four books of experimental writing and an encyclopaedia of imaginary languages. Inevitably, her next book of poetry will focus on her avant-garde family.

mama is proud mama is so stupid mama is so old mama is going to law school before you mama is lively mama is so ugly mama is sick now mama is so big mama is back mama is sooo fat mama is watching you mama is the star mama is just in pieces mama is so fat; yo mama is so stupid; yo mama is so greasy; yo mama is so skinny; yo mama is so lazy; her head so small; yo mama is so poor; yo mama is jong mama is going to have a baby mama is so hairy mama is so old that her social number is 000 mama is so nasty mama is down for an annual visit mama is the chinese government ma thesis supervisor mama is so funky she used secret and it told on her mama is so poor that she thought a quarter back was a refund mama is so stupid you can make her eyes twinkle by shining light in her ears mama is a tax mama is so fat last time she saw 90210 was on the scale mama is so slutty that when she sat on santa's lap he said ho mama is like a television mama is so dyslexic mama is so fat that when she sits on a quarter she squeezes a booger out of george washingtons nose mama is so fat that she was baptized in sea world mama is the dumbest mother is me mother is overbearing mother is watching you mother is just another face in the crowd mother is great mother is depressed mother is driving me crazy mother is disrespectful mother is forcibly sedated mother is mine mom is a survivor mom is love mom is sick mom is at wit's end mom is glad mom is punk rock mom is a gearhead mom is home from the hospital mom is a lasting tribute mom is still mom mom is interested mom is out of control mom is blessed with two babies but is besieged mom is ill mom is the nation mom is cooking mom is a fraud mom is different mom is gone mom is cuter than the dalai lama mom is beautiful but don't tell her mom is a painter mom is driving me mom is no longer 53 mom is a bitch in d minor mom is in the hospital and is not expected to live mom is outraged mom is teaching me now mom is a vampire mom is bald mom is the best mom is coming mom is sitting naked ready for you mom is busted mom is mean to her children mom may not be reproduced without express permission mom is proud of you mom is going to stay Lutheran mom is my hero mom is there for me mom is so phat mom is a vet mom is a working mom mom is a prostitute mom is strep carrier i have had strep throat at least once a year for the last 10 years mom is so lucky mom is an exhibitionist mom is thrifty mom is a witch mom is so ugly mom is so stupid mom is y2k ready mom is 16 mom is more than a bus driver mom is my slavegirl mom is charged in her son's truancy mom is in mommy is insane mommy is in a wheelchair sometimes mommy is from mars mommy is an angel mommy is a welfare mom mommy is great mommy is so sick mommy is tired mommy is crying mommy is half Cherokee mommy is a maniac mommy is lower than your mommy mommy is lower than your daddy mommy is a mutant free mp3 download mommy is an apple pie mommy is buff mommy is an angel my mommy is an angel mommy is the best mommy is so proud of me mommy is a delta mommy is waiting for you mommy is nursing me mommy is pretty comfy too mommy is on bedrest mommy is human and will mess up a lot; however mommy is dressed in a soft pink top with a pink bow mommy is here for you mommy is fulfilling and relates more to her needs than yours mommy is formerly fun mommy is loving and affectionate mommy is 6 months pregnant mommy is always crying mommy is getting it fixed today mommy is for hugging mommy is typing this for me cause i can't read yet mommy is crying as she lifts up her hand mommy is home more than daddy is mommy is expecting mommy is home all the time studying for school mommy is a man mommy is brought into the room where i am to be born mommy is the hardest mommy is feeding her one half can of soft dog food in the morning and one half can at night mommy is in heaven but she's not far away mommy is a really sweet person and i try and "humor" her when she wants to hold me mommy is so sorry

KATHLEEN OSSIP

was born in 1959 in Albany, New York. She is the author of one book of poems, and of a chapbook of movie poems. She teaches poetry workshops at The New School, where she serves as Editor at Large for *LIT*. Her daughter Muriel was born in 1998.

A CONCEPTION

Who wouldn't heave
a careless sigh?
A terror upheld
in sorrow, in rye,

invaded the heart.
The brain took a rest.
The homeopath
proffered his best.

A mystery!
It *did* hurt to try.
It happened then
the usual way:

I got out of bed.
A traffic light blew.
An artery flushed,
a ventricle grew,

lanugo hair
invaded the bog.
The female form
became the norm.

I had to laugh.
The heather went dry.
The grandma cracked
and so did I.

What blare, what bliss,
upturns me so?
Who'll cozy to
a mohair throw?

I altered the sauce,
I tasted the bay.
A style was lost
the usual way.

I whimpered past
the printed page.
I counted my toes.
I did know my age.

The grasses pealed
a tiny reprieve.
I started to read
Emily D.

and waiting for
her stern reply,
the outcome loomed
and so did I.

NURSLING

Over there, a fly buzzed—bad.
All ours: the bra, the breast, the breeze.
Starlet of the reciprocal gaze.
Something about her rhymed like mad.

And ours the sigh, the suck, the sing.
We forgave everything we could.
Ravenous palmist. I'm gone for good.
At last I gauged the brash, brash spring.

The skin fiend folded like a fawn.
Torso Magellan. Time's own nub.
Here at the center of the dimmest bulb.
A mouth hovered before latching on.

BABYLAND

Enter warily: here suavity reigns.
Enter solemnly; enter with great thirst.
Under the banner of the splayed lips, the first baby
staked a claim where the ravine crested and the wax-
white cups of the May flower never shut up.
The second baby failed to live up to its potential,
becoming a charmer who embodied the comic spirit.
At midday, in the dappled thicket,
the third baby simply poured out of you.
The fourth baby, nothing more than a figurehead,
broadcast, in Baltic languages, his many moods.

Step aside: now they come faster and faster.
Newsboy baby delivers the morning paper:
Confessional baby tells all!
Daughter-in-law baby disapproves
and hermit baby is just plain weird.
Sculptor baby lingers over the naughty parts.
A chorus of art critic babies whimpers,
"Why'd they take the tits out of all the pictures?"
Here censorship reigns with its attendant amnesias,
in the desert where the gardenia blooms and in the fen
where vegetable marrows sop up a nutritive fluid.

When night comes the babies scamper into their burrows,
deep under a moonscape of white plains.
Even town crier baby turns in. Nevertheless,
the abandoned square is dominated by a screen
where favorite movies play in an endless loop.

Here reign the sneaky essentials: tread softly
and with respect for the perils you will suffer or cause.
In the blackening copse, for example, a mystery is unfolding---
who, oh who, dropped the final baby?
Little matter, my darlings. Her unrelieved preciousness
would have slain you, just as nature intended.

JULIE CARR

lives in Denver and teaches at the University of Colorado, Boulder. She is the author of two books of poems and the co-publisher, with Tim Roberts, of Counterpath Press. Her children are Benjamin (8) and Alice (5).

from Wrought

4. *Time Paper*

Why does the philosopher call the "time of the now" the "technical expression of messianic time"? What use the word "technical"?

Turns to face me, but its features are transparent, empty as a spill of foam.

My boy walks—almost steps on—the carcass of a bird.

—

"I grieve that grief can teach me nothing." Emerson: choosing redundancy to reveal emptiness.

To think is to describe with indifference: feasters on a holiday in any country, the breath as it freezes just beyond the mouth.

Fallen leaf: one side pure black, the other yellow as a feline eye.

Oh continent less imagined: manhood begins in the womb.

—

I am nothing, writes Pessoa, I am the extended commentary on a book that doesn't exist.

In the center of me is a vortex like the crawlspace in a house never built.

The morning comes according to its numbers, which means it is safe to rise.

The family that shares my DNA, my name, and in some cases my memory,
is getting out of bed, peeing, putting on slippers, walking out for the paper,
beginning to play.

Emerson says the private thought is the universal but it must never be construed as
the universal lest we kill its difference.

She's made the bed, stretching the sheet over the blankets, which doesn't work.

She errs not because unable to hear the spectacle of humankind's oblivion but
because time and its order is not.

"Technique" from Latin texere means "to weave." "The tapestry of now is endless"
would be another way to translate the philosopher.

The child walks upstairs on all fours like a cat.

5. *Wrought History*

In the history of the child there is always an account of her beginning and she
knows herself to be magnified by the tale.

Gathering the stones into a circle, each one turned inward as if they have faces.

She walks through the zoo with notebook and pencil like a reporter from the New
York Times.

Like other mothers, I say no to desserts, noise, and spitting, but I am not a mother
and I am not like anyone else.

I and a prairie dog meet "in person."

In the rental car she says, "I like rental cars. We should buy a rental car. If we clean
our car, we will have a rental car."

I speak exactly as everyone else speaks; fall asleep exactly as anyone else falls asleep.

There is no greater expression of pride than to refer to oneself as nothing; no
greater claim for one's centrality than the claim that one has none.

It was raining, I tell her again, a man drilling a hole into the avenue below.

ILIADIC FAMILIAS (WITH INSERTIONS FROM HOMER)

I.

My mother used to cry in the car while driving. This was terrifying to me in the
back seat. Not only was she responsible for my safety, but I could not see her face.
And now I cry in the car while driving. My children behind me fight over who gets
to hold the twist-tie. This is a particularly deadly fight. I turn the news up so as not
to hear them. I want to hear the mother who is talking about her dead son so that
I can cry. Sometimes they ask me why I am crying. I always say, "The war." This
is how they come to be against the war. This is also how I came to be against the
war that made my mother cry. She used to say, "It was not politics that got to me.
What did I care about politics? It was thinking about the neighbor's son." This is
the famous fierceness of mothers. We do not want to listen to our children fighting
because it will distract us from the war, which is making us cry. One mother says
she opens the newspaper and immediately begins to cry, even before she reads
anything. Another cannot watch child-in-danger movies. This is also true for me to
an extreme degree. Once I was kept up more than half the night worrying about
a girl in a movie who'd had her appendix out. The surgery was not dangerous, it
was very simple and she emerged from it perfectly well. In fact, the surgery was
placed in the plot in order to bring her uncle and his boyfriend back together. Their
mutual concern and love for the girl was a sign of their continued love for each
other. All of this I knew. I also knew, incidentally, that it was fiction. However, I
could not sleep because they never showed the girl back home. In the last shot
of her she was asleep in the hospital bed, resting peacefully. We were supposed
to be thinking about the two men who loved each other and who were watching
over her as if she were their child. We were supposed to be thinking about love
and how it is not the exclusive property of parents or heterosexuals, but belongs
to everybody. But I wanted the girl to wake up. She never woke, so I never slept.
In the morning, I told my husband and he was furious with me. He wants me
to be able to watch movies and it is more and more evident that I can no longer

watch movies. This, according to my husband, is a pathetic failure to be objective, rational, and to have fun.

II.

My mother used to cry in the car while driving to stop the sorrowful fighting. This was terrifying to me in the back seat. We shall fight again afterwards, until the divinity chooses between us. Not only is she responsible for my safety, she gives victory to one or the other. And now I cry in the car while driving. By this time the terms of death hang over us. My children behind me fight. There is no sparing time for the bodies of the perished; this is a particularly deadly fight. Standing there in their midst, I turn the news up high. Now the sun, rising out of the quiet water and the deep stream of the ocean speaks of the mother who speaks about her dead. As they wept warm tears they lifted them. Sometimes they ask me who I am crying. In the same way, on the other side, their hearts in sorrow. She used to say, "It was not politics, what did I care about politics? Is there any mortal left on the wide earth who will still declare to the immortals his mind and its purpose?" This is the famous fierceness of mothers. "Why then are you crying like some poor little girl, who begs to be picked up and carried? Who holds her mother back when she tries to hurry?" We do not want to listen to these children because it will distract us from what makes us. There is little breathing space in fighting. This is also true for me to an extreme degree. My desire has been dealt with roughly. Their mutual concern and love for her was a sign of their love for each other. Said one to the other: "Obey to the end this word I put upon your attention so that you can win, for me, the lovely girl." But they never showed the girl back home. Tell me now, you Muses, how fire was first thrown. We were supposed to be thinking of love as property, but wanting the girl to wake up, I never did. Drinking from a spring of dark running water, willing her to wake, in the heart of each one was a spirit untremulous, and he wants me to watch, he is furious. Your mother nursed you on gall! You have no pity! This is a failure to be. You would gather in groups to have fun, to be rational, yet the desire in your heart is to watch the grim encounter.

III.

My mother, an unearthly noise, I could not see her face as wolves make havoc among lambs over who gets to hold the black earth, burdened, so as not to hear

them, by the works of men, I turned to the neighbor's son huddled inside his
movie, he in the dust face downward was also true for me, mouth open to the
bright spear, willing him to wake, the heart in my breast was balanced, between
two ways, was pathetic, as if he were my child, as if where the beating is enclosed
in the arch of the muscle is a failure to ration, to be, a lowing bell, a bellowing.

MOTHER POEM

Ankle-blood &   bit lip

            the only way you'll think you'll

footstep up to the curls at his neck

                        is stealthily

Starred and starred again

            they're running wired like squirrels

The ice-cream man's a woman

                        nine-month belly getting air

                        deep purple tracks hip to navel

They chew Sponge-Bob's popsicle eyes.

RACHEL ZUCKER

was born during a blizzard in December, 1971. She grew up in Greenwich Village and returned to New York City after attending Yale and the Iowa Writers' Workshop. Zucker is the author of three books of poetry, including *The Bad Wife Handbook* (forthcoming in 2007). Zucker and her husband, Joshua Goren, are raising two sons: Moses (born June 8, 1999) and Abram (born December 11, 2000). Their third son is forthcoming in late spring of 2007. Zucker has taught poetry and writing at Yale, NYU, and Fordham and is also a certified birth doula. For more information please visit: www.rachelzucker.net. "I can't remember a time in my life before I wanted to be a mother or before I knew I was a poet, but it was not until the birth of my second son, 18 months after my first son was born, when I was so severely pushed beyond my physical and emotional limits, that I was forced to reckon with the reality of these two choices. A serious crisis ensued in my mothering and writing, a crisis that has (re)shaped my sense of self, my world view, my relationship to others and to language.

"And some writing advice: Write anyway, in an empty bathtub if necessary. And: Beets are a good early food. To prepare: simmer beets in their skins for 20–40 minutes or until they yield to slight pressure. Run beets under cold water and slip off the skins. While beets are cooling undress child completely or at least down to diaper, and place in high chair or, preferably, in a plastic travel chair in an empty bathtub. When finished rinse child and remove, then shower down the chair and tub."

HERE HAPPY IS NO PART OF LOVE

(birth of the second son)

o

she is not   (in the end)   denatured   (but begins to)
like acid body-away some under, subjacent revealed

a catalytic sizzle dissolves solvent the picture the sky with atomic bomb
cloud suddenly black, blank then

Someone shouting,   (a woman) she

        "go through"   "circle of fire"
"through go"   though death *go-go-go* she says *breathe*

        breathe

I————oh no what is that I collect, try,   I
lift want to set down but in parts
pieces no longer I *lift* want to stop
sit down lift I *want*   burden
burden burden burden   *breathe*

Organic: I cannot move.

A woman, some screaming—they say less screaming—breathe! they say—she
    wants to say
I am but is not hears screaming is that her? what is that *fire?* peeling away each
    sanity: skin,
bone like bark stripped off a slender branch inside screaming cardiac smooth
    muscle "you
            must breathe"

                                but who? and how to with all this screaming

it

            explodes

my body opens-in one cannot witness   is

    o

    o

At some point I started begging.

Each time in that place thinking "I must tell them" thinking "the difference
between saying and thinking is they can't hear me," and would say, "I can't do this"

then would sink again drowning again desperate.

Decisions were made in both places drowning and living and a woman sent out
for Demerol. It was long and I went back and back and back to the place I swore I
could not go. Before I knew I was there again. It came to me, became me.

And here she was fiddling and fixing the I.V. Bitter, chiding, I'd used my strength to
say "enough!" "We hear you" they said, "we're helping." And a woman was sent
for Demerol (it had been fluid). Oh I was faché and told them, told them off but
the place came to me and I could say nothing.

No position, no angle, "way to manage."
Someone said "this is the crescendo" and I thought:
fuck fuck fuck fuck, fuck-you.

then: the syringe

In snapshots—as if a disco or strobe is the syringe and I.V. suddenly tired—
snap-shot: hope,   snapshot:rest ,   snapshot: I . . .

                       —a muzzle descending.

              (not a word thought had no word snapshot: [I *will* die])

And everywhere an explosion I am inside myself which is molten clear view: there
is no help shade overpass, monumental desert.

Fear, a pure thing, is not acceptance.

o

Behind the curtain of Demerol which made them suddenly impervious to my
suffer unlike anything and made me incoherent scream no sound to say this ocean
you have poured over me is not cooling down this one bit drowning but only some
plankton morgue you thought would shut me up—

                          they said circle of fire so many times it
              seemed stupid I had no
choice but burn and burn and then something ungodly——what was *that?*

                              someone said, *I see it*
                        someone said, *crowning*

An explosion that would not move.

Circle of fire, they say.
Push, she says.

Something——the room—shifting———

                                                        " . . .get the doctor."

o

[   ] is faster than I can recount what I saw was strobe again blinking series of
frames in their faces and bodies a sudden new weather in the room people moving
pressing a monitor to my side and a woman rushing in in street clothes everyone
else in scrubs the room moving alive around me as though they have forgotten I
am here dying and no one saying push it is over I think I am finally dying I . . .

        ("get Dr. Mondoni")

                                                                then

"LISTEN TO ME," she says, (she looks like my midwife my husband holding my
left leg just like he did for my first child and who is that stern woman purse tight
across her chest like some pageant ribbon or breastplate) "you MUST push"

and I know this is not the circle of fire.
is fire. Out of, chaos.

—Perhaps a woman wrote the image of god contracting to create the world before
she died as Rachel died in labor with Benjamin she named him *Ben Oni* son of my
mourning a midwife herself perhaps she knew she would not breathe this fire as
they tended and she screamed how Jacob had the nerve to change the name to son
of my right hand—

They lower the side rail. They fumble.

And the woman: *get Dr. Mondoni!* and someone pushes in a baby warmer I think my husband says "the head" I must push I must I hear a hot sound inside the body, a moment liquid / vapor— *Stop Screaming* someone says and I realize for the first time I am screaming—

you—   must—   she says

and I did did not want to die I did and feel a ripping deep turning something in what should be out this is not the circle of fire something else this is in in in a burrowing when nothing left to burn

and the baby slides

o

o

"The truth is I did not want this baby though beautiful it almost kills me and bleeding waiting I am not safe even my bedroom ipso facto the post partum a nest like a bird with only plastic or glass slivers to build with makes one sit gingerly alive I'm not safe here there was I know technology for this for even a woman with one young child wanted more but not so soon but how can we have everything I thought it's not my place to make this absolute fuck you to whomever sperm egg zygote (God?) I can handle this but cannot, barely not, rock/rock and cover my breasts on fire with chilled cabbage leaves these monstrous bosom-rocks with carelessly cut-out holes for the huge bruise-colored nipples . . ."

is not a metaphor for, is

o

o

When they brought the baby his was my own face.

My face, survived.

Is he OK? I said a hundred times is he? where is he? why is he? yes, they said he
is. He is. They just want to—he is, they said. Beautiful, they said. Big! they said.
Your husband weeping.

The face of course it is not yours, perhaps the Demerol, but that moment and even
after when your husband said what's his name? and only my own name came to
mind.

Myself divided, severed,   everyone smiling.

o

5 am, snow, a low mustard light.

"dying is better than this" someone says in your voice no one hears

        Birthing is no— metaphor?

Lest the suckler hunger. Least.

bones under the bedclothes suffer. I every day age three and don't recall

and there is that sharp taste again like the smell of by-products, a released
   consequence

The smell, the mess, the literal place, on all fours like an animal—you remember
   nothing.
And too much.

And am I now one with other women? hardly except perhaps my shattered
    this and this happened then   this   the is   so now you know

everything—in and out of the room see a body splayed and naked giving up—and
   you?

I'm sorry but there is no new place for anyone to touch me.

LAYNIE BROWNE

was born in 1966 in Los Angeles. She is the author of five collections of poetry and one novel. She has two books forthcoming in 2007: *Daily Sonnets* (Counterpath Books) and *The Scented Fox*, which was selected for the National Poetry Series by Alice Notley (Wave Books). She has taught poetry-in-the-schools as a visiting artist in New York City, and Seattle, and has taught creative writing at the University of Washington, Bothell, and Mills College. She lives in Oakland, California, and is the mother of Benjamin (born May 22, 1999) and Jacob (born August 29, 2001).

from FIRST SEA

Body becomes sound

Each morning there is the drift
a cutting keel

The wish to marry time
to steer precisely despite
increasing blood volume

Indentations where I press
my wrists to calm the tide

Days immerse themselves in silence
and pass weatherstones
This tiredness is merely that—
dressed in cartilage and bone.

+++

Dressed in cartilage and bone
morning awash in mist
Detail will be added
(toes, joints, toenails)
2nd century A.D.,
Galen's theory of "emboitment"
Existing in embryos "female semen"

Later enveloped in "amnion," little lamb
Blood islands form channels

+++

Blood islands form channels
stepping through a fluttering guise

The body island surrounded—
mast of spine, shudder swells

We have been taught to recognize these signs:
illusion of sight, discursive season, denial of gravity
and other myths—

With two hearts I proceed

ZHANG ER

was born in Beijing, China and moved to the US in 1986. She is the author of three collections of poetry in Chinese. Her poems have also appeared in English translation in many poetry journals. She has six chapbooks in translation. She has read and lectured at international festivals, conferences, reading series and universities in China, France, Portugal, Russia, Peru, Argentina, Canada, Singapore, Hong Kong, Taiwan, and in the US. She currently teaches at the Evergreen State College in Washington. Her daughter Cleo was born naturally on June 26, 1999, 8 lb 6oz. Zhang Er has written many poems for/about her daughter, which are collected in *Mother Event,* an unpublished manuscript in English translation.

FEMALE CODON

Uniform from head to toe
you in black weary of the barren
rise from the bottomless core of your flow
for a long long time

We always young and always worried about you
running among the snow flakes in the streets hawking
steaming dumplings and frozen porridge
for a long long time

Absorbed in bearing the single child
bawling at the emptied square, no roadblock
here, trees should here, wind should
for a long long time

Squatting in the garden smoking then sat inside
talking about your lineage and ordinates
watching your slender tips once more
soaked in ink

translated by Arpine Konyalian Grenier

LECTURE ON THE MOTHER IMAGE

Interrupts the hot summer post lunch somnambulism of the museum tourists.
When is it best to become a mother, at fourteen like these Middle Ages, or today's
thirty-four even forty-four? A particular consideration of respectable motherhood
following the overpopulation that tightens habitable space until we ourselves pose
the threat to ourselves. Immaculate conception, then virgin birth removes mother
from lust, then rational thought, then selfhood. She's forewarned of the crucifixion
of her son, her fate eternal loss, her position hanging, imposed from church
walls, bleeding all over the world, face, breasts, palms, yet loving without fail.
The pinnacle of maternal love. Not human, not sexual, untiring in self sacrifice,
uncontrolled and irrational despite the augury of doom. Her appeal is in the
beastliness coming from the face.

A father coaxes his son to be quiet for a few minutes on the opposite bench, letting
mother take a nap.

translated by Rachel Levitsky

LESLIE BUMSTEAD

was born in 1967. She was raised in Washington, DC. She holds an MFA from George Mason University, where she was a founding editor of *So To Speak: A Feminist Journal of Language and Art*. Bumstead's poetry, prose, and translation have appeared in numerous journals. She lives in Takoma Park, Maryland, writing and raising her two unschooled children, Jonas (7) and Gillian (5).

"My first child was an infant when I moved to Ivory Coast, so my experience as a new mother involved a confusing and surreal clash of circumstances. I tossed between the tenderness of this exquisite mother/child love, the daily poverty surrounding us, a bizarre expat scene, eruptions of political violence, and the wretched and otherworldly state of sleep deprivation. In this environment, I wrote 'Abidjan Notebooks.'

"We were evacuated from Ivory Coast when I was 5 months pregnant with my daughter. I gave birth to Gillian in Washington, DC. The madness of attending to the mostly contrary needs of an infant and a toddler began. There was no time for writing, no time for reading; I yearned for sleep. The sheer physicality of motherhood took over my days. And there was nothing more interesting to me than my children.

"Some months after Gillian's first birthday I saw a small notebook in a shop in Takoma Park. I bought two: one for me and one for poet Jean Donnelly, my closest friend, who also appears in this anthology. My New Year's resolution was to fill one page in this notebook (it had small, dated pages), every day. I did not care what it was filled with. I just wanted to write again. This later turned into "Between People & Living Things," a collaboration with Jean that went on for over 100 pages.

"Things have changed: this year my children bought me a notebook for Christmas. My writing is as natural to them as my morning coffee."

from ABIDJAN NOTEBOOKS

On December 24, 1999, Côte d'Ivoire suffered its first military coup d'etat when enlisted soldiers mutinied over pay. President Bedie was ousted & General Robert Guei became Chief of State. The international community spoke of the "bloodless coup" because few people were killed, & everyone expected Côte d'Ivoire to remain the oasis of stability it had always been in a poor, war-torn region. Three months after the coup my husband Doug & I moved to Abidjan with our 8-month old son.

At first General Guei assured everyone that he was only here to "clean house," had no interest in power, & would soon hold elections. He surprised few when he decided to run for office himself, & has slowly but surely turned into a thug, implementing summary executions of petty criminals, having unarmed protesters & journalists whipped & beaten, & arresting or exiling junta members he suspects are no longer loyal to him.

After 9 months under a military regime, everyone is speculating nervously as to what will happen next. How long will Guei manage to stay in power? Will his opponents respond with violence to his aggression? His main opponent is Alassane Dramane Ouattara (whose supporters call him "ADO"), over whom there has been much contention as to whether or not he is in fact Ivoirian, which is really just a way to keep him from running for president.

Foreigners have been leaving in droves, some because the economy can no longer support their businesses, & some because they fear civil unrest.

September 20, 2000

my stupor & birds
at noon
then dusk, dawn
& my stupor
at the entrance
political magic
a cartoon
autobiographical
stew

there is no reconciling being white
in Africa
just be yourself
just *don't* be yourself

being a mother is so hard sometimes
it makes me want to smoke & drink

Dinner with a crowd of journalists last night. I was the only spouse. Purnell defended Luis, saying, "I think he'll find his legs. He's got some stories—he was telling me about being held at gunpoint, having his life threatened when he was working on the Mexican border." I wanted to say, any old sod can be held at gunpoint or have his life threatened, that doesn't make you a hero it just scares the shit out of you & gives you a story to tell. What I worry Luis won't be able to handle is the more mundane stuff—the constant hassle, the lack of comforts when he travels, a violent bout or two of diarrhea, maybe malaria—& worse, his own defensive response to poverty, repression, insanity, violence done to *other* people, not him.

May 10

the trees lining Blvd. de la France have been cut down
ten feet up their fat trunks—huge branches summarily lopped
off, & now they make me think of Foday Sankoh.
I don't want to think about him 9:00 a.m. Friday.

after a mutiny, the dove
hoots & snails eat the rabbit's
carrot. no shooting, cars
circulating normally, people
having evenings

all over Africa, white people carry on as if.
& it's if.

the wood-carved Baoulé couple in the corner,
looking so good. wisdom & fertility. so many
ways to consider a family. art's
the means & the baby looks fabulous
in a sleeveless orange sport shirt.

pile me up a guru,
& disconnect me from my filter!
exaggeration's a distinguished seat in my beach-
side bungalow. death is always scurrying
about, obsequious
riverman in white linen.

history means to pass us by
& will hate the innocent
a cemetery singling out the disease

Monsieur le "President" arrested 3 of Ouattara's top men, one of whom Doug
was supposed to interview today. Grey morning, 7:35 a.m., Jonas still asleep after
a semi-fitful night. I had a dream: I am on a subway in the States & I notice 3
teenage girls looking at me & laughing. They're pretty & fashionably dressed. So I
look back at them & laugh at them defensively. I realize they're making fun of my
clothes, so I stand up & say, "You know, it's not really as bad as it looks—the clothes

individually are okay, if nondescript." And I point to the clothes one by one to prove my point. "The pants—regular khaki pants, the shirt—the neckline is ruined from washing it too many times, but for the most part it's fine. The jacket is really what's messing everything up & making me look stupid." The girls seem to accept this.

July 14

what stops a line
blue ink on my arm
my child eating mango
& yogurt & speaking of it

be thorough in your thoughts
so the thought police can't
steal you. stay home
this evening with the yellow
blooming orange blooming
flowers on the vine

child at the door, reasons to greet him
fondly, my darling, your grins & decisions.
which tower should I knock over?
lovely ancient love. my dear in great pants.
blocks & puzzles & colors on shapes—
I've written it all down.
the last living polka dot.
purple & blue. yellow & white.

There is this white guy writer, Robert Kaplan, who claims to understand African people because he has traveled throughout the continent on their buses. This man writes that a woman breastfeeding her baby in a public place does it for the same reason another woman urinates in a public place—squalor. This man wrote a long book & westerners bought it.

August 15

one day in tatters
flat, thin, no good
words on strings
my dead bread—I mean,
my dead dog brain

pause & give up
fingers tuned to leap
in this place, unwelcome
furnishings
a month passes like that
hurtling into stem life
dreamy the nation's
oldest socks. what will you give
a place so far gone, the humans.

Didn't sleep well. Kept hearing some strange dog. Jonas slept in his own room for
the first time, & I worried about that. Last night some people were arrested. The
government says they're Madame Ouattara's bodyguards, & they were caught with
weapons in their cars, but Imke just called & said some of them work for Nestlé, so
how can they be her bodyguards? They're accused of plotting to foil the elections.
We saw them on the evening news, standing there looking pained & vulnerable.
They were probably thinking about the hours of torture ahead of them. Then
the minister of interior mentioned the Washington Post several times, denying
outright that the government falsified Ouattara's marriage certificate, & called the
State Department official who backed up Doug's article a "clown." We are nervous
& irritable.

October 4

Silence. Strangers. Lunch.
I've got a hunch. Echo in
the milk, like the Ukraine
in a book.

Stories & speakers, rumors
& real life building pieces
sway my red brigade Liberian
mercenaries in 4x4s photographed
at gas stations

Moons on the table
blue, yellow, green, purple
bare feet slapping to me
coconut tree fabulous

Maybe Guei was successful with the arrests & the torture & the state of emergency
& curfew. Ouattara has told his people to remain calm, & they have. Everyone is
walking around saying, "Is everything quiet chez vous?"

October 7

OLENA KALYTIAK DAVIS

was born in Detroit on September 16, 1963 to parents of Ukrainian ethnicity. Her son, Avgustyn Roman Kalytiak-Davis, was born on October 19, 1999 in San Francisco, and spoke fluent Ukrainian at two, which at seven he has completely forgotten and replaced with much scientific information. Her daughter, Olyana Esme Kalytiak-Davis, was born on May 28, 2001 in Anchorage, and by three could recite Hamlet's entire fifth soliloquy while substituting the letter "P" at the beginning of every word. Now five, she will not speak to anyone at kindergarten, but can read at a Lear level. They don't give a shit that their mother is the author of two books of poetry, although sometimes refer to her as a "famous fish." The poems included here are from a third manuscript, *on the kitchen table from which everything has been hastily removed*. Literally.

LYANA SICK AND NEXT TO HER

lyana sick and next to her i lay
as if myself in fever fretted head
and thought on him that i recorded dead

as if laudanum as if claret
as if it weren't over yet

brought him to mind again and again
beseeching him like thought to stay
then move do something that i could and did not will
live a little while i held him there

but again and again he overclouded disappeared
(he lives aftermiles and afteryears away from here)
i had to keep incanting him from scratch

i loved him once or didn't
get a chance so i resurrect him as i laid
with my sick child and dear small she
stroked my hot and poisoned head

the dream went on all afternoon
so glad was i with her alone to dwell
in that sick and sunny afterroom
where we would aftertime be well

"HOUSE" IS BEING CLEANED

house is forever— being cleaned—
the children hate to watch it go—
every scrap to them is treasure
loss found the second time— anew

house is forever being— cleared—
to help me decide— who—
i make high heaps of harbored stuff
then watch the rick fall— through—

collide with floor— strike the board—
"less fell" i make into our daily bread—
then again i wait until
i can heap store speak— again

house is— forever being moored
to unmoorish moony things—
like springs from toys—
and spring—

pestilence too— i thought i liked
my poisons in pretty little cups—
but the mouses in my closet
have put me on— the cusp—

house unhoused itself this morn—
the way it does when i like that do sing—
beneath the fingers of a man—
i didn't quite ask— in

house refused to sail away
it stayed with me— within—
together we used the windows
to count macaws— and sin—

house is settled— mine—
he's learned to send himself— away—

knock later if you must, you will— persist— now
empty only looks and sounds— to the amateur— amiss—

LOOK AT LESBIA NOW!

and look at lesbia now! she's said farewell
to her face: dark circled
nipples down and dark
she's even let the hair grow back down there.
right, she's not a real blonde, and
no one's knocking at her door anymore.
we all knew it would turn out like this.

o lesbia, daughter of _____ and wife of _____ and mistress of _____
mother of _____ , ha! ceded what? the one so valued
what she had on her once pretty mind
she traded in everyone for that? did you hear
she wouldn't have a baby with her lover
even if he promised to keep it in a tent out back?
so he left.
have you seen her walking alone thru this black and white town
her pink i-pod playing ryan adams, spoon, rilo kiley,
lucinda, arcade fire, the silver jews, mark mulcahy,
yeah, dylan; sufjan stevens, even,
wearing her usual yellow-pink-blue woolen cap?

let the kindergarten parents talk:
yeah, you know, the divorced one, the "poet,"
the one who wears "the jeans,"
circles under her pink eyes, her young boyfriend
just moved back to new york.

IN PRAISE OF MY CHILDREN

i sing my childrens' lovely dirty blonde heads
i sing their hands, their fingers, their widely spaced teeth
i sing their limber limbs, their fish white rumps

i sing their complicated lives
i sing their simple feet:

once a pants a time
my grandpa had a tree
and ants ate out its heart

i sing their knowledge of marine mammals
i sing their apprehension of the dinosaur and bat
i sing of their enlightenment; their having lighted on
the spider and the many eyed fly

the wings of nymphs and butterflies
the mating of the octopi

i sing their love of sugar
and, of love

glory be for the ability to laugh and one second later cry
glory be to those that hate and love their brother
want to pinch and poke him in the eye
glory be to those that suffer their sister

i praise their sorrys, their beg-a-pardons, their 'kooz me, 'lank you
and their mama, please
i praise their growing slowly up
and their lying reluctantly down . . .
their imitation of sleep:

ah speepy speepy speepy
ah speepy speepy speepy. . . .

somebody take that apple off my son's head
the arrow from my daughter's bow

o alate, though their shoulders bare be
o fucked up, though without a fucking care

SUSAN M. SCHULTZ

(10 October 1958) "My children are Sangha (7, adopted from Cambodia, July 2000) and Radhika (5, adopted from Nepal, December 2004). My husband is Bryant Webster Schultz (44, born in Illinois, adopted by his then-stepfather at age 1). I have taught at the University of Hawai'i at Manoa for 16 years. My poetry, since just before the advent of my children, has often taken on definitions of family and tried to expand them to include adoptive ones. This project has proved more difficult than I ever anticipated. And also more rewarding."

NO GUNS, NO DURIAN*

> *on reading Angelina Jolie's Cambodia diaries*

In the countries with no diamonds, they are not getting their hands on good weapons. This is no land for oboes, for the frail reeded ones. *He was our Elvis, but Pol Pot killed him.* Old man meets quiet death. *I was complaining that my feet were sore and then I met a man with no legs.* Roads rutted, but the orange-togaed monks are sweet. Above all, a sense of gratitude, not for what is here, but what exists in the place one flies to after. *Where do I pee in the middle of the night?* The author-accumulator of this poem intrudes to say her intent (on first blush) was to write satire: the vocabulary for this poem comes, after all, from a starlet, one who "just keeps on giving, gossip-wise," according to Salon. com. The method lends itself to sharp contrasts between evidence (stifling concrete room of men, women, children with amputations above or below the knee) and language (the tattooed lovers say *see you soon!* as they depart). And there is the question of the baby: where did he come from, how did he get to her, what was the cash amount?

Our informant is prone to writing sentences like the following: *It never dawned on me that I was raised in a city,* which might qualify her as unreliable, were she novelized. But how to handle the *man with no arms who raised six children and whose face is so sweet?* The *very little dirty boy with brown eyes who clings to his father?* The children singing about landmines, how to avoid them. The drills in the head, the skulls. Even the starlet's nightmares, her desperate cliches, the ill-fitting self-references (for whose self-reference fits?), even these cannot break the narrative apart. She has found her subject. The starlet cannot be silenced. *It was all so beautiful to see.*

*an exceedingly smelly fruit

KASHMIR

And the Verisign said: "this is fragile, even when broken."
The boy with a box bore a gift of shattered telescopic glass.
Unaware, as yet, of his problematic heritage, he belly laughed
when the Tubbies spilled their custard. We talk of identity, even
as nuclear holocaust looms. Get under your desks and cover
your heads with your hands! In our corridors, the ghosts are
reversed; we see the dead, while the living pass by unnoticed.
Running down the hallway produces time-outs. Mowgli and
Tarzan were both orphans raised by animals. *He is not my son,
opined the chief gorilla. He cannot replace what we have lost.* Either
Mowgli leaves his single father, the bear, because he wants to be
with *his own kind;* or, he enters the man-village because he finds
a woman with whom to have a child; or, he's a teenager fleeing
hearth and home, albeit jungle. Having studied to be a gorilla,
Tarzan is faced with the necessity of learning to be human.
That means acquiring manners (personal space) and enough
words to seduce Jane, who stops running when his syntax
straightens like newly combed hair. Ms. Manners' ill-advertised
lair. The narrative posits *choice,* even where there is danger,
a vicious tiger thirsting for human blood. *Our* crops may be
dusted with radioactive matter, because the wind is general over
us all. What breaks, finally, is blood and its thickness.

NATIVE SON

The mirror dawdles before (at *best*) a family resemblance. *We live in an age of genetic determinism.* His "father" (as opposed, in this instance, to "social father") a Nobel laureate, he dreams of becoming a pro wrestler. Moniker: THE SEED. I seed what I seed, before I turned back. Sperm bank children lack many adoptees' anguish. Once her second divorce is out of the way, she says, she will have a child (in-vitro) with her first ex-husband. All women giving up children for adoption in the state of Florida must publish the names of their sexual partners in the newspaper. He collected *verités* before most wanteds hit the small screen: a rat, an alarm, a cell. Scrap that. Haiku he set in the snow. Hold up your small glass shard and wait. What is in the one instance a matter of privacy (the laureates') is, in the other, one of publicity. *In the name of the biological father, the biological son and the biological holy ghost.* Sunk in his red chair in a darkening room, a teen-age boy glances at the evening paper. Whoso hunts these lists. Seeing her on the street with her nine year old daughter, he wrote a postcard, acknowledging paternity (after the lies, the lawsuit).

BIRTH STORIES

Questions of priority, privilege. As if the long trip back were a race, and firsts its winners. A baby bird finds its mother is not cat, dog, airplane or snort, but another bird. A wolf in the suit of a white businessman crowns the food chain. If the left wall is unmoving, the gutter welcomes chance visitations (a drunkard's bob and weave); if it be the right, the narrative of progress knocks the businessman off his pedestal. Bread and tulips, housewife on holiday. *I have come to reclaim your mother for love,* says the Icelander. Remembered capitals, like Helena. The four line stanza stands, along with hidden line breaks. Empty backpack beneath the Brooklyn Bridge. Keep them scared, lest they remember the past. *Americans have no memories and that's a good thing.* Bunk. Bridge across the river Cam. There are two narratives. According to the one, she is ill at ease in her family, and so begins the search; the birthfamily she discovers not only resembles her, but shares her interests in flora and fauna. According to the other, she feels no pain but curiosity, locates her birthmother in a cellar in Iowa, typing. The woman shares only her nose. Nothing lost but the fantasy of a wealthy Hollywood tycoon whose birthdaughter got in the way of the next shoot and was relinquished to the middle-class. Call me Mom. *But you're not going away.*

THE NEW YORK SCHOOL

The email from Hanoi reads: *Babar was a colonial foil, beset by pygmy riff raff, whose trunk was the family tree of empire.* Postcolonial theory adopts the unexamined rhetoric of adoption, *bien sûr.* Purée of Khe Sanh and oyster sauce, Tet and the cake they also ate. Which was bread (to the bone). The father of country X, Y, or Zed is never *natural,* is presumptive, author overseeing his text (like Washington his darkies at the Manoa B&B). The author is not dead, is simply fictive. Least original is the question of origins. She said she met Ho Chi Minh's double at a party in his city. Consider that the ostensible subject of this paragraph is not its actual subject, that it has yet to come up, that it might not. That the schools of poetry you distinguish (one reads the other, while the other does not) in fact collude to corner the market. That there is little difference between the 80s and the 90s, at least geographically (a New York poet is always already one). We've been taken off the track, but it did come up, this *vexed issue* of kinship, which poet gets assigned which number and waits her turn in line, my mother myself. But to return to Babar (aka Mary Rowlandson), beset as he was by *savages,* yet saved by the French army, their funny hats. Please adopt this book for your course.

Blows on my owie, asks if it's butter. On waking, he enters the
naming stage. Nak! Nak! means he's hungry. Adam, according to
Milton's diagnosis, did much the same. It's the blind leading the
blind, he says of a prospective psychotherapist, but ATMs have
begun to talk. She wants me to put Steve Evans in a poem, but I
can't find a place for him unless I perform a critique, pronounce
this less avant-garde than mongrel, less pure than pastiche. His
alleged victims were buried in white caskets. The rhetorical
trope you will find yourselves using more than any other is
metonymy; I will defend metaphor to the death, but rarely
use it. There's that problem with the epic, that it's imperial,
that it classifies everyone according to another's station, that
its metaphors disable through repetition. Inspires one manner
of decadence, the channel whose experts are all blonde. One
category I've developed is the prose poem as essay (comes after
description, story, parody, memoir and the rest). You might
consider your poem a place in which to develop ideas, rather
like a stadium in which you're seeking out periodic curves and
finding them beneath the sine wave hills. He showed us on his
memo pad. A vegan from birth, he can't judge the artificial
ham. Which is to say you'll be drawn more to some genres
than to others, according to an algorithm of temperament, one
you could spend a summer describing, only to pronounce it
pure math rather than the actual experience of an experiment.
It helps to know what you're doing, even if you change your
mind later. *I went into therapy to create the problems I never had
and then solve them,* I heard a classmate say. The problem is
that poetry is spent, there's no romantic spark left, no skylark
to spread the news. You could write a poem so deliberately
unambitious as to please our instinct for the banal, yet another
in a long line of anti-poems; what used to be considered insult
is now the inevitable surrender of a good writer. I prefer the
synthetic method, pulling voices from the wallpaper, changing
their accents. Jonathan Edwards woven into the new powerball
winner, with his Kentucky twang. *I had no money left, so I bought
a lotto ticket.* *Song, song* he trills, and I turn on the Wee Singers.
Artifice of campground emanating from a boom box. Aporias
do happen.

REPETITION COMPULSION

An aesthetic of joy. No, not the aesthetic, but it itself, the
expression of it, what comes before expression, which is fact,
if untranslatable in speech. *Where dada go?* means he speaks
in full sentences, questions. Having pencilled a "gecko" on a
legal pad, he raises his arms as if to denote touchdown or field
goal. Throws right, bats left. Swings his large plastic spoon at
an invisible b-ball, then runs around the living room, catches
his own pop fly. *I used to be able to write for 50 hours at a time,* the
historian says, who now tries hard to remember plots to daytime
soaps. If he prayed, he'd ask for an end. But the boy says *gain,*
gain and the television complies, at least this once. Is the joy *in*
repetition or in what is repeated? I was on a bus and feared I'd
forgotten how to tie my shoes, so I watched as a student kneeled
and tied his. The memory function was all repetition, obsession,
re-runs, but it left out the details. I did too, until—as Ashbery
notes—the world acquires a sheen in one's late 30s, a post-
meditative rose, beauty in both thorn and leaf. I ask him where
he flies his airplane, and he says *up.* I ask where he drives his fire
truck and he answers, *ome.*

AND THEN SOMETHING HAPPENED

London, November 2002

What to make of the pastoral even where it's apparent
hills are covered with tank tracks, where sheep contrive
to make this landscape hegemonic green and white,
connecting the dots into a tender portrait apart from
any pre-war sense of these fields; what will have been
shadowed by violence is still an open space, grief
mortgaged to a later chaos. *You cried yesterday*
over the lost child; do not cry again.

"I didn't mean what I said," says Thomas, the doubting engine
(who could, if only he'd say so, but he can't). Sincerity over-
defined as meaning without skeptical admixture, dare I say
the trope Americans cannot do? The Fat Controller's persistence
demands an on-time schedule that resists compassion and/or
ordinary breakdowns. This last "person under train" was
surfing at Chalk Farm, name so bland it hardly merits tragedy.
No meaning, no irony. Cast them while they're hot.

Pavement strewn with brown leaves, like lost italics
from a forgotten passage. Romantic forgetting gives way
to contemporary excess, access to random configurations.
The more you ask of us, the dumber we machines are, as if
shedding lives were more crucial than recapitulating them;
capitulation the art of what's possible, framed topologies
so strictly zoned nothing more can be built, not even by Bob
the Builder, the man who can. The litter of that drawer
became ash, as what is lost returns to us as meaning.
She squares her shoulders to a new world, in whatever form.

[John Ashcroft, he do the police in many voices.
The enforcer, Miss Clavel, goes faster and faster
as her minions gather before the first with the heroic
dog who saved Madeline's ass from the Seine.]

"Is it real?" "No, the airplane is paper."

Today's question is whether or not a toy is *real*.
Its frame borders on nonsense, except in the tone
in which he asks. His yellow plastic hammer fell

from the third floor of Gonville & Caius College
onto paving stones. Bryant retrieved it.
Whether or not it was real, it existed
in the mind of a boy. This is mommy's
baseball and this and this and this is
a baseball. You hit the ball again and again
and again and then you leave. Full sentences
suggest the sense of an ending that closes,
if not closes off, possibilities for future wrecks.
Bob would fix them, his hard yellow
hat gleaming in the English sun.

In theory, an anti-theoretical poetry is possible. If career is
construct, then why not take it apart, keep it out of reach of
Bob the Builder's yellow hat and hammer? Fear's a construct,
created, then joyfully demolished. The boy runs in and out of
the room, exploring terror and its recovery as sound. Sings the
song of the strange British optimist. *Yes we can.* Optimism goes
against theory; pessimism is pure. "That's not a monster, that's
a pig!" If family is resemblance, then this is none, is horror.
Language as the imitation of same, his "letters." Wrote one
to his "sister": it was the letter z. Shapes without the expected
content. Like mummies. Afterlife in a glass case, given water
and food for the journey. Or in a tape machine: "hello, I love
you, I'm trapped." She did not ask for my stories. He was ill, as
his cough testified. The poetry of testimony depends on true
statement, yes? His neck held back so he could not swallow; his
penis nailed to a table. These are not my stories, yet they are
true. Where scale no longer matters, the torture of a boy or a
nation. I believe in whatever moves away, but in nothing that is
fixed. No monument but in sound.

We can't get past reach of the Bureau
of Homeland Security, for *this* is our
homeland, this wanting to be good

in our skin, at ease with syllables, sounds.
Babies learn phonemes the first year,
and then he switched to English,
vowels altered that first week.
If description is sound's outcrop,
then how he sounded changed
where we were. Old linguistics,
surely, but fresh poetry. Odd angled
accents re-call empire from its
closets, street to street battles
about a vowel, some of them
transported to antipodal prisons,
others flattened across frontiers.

"A creature of uncertain race" was loose in the woods
wearing only empty pants; when I saw him, I screamed,
although I'm rarely frightened. Them without stars
clustered on beaches, self-pity bringing them home
to themselves. Meanwhile, the French army held off
pygmies with straws, poison arrows, (cannibals, no doubt).
Elephants stood aside, lusting after that Riviera cruise.
Her bellowing offended or confused shoppers
at the estate mall, but we ignored pinched faces
in our push and shove. Thin and thick robots joined hands
with yellow and green ones; it helped that everything
rhymed. Agency always belongs to someone else, though
we want not to say it. Yes, the author knows what she's
doing, where we encrypt our tongues. Microsoft Word is
an agency of capitalization. Let these pale green pants
be my homeland security. "Can we fix it?" "Yes we can!"
Not the car story, but a better one, like a good joke
that follows a weaker. This is the beginning and this
the end of the story, but he refuses them both, wants
fact, story, the car, pants, the star-bellied sneetches.
In two pages we get to where we've always wanted
to be, where the story is itself and not a metaphor
to fill a poem, like the diver's tank before waking.

Institutions forgiven by instance, or instance of forgiveness
authorized not by the Institute of Kindness but its analogue
in what space is left outside suburbs choked with graffiti
(*personal* inscribed as *public* obscurity, the artist formerly known
as reduced to abstraction, writing contentless messages on the wing
of a Metro tunnel). She asked where to find the Bastille. Pressed
for directions, she proferred them laboriously in French, only to
realize the question was put in English. These are now my memories,
renovated by rubber squawk, unpredicated as letters of recommendation
sprung from angry foreheads, or false translations, the irk of name
changes. I cannot hear your poetry, says one to the other anglophone,
as if the demotic were a text generated by the person on the street
who tells the butler he's bored by revelation. Those white horses
and winged things outpace boxes holding the royal secrets, injuries
against the body. His blue glass box contains a butterfly (is moth)
that landed on his dashboard in France the instant his friend died
in New York. Know happenstance from truth. What fades is need.
One wants to say desire, but that seems too intimate, so I write need,
just this side of it, active lack as the hope for sustenance, the knowing
we recover from with age. Twenty years on, the Eiffel Tower!
Replacement therapies for agitated states, the body a projectile
armored against any but its own future. What is not outgrown
can be admired, if not emululated. "I'm a shark!" he says in the tub,
when he's not surfing or fishing. By the river Cam he sat and fished,
his pole a broken stick. Happy echoes of earlier laments. Private
grief megaphoned as public anger against the state, any state.
That Donald Rumsfeld stars in my friend's poem is not a good thing.
What revision could not do for this regime. What fear will not do
to remove itself by removing its shadow. He "writes" to his "sister"
in shapes that are letters only to his eye. Order is a private matter,
even in language. The glider flies solitary over no daffodils but those
the pilot sees in the eye of his night goggles. A poetry of nature
might be recompense, were so much of it not a trivial lament for
passing things; though to see veins run "the long of" a fuzzy leaf
is perhaps miracle enough. Concepts like "racial lesbian," based
as they are on misspellings, shift angles, angels, wings one hears
late nights amid the nerve rush, when you can afford it. Her words
clotted like prose or resembled a collage without hinge, air rushing
through the "sortie" from which another frantic word arrives, scarf

tossed around its neck, supporting the grieving widow who leans
against the yellow tiles of this piss-smelling place.

I done seen about every thing
When I see an elephant fly!

Dumbo falls and falls, his house a bubble, lest it break—and it
does!—to the boy's deep belly laughter. Destruction's sweet
when you're three; Thomas smiles to see his trucks fall the
length of *vadeen* ("ravine"). *I am sweet today* says Pan. I know
the sweetness of a boy's violence against his imagined world,
soft voice singing. Pan with flutes, not panic, Pan as in Peter,
unformed man in bronze, perpetually boy, never father to the
man. I cannot argue with my son's violence. The honey in my
throat is his.

Needless, like art, like terror: do not confuse them.
Sangha says his curled potato chip is the tunnel
where Gordon got stuck and the diggers came
to pull him out. Not where the bus, Bertie,
jealous of the engines' speed, trapped himself
beneath the train bridge, was later abandoned
to the hens. *My bus* literalizes an exchange
that usually resists ownership. The child resists
paradox, where outside is not outside, is inside
the loving parameter of his hands, even
when they pull down the tracks, the trains,
scratch out his hieroglyphic letters. Mandalas
last. It is we who are the real, alarmed
by a black man in yellow wig, but not
the white guy who can't stop scrubbing.

Fragment within what is least fragmentary,
bird singing this Saturday on Addison Grove,
Sangha in the next room talking about baby birds.
Dull brick houses, the drying pavement.
Bells rang yesterday, too few; when you stop,
the disjunctions come clear, leaps between poles
(A polar bear says "we love you, even if you're brown.")

Caffe Nero, Chiswick High Street: Sangha and I duck in out
of the rain. Plant ourselves across from a man who yells *Get
some sleep! Get some sleep! Good night, good night!* at five minute
intervals. He says I'm blocking his way out; I move my chair.
There are two blue take-away cups on his table, torn sugar
wrappers. The social worker told him this morning he'd have
to move to a group home. If he keeps doing what he does at
night on the street. *Get some sleep!* He doesn't want to leave his
neighborhood. His father *worshipped* his flat, he keeps saying.
Furnished? He'll try the group home for a couple weeks, but he
wants back. No more services. *Good night!*

NICOLE COOLEY

was born in 1966 and grew up in New Orleans. Her books include two collections of poems and a novel. She is an associate professor of English and Creative Writing at Queens College– The City University of New York and lives in New Jersey with her husband and two young daughters, Arcadia (12/23/03) and Meridian (12/03/00).

AMNIOCENTESIS

           the sky a lake in the New York barely
dark outside the bedroom window
the willow is all
        clusters bubbles foam disappearing

      like the body I've convinced
                myself—chromosomes rearranging fiction
into fact   the hollow needle will reveal

        shuttered like a window   I wait

     let the world beneath the skin be pure astonishment

O Body no matter what the sky leaks through

PREGNANT AT THE ARCHIVE

where you are not supposed to have a body
in Special Collections, in the reading room, in the straight-spined chair

where all afternoon you study portraiture, Cassatt's late prints.
Directions: open each folder slowly, remove the proofs.

So many bathing scenes. All the private actions.
Inside your body a ring of cells divides, divides.

Each image is a reprise. Sanguine, fugitive red,
fine drypoint hatching to expose the mother's inked-in hair.

The child always underscored by a lack of detail.
Directions: study the careful incision of lines.

Inside your body the other is still safely other.
Most often Cassatt prefers to leave the background blank.

Directions: don't look down at yourself below the desk.
A pencil study. Drypoint outline. Aquatint.

Directions: will you even remember the occupation of just one self.
Cassatt reverses the terms of reproduction, copies her finished oil.

Directions: will you remember.
Only the friction of two bodies that share an outline.

All the conflicting voices.
The body backlit. The body incidental. The body reprised.

Directions:
Pencil study. Final print. Slow, familiar dissolution.

A Mother's face obscured.

CESAREAN

Now the irises rage light, spiked tongues
at the hospital window

Inside the body's solarium light shrinks
to cold flat stone

How I would like to just unravel

Through glass, cut leaves curl like fingers
in my throat

I once wished to take myself apart

There is no space between us: body caught in my body

There is the voice telling me there are many ways to give birth

The lesson chalked on the sidewalk like a missing
body these lines the surgeon sketches—

to save her, cut here and here and here

MARTHA SILANO,

born 09-02-61, has two children, Riley Francesco (12-07-00) and Ruby Josephina Cook (03-24-05). After the birth of her first child she spent a month in a mental hospital recovering from postpartum psychosis. Four-and-a-half years later, the birth of her second child brought on manic symptoms within hours after delivery, but this time she was given bipolar medication to stop a full-blown psychotic episode. "What Little Girls Are Made Of" was written during this time. Silano has published her work widely, including in two book-length collections. She teaches at Edmonds and Bellevue Community Colleges near Seattle, WA.

WHAT LITTLE GIRLS ARE MADE OF

Tapir, pure tapir—all wide,
delicious ass. Herbivorous

to the core, union of fly rod
and shad roe. After hiking all the way up,

then all the way back down Mount Kinabalu.
In the month of pastels, fluorescent pink grass.

As American as a forest fire enveloping
your god-given home on the range.

With wheat berry eyebrows, resides
in the batter of Proust's madeline.

Also of the sorrowful women of Durer.
Of cantaloupe rind, of gargantuan zucchini.

Of Athena—all brains from the get-go, over-
brimming, teeming, full of knowing

hare-bell from bluebell, every genus
and every species, all brushed up

on conifer know-how, reminding us
spruces have papery cones.

Of granite, with meteor shower
skin, her nose, when it sniffs,

pre- and just- rainfall, her voice
a synthesis of Ginsberg and Plath—

"A Supermarket in London," amalgam
of nasty boy love and honey,

Lorca chasing her down the aisles hissing
Bees! You must devote yourself to bees!

"Babies in the tomatoes," yes,
but also of baby tomatoes. Of those believing

the world held up by a turtle. She's
the Thinker, Ye Olde Tick Tock.

She's the patch of geraniums
in full throttle, all wrists and sucking fists.

She's what glows and glows.

BETH ANN FENNELLY

was born in 1971 and currently lives in Oxford, MS, with her husband, the novelist Tom Franklin, and their children Claire (born May 19, 2001) and Thomas (born June 11, 2005). Fennelly received a 2003 National Endowment for the Arts Award and a 2006 United States Artist grant. She's written two books of poetry as well as a book of essays. Her third book of poems, *Unmentionables*, is forthcoming in 2008. She has three times been included in The Best American Poetry Series and is a Pushcart Prize winner. She is Assistant Professor at the University of Mississippi.

ELEGY FOR THE FOOTIE PAJAMAS

No snap between your legs,
for months. But how? When did I last
gnaw sausages cased in terry cloth?
When did I last un-snap-snap-snap?
I've gone to the door and I've shouted.
I am missing some-ping. Hey, you,
in your big-girl PJs, don't you have
a little sister? You're giant,
lying down, dreaming of beanstalks.
I have no cows for you to sell. Not now.
What is Mommy doing? I am reading
in a disco. No, it's not a disco,
it's my office with your finger on the switch.
Two years lived under a strobe light—
when I look up, you're there
then there and there. When I look up,
you've nailed the cha-cha, the fox trot.
What happened in the in-between?
What is Mommy reading?
A book with pages torn out
by Kenny Mullins in grade four.
Kenny Mullins why do you do that I said
he said Because you're fat.
Twenty years later in Starbucks
Kenny Mullins says Sorry about the book
it was a joke! He says Don't put me in a poem!
He says Ha ha ha! Now *he's* fat, and also bald.
Oh, yes, now I say Ha Ha Ha.

I don't like myself like this. I am leaving
some-ping out. Like me. Do you? Tomorrow
you'll ask for the keys. Answer's No.
Buttering me up, you say, Let's play,
Mommy, I be the snake, you be the dark.
Fast child of a fast mother,
it's been years but I haven't forgotten
being the dark. It comes right back. It's like
pushing someone off a training bike.

BITE ME

You who are all clichés of babysoft
crawl to my rocking chair,
pull up on my knees,
lift your delicate finger to the silver balloon
from your first birthday,
open your warm red mouth
and let float your word, your fourth
in this world, *Bawooooooon*—
then, delighted, bite my thigh.
I practice my stern *No*. You smile,
then bite my shin. *No*, I say again,
which feels like telling the wind *No*
when it blows. But how to stop you?
This month you've left your mark on me
through sweatshirts and through jeans,
six-teeth-brooches that take a week to fade
from my collarbone, hip, wrist.
What fierceness in that tiny
snapping jaw, your after-grin.
You don't bite your teething rings,
don't bite your toys, your crib,
other children, or your father.
It makes us wonder.

Daughter, when you were nearly here,
when you were crowning
and your father could see your black hair
and lifted in his trembling hands
the scissors to cut your tie to me,
when a nurse had gone to the waiting room
to assure my mother *Just a few more pushes,*
when another had the heat lamp
warming the bassinet beside my cot,
then held up the mirror
so I could see you sliding out—
you started turning. Wriggling
your elbows up. The mandala
of your black hair turning and turning
like a pinwheel, like laundry in the eye
of the washer, like the eye of the storm
that was just beginning
and would finish me off, forever,
because you did it,
you got stuck, quite stuck,
and so, they said, I'd have to push
head-shoulders-elbows out at once.

And Lord did I push, for three more hours
I pushed, I pushed so hard I shat,
pushed so hard blood vessels burst
in my neck and in my chest, pushed so hard
my asshole turned inside-out like a rosebud,
pushed so hard that for weeks to come
the whites of my eyes were red with blood,
my face a boxer's, swollen and bruised,
though I wasn't thinking then
about the weeks to come
or anything at all besides pushing and dying,
and your father was terror and blood splatter
like he too was being born
and he was, we were,
and finally I burst at the seams
and you were out,

Look, Ha, you didn't kill me after all,
Monster I have you,
and you are mine now, mine,

and it is no great wonder
that you bite me—
because you were crowning
and had to eat your way out of me,
because you were crowning
and developed a taste
for my royal blood.

THE GODS TELL ME, *YOU WILL FORGET ALL THIS*

You lie, I answer. I remember circling the Q-tip dipped in alcohol around the stump of her umbilical cord. I remember the newborn diapers with the half-moon cut out so as not to chafe that black knot. Those hips the breadth of my hand. I remember the terror of trimming her nails.

No, they say, *you are forgetting. Already you have lost the trip to Indiana, when she was five weeks old. Tommy drove, you sat in the back leaning over her car seat because you needed to look at her as she slept or you would disappear—*

Sometimes even now I sit in the backseat with her—

It's different now. You sat in the backseat with her and you were sucking on a Tootsie Pop—

Yes it was a cherry Tootsie Pop

and although you knew it was wrong you touched it to her tiny mouth

I remember her tiny mouth

and she who had never tasted anything but breast milk

My breast milk

got the scent of that sweetness and her blind blunt tongue emerged and bumped against it, withdrew, bumped against it, withdrew.

Yes, that's how it was.

And you were fascinated at your own bad hand, holding the red ball there to her red tongue.

Yes, I was fascinated. Tommy heard my guilty giggle and looked in the rearview, so I lowered my hand. Later, we pulled over at a rest stop and I sat on a picnic table and suckled her, the yellow waffle-weave blanket over my shoulder, her tiny tummy warm against my own warm flesh. Afterward, I hesitated, but showed him the Tootsie Pop. He hesitated, then took it, held it to her lips and we giggled together. For months to come, when she was asleep and we missed her and it was all we could do to keep from waking her, he would imitate the tentacle-tongue slipping between the lips, not pointed with intent but flat, world-free, allowing the pleasure to meet it. Then retracting. Then emerging again. Ah, it was sweet, because she was so very small, and because it was our secret, our original sin, Claire's first solid food.

It was sweet because you understood you could hurt her and that made her more yours. And just yesterday you realized you hadn't mentioned that for several weeks so you said, "Do the tongue," but his imitation was off somehow. Though you both tried, neither of you could quite correct it. And so it is gone forever.

That's not true, I say. We'll recapture the tongue. Besides, I'm writing everything down.

That old lie. You'll look at the words and they'll crawl off the page. But take solace that the pain fades too. You can't relive childbirth.

But I *want* to relive childbirth. I want everything back, every blessed thing.

It's too much for one person.

Let me try.

You're too greedy. And it doesn't work that way. The infant is disappearing as we speak. She is more ours than yours now.

Fine, I say, not meaning it. I'll have another.

HOA NGUYEN

was born near Saigon in 1967, grew up in the DC area, and studied poetry at New College in San Francisco, California. She now lives in Austin, Texas where she edits the poetry journal *Superflux* and teaches creative writing. With the poet and husband Dale Smith, she operates Skanky Possum, a book imprint, and curates a monthly reading series. Their sons were born in Cancer (07/12/01) and Pisces (03/13/04).

WORE A HEMP HAT   ATE GRAPES

Wore a hemp hat ate grapes
A list of future baby names:
Waylon   Angelica   Martin   Lucia
Rhymed some words & read a poem
Still damp   the laundry   Come on sun
Swished the toilets and watered plants
By March I'll have gained 2 extra pounds
in uterine muscle   Ate gross cinnamon bun

"BY GOODS WE DESTROY GOOD"

> *what is good   how*
> *is it clear of ruin*
> *what is at the other end*
> (C. Olson, c. 1952)

The possum haw hasn't berried
It is good but no good   twiggy
bent limbs   greening

He came to the door
and asked for money
"I'm stoned," he said   (cracked)
and also something sad

in his face about his family
We gave him $10

The "twin of totality"
that writes the poem
The twins Jennie lost
in a swirl of tears and blood
Angelica root   Charcoaled ginger
Infusions for building back the blood

Worried about the work horse
drawing the open carriage
and breathing car fumes

Now alive life   What good
is my worry
cutesy in drawstring pants
pom pom hat

      O I could scream
and scare the baby   and move roughly
Roughly move him   And would you

like some food/to nurse/ a book?
Rumpus   tickle   new little boots

THE EARTH IS IN ME

The Earth is in me   I am old
and clay   nameless
"grass" with tiny yellow flowers

More mucus this morning to feed warm sperm

The Earth is capable and heals you
You have friends among the weeds

Reddish "sugar ants" next to the mugwort

I had this idea   stubbornly
Dog still barking

Write something "new" about the national tragedy

UP NURSING

Up nursing   then make tea
The word war is far

          "Furry" say my boy
about the cat

I think anthrax
          and small pox vax

Pour hot water on dried nettles
Filter more water for the kettle

Why try
to revive the lyric

EURASIACAN

No mother in body   no
body   when on the phone
meatballs simmering in sauce

Maybe my baby
whitens me
Turtles and blue eyes

"Pet" turtles discarded
in the pond
crusty deformed shells

Ground deer
meat balls mixed
in my mutt hands

Ma = horse
Ma = rice seedling
Ma = graveyard
Ma = mother

My boy walks
arms out   pointing
at the window

Yes you saw a lizard
there once   Yes you rode
a dolphin   and a seal

MARIE HOWE

"My daughter is Grace Inan Howe and she was born March 5, 2000 in the year of the dragon in Hunan China, adopted in March 2003."

Marie Howe is the author of three volumes of poetry, including the forthcoming *The Kingdom of Ordinary Time* (W. W. Norton 2008), and the co-editor of a book of essays. Stanley Kunitz selected Howe for a Lavan Younger Poets Prize from the American Academy of Poets. She has, in addition, been a fellow at the Bunting Institute at Radcliffe College and a recipient of NEA and Guggenheim fellowships. Currently, Howe teaches creative writing at Sarah Lawrence College, Columbia, and New York University.

NONVIOLENCE

My daughter doesn't like the fly that keeps bugging her

As she eats her Cheerios this morning

—But we had a talk about the ants yesterday so she says,

The fly is alive, and I am alive, and covers her cereal bowl

with a dishcloth which she lifts a little every minute or so

so she can slip in her spoon.

But 6 hours later I want to murder that fly—landing on my arm

as I write this, on my knee.—the same fly spared

I want to find a book and flatten it.

The morning newspaper says the British Policeman checking

Through the rubble of the bombed subway car thought—because she

was moaning—that the woman was alive. Then he saw she had no
arms or legs.

I don't want to think about Donny who hung them from the open top of

His desk—where did he get the thread? Or the tape?

Or his gentle younger brother Bobby, who killed himself when he lost a lot

of other peoples money in the market.

My mother made a point as she told the story—or mentioning he was

so considerate he pulled a plastic bag over his head before he did it

A full summer day outside humid, hot,

The fly that was bothering me—gone—who knows where—

Now some detritus falling through the trees and air outside this window

Blossoms and seeds. Blossoms and seeds

COURAGE

I'm helping my little girl slide down the pole next to the slide and bridge
    construction

when a little boy walks up and says, Why are you helping that young person

do something that's too dangerous for her?

Why do you say it's too dangerous ? I say

And he says, She's too young.

And I say, How old are you?   And he says, four and a half.

And I say, Well, she's three and a half.

When he comes back a little later he says, I'll show you how it's done, and climbs

up the ladder and slides down the pole.

Then he says, She's too young. What happens is that when you get older you get
braver.

Then he pauses and looks at me, Are you brave?

Btave? I say, looking at him

Are you afraid of Parasite 2? he says.

And I say, What's Parasite 2?

And he walks away slowly, shaking his head.

ELIZABETH TREADWELL

is the author of seven books, the most recent of which are the poetry collections *Wardolly* (Chax Press) and *Birds & Fancies* (Shearsman Books), both 2007. She is currently working on a long poem of American history, centered around the figure of Pocahontas and titled *Virginia or the mud-flap girl*. More information about her books and projects may be found at elizabethtreadwell.com. Treadwell has been the director of Small Press Traffic Literary Arts Center in San Francisco since 2000 and is the founding editor of its journal, *Traffic*. Treadwell was born in Oakland, California in 1967 and lives there now with her husband and their daughter, who was born in 2003.

THE FALSE TRANSGRESSIVE EVANGELISTA

(i.)
until the world needs women again,
I live in the woods with my sons:
the saints' talents, and the birds humming
and the birds not humming,
under the bone tree,
by the dinghy, the oaks dark
against the gold.

the new usual,

the empty word-hut.

sometimes nasty witnesses,
the resort colts, mine & others'
shell-bright memoirs—
here in this landscape we've bitten—
the original lawlessness;
low-rent trees
in the foreground
(we're advised to hire more trees).

the big-wig carry-all of yore;
that large, differing hand;
sweet, flip echoes
(his thousand petticoats).

storm choirs with simple english,
the sacred follow-up.

(sleep like riverbanks holding us in.)

the cruel laws of the throne,

undone the churchstep:

(ii.)
the prison of no past,
a christ in every literature.

the floating grimace
of personal despair.
it's just perspective
that's all
it is

(thanks, thin goons of the mood police.)

in the curse lots
foreign words like little pets,
with genders,
& curls.

the little words step down,
garden-heavy
in the windows of a church—

rub the idealist,
the bulbous theme:

(iii.)
its face-splashed
news apparel,
homemade rotten filmstar,
or thuggy celebrity gelding.

the house motions
of animals at night,
like a character
stuck to a scene.

(these treetop hormones
older than   our brains.)

here in this landscape we've bitten
the train, the watertower,
& the mail. tender finger-stubs, offspring's
feats & qualities.

until the world needs women again,
I live in the woods with my sons.

the country moon, the fat orange jewels of winter;
all our gliding, loose particularities—

sweet protectorate,
and broody.

CRÈCHE

I'd meant to solve the universal her,
and here I've been a wreck
sometimes and sometimes ambling
up a firm familiar mountain or the seas
to small geographies unmeasured
and unmapped, you'll find them

LEE ANN BROWN

born 3:15 AM, 10/11/63 near Tokyo, Japan (Johnson Airbase in Saitama prefecture), mother of Miranda Lee Reality Torn ("only Miranda"), born 4:27 PM, Sunday, 12/08/02, St. Vincent's Hospital, with Tony Torn, mother Dora Lee Wiley Brown, sister-in-law Angelica Torn and midwife Maureen Rayson, in attendence.

Poet, performer and filmmaker. Author of two poetry collections and a chapbook collaboration with Laynie Browne. Wrote and performed in an a capella song cycle for 5 women's voices, *The Thirteenth Sunday in Ordinary Time*, directed by husband, actor and director, Tony Torn, with whom she has also authored *SOP DOLL! A Jack Tale Noh*, which will be featured at the Yockadot Poets Theater Festival Spring 2007. Has received fellowships from the Howard Foundation, the New York Foundation for the Arts, The Fund for Poetry, Yaddo, MacDowell Colony, Djerrassi Artists Residency, the Rocky Mountain Women's Center, the Virginia Center for the Creative Arts, Foundation Royaument, Centre International de Poesie Marseilles. Has taught at Naropa, Bard, Barnard, the New School for Social Research, now teaches poetry, cross-genre writing and visual culture at St. Johns's University in New York City. Recently participated in NEH Seminar on Appalachian Studies, and is on planning committee for Asheville Wordfest 2008, to be held in Asheville, NC and surrounds, in April 2008.

"Mommy I Am Now: It is appropriate that I am writing this right after Miranda has just gone to bed with the cricket machine on—(why didn't I think of this before) wondering whether I am really dysfunctional or if it's "like this for everyone"—as Ellen Pearlman says "Who Knew?" well not right after she went to bed—I did unstop the sink with the plunger and take out some of the trash—with seven other pressing matters tugging at my coattails—it takes a strangely fragile mixture of the belief in the hedonism of the poetic moment to allow myself the luxury to go into poetry mode—but it's not like a Calgon bath ad—it's a difficult pleasure that comes of trusting it has happened before in new ways now because of the impossibility and groundedness of it all—major features of the landscape of motherhood the past 4 years: the waiting, the abstract and concrete knitting, the filling and feeling of polyrhythms of the becoming other inside + the sideways eye of the mandala the universe revolves around for an extended timeless waveform pressing out a new head you don't know that way yet + the bizarre and time-warped time right after birth, the dream recurrences flash and then gone during daily detail—hard to "record" or represent—Life really becomes Art—think of Mary Kelly's *Post-Partum Document*—or Carolee Schneemann—wonder what she would have done around mothering if she had More Than Meat Joy—the totally gaga in love with this being who is your Other but part of your own aura, attached in the truest sense + this being actually coming into Language and going from represented co-experiencer to dialogic collaborator—dictating formative—traveling stretch—or as in the call for work for a book called *Mamaphonic*, "Do you have a toddler seat strapped in the back of your tour van?" I am still formulating the answers to the questions of reciprocity within the artistic community—we will see and be a part of a shift I feel of an expansion of content, consciousness, and formal ways organically wrested from new waves of mothering verbal and gerundive diving into the flesh of the language like a barb that's soft and needing to be articulated out."

SCRAWL

I rail against the powers that be that burn the innocents in the streets of Rome
zoned for the future milk leopard Chibachrome. Her back was strapped with
unseen claws foundered on the knight ridden parapets of dismal swampish
hugeness. The baby's skull is knitting together. She is separate and I am a hollow
reed unable to bring myself to the table, unable to feel it all. Hungry so hungry
then I engulf myself unable to eat right. Free masons I don't care about you. Want
to return home with my bootie but where's the black beauty when I get there?
My dreams slide by, dreamed transparent baby milky glass. What is it called—yes,
frosted. Alive and pulsing but no veins, I dreamed my darling baby's head was
separated from her body, cleanly. It was round and I winced to see the she the
underside with the neatly sliced round red vertabrae. Music from a time when I
was very sad brings it all back from long distance. Inoculated by happiness, I called
the pediatrician who was Elizabeth Murray to plead with her to put the baby's head
back on right. After all, if I fed her head, how would the nourishment get to her
body? Roller cosier coaster joy pure Joy then horror vacui. Don't let myself feel the
dark organs. Elizabeth Pediatrician said she could do it after Christmas, but that
I could really just do it myself. I am terrified by infection. I'm sick of being legit,
itemized as sweet. O my infant's face is so much more divine and full of radiance
than I ever imagined! I have not been able to write the infanta the luminous One
who is so lovely and her little voice sings to me already and she is already almost
seven weeks old and time is speeding past and I have not represented all of the
time I thought of her inside of me before she was and then when she was   there
and unrepresentable yet totally daily meant to be She is sleeping now. Who am I
writing this for?

8ᵀᴴ MONTH COUPLETS

another letter from the wondrous field

So that you may remember pre-language events
and not bump your head as you crawl across the alphabet

You've had plenty of adventures already to be sure
though All of culture lies before you to be unglued

You can dance in a roundel in your romantic phase
amongst hostas and hearty begonias bedecked

Without irony and then throw it all over for Apollo
then again subvert the third term beneath the Dionysian
Tread of trees. When I was pregnant I had a vision
of lying back into the lap of the earth supporting me

From below as I was holding you on a conch couch
at my sweet shrink's. The other day I envisioned a huge

Breast I suck on from above as you did just a moment ago
I let you down on the floor so's I can write this line

on the Think Pad you are reaching up to touch
the table matrix You have never tasted African Slush Punch

from Vicksburg or seen a folk art cat birdfeeder inscribed
with "Free Birdseed" I write today from The Springs, Amagansett

where we swam in an L-shaped pool at Carol's place and ate
striped bass fish tacos but you ate strained green beans and

bananas and are playing with Laura and shells on the white carpet
You are dressed all in white as am I "It's going to be hot today"

she says you are a superstar because you are crawling now
with two hands planted before you and pull your body forward

undulating like a worm "make you backbone shake" you are
a Brown Torn girl in the ring tra la la la la and you look like a

Sugar and a plum plum plum. A red and green hose like a snake
spiraled in the sun. A globe sun black spins as he lied and upped

the date of his death Jackson Pollock. I am a permeable membrane I think more or
    mortality
and immortality as when in labor on December 7th and it was surely

to be your birthday on the 8th it was determined so I said "The 8th!
That means Infinity!" My mother was impressed with my articulation

and that I could speak at all much less make poetic conceptualizations
about your birthday. In fact I was obsessing on what it would be

in the Big Birthday Book.   You almost made the Day of Eccentricity
along with Emily Dickinson but you passed that over for The Day of

Abandon   Total Freedom   same birthday as Sinéad O'Connor, Mary
Queen of Scotts, Jim Morrison, Flip Wilson (alter ego: Geraldine whom

your grandmother of the same name was purported to have loved), and others
of wild nature unable to be contained   You are also born in the Year of the Horse

and as a Sagittarius you are double horsey ready to run and travel free
but I hope you'll stick close by me for quite a while because I love it

and even though last month you supposedly finally figured out we have separate
bodies and identities (You were your own self from the beginning, a focused

discerning light so calm for a baby) You did cry though not as often as most
we hear and you did not have any choler or colic but are of an undeniably

sweet disposition. Anyway, as I was saying I love you close by me and when
we are together in bed you nursing in the crook of my arm I can imagine you

are still attached to me as you were in the inside and your fine smooth body
exceptionally phat fair and pure is covered with a fine patina of sweat

it is like you are still swimming in me One time when you were kicking up a storm
so strong in Vienna when I was walking one night to catch the tram to meet your

father you kicked such a complex rhythm that I had to stop walking in order to
    process
the polyphony   I notice these couplets lines are growing longer and longer it's
    because

I have so much to say to you and the headlong rush seems the way to go if I am to
attempt to catch up on all the varied strands of thought and experience that have
   transpired

since your birth making everything richer and more layered I even had the feeling
   yesterday
that you had always been here even though you've only been outside a little over
   half

a year Maybe you were always there in eternity or infinity   You met Destiny on
   the street
the other day and I said Destiny meet Reality and Reality meet Destiny and
   Destiny's

mother laughed and told her friend how I looked around as she was calling out
   down 8th Avenue
"Destiny! Destiny!" So many little happenings since you were born and before
   now that art

and life seem even more enmeshed think I'll go take a swim with you and your dad
   now in the L
shaped pool with you in your bright pink swim diapers given to us (unused) by
   Stella so many

lovely hand-me-downs, and new things too.

UP IN ARMS

We're embarking
on another adventure

You face the other way
Travel to the speed of sound

Eat your foot
And Peas porridge hot

The Queens of all we survey
My Hands free for a brief moment

Until you can't stand it
I will write you this poem

You're breathing faster
Excitement or frustration

Arching your back against the plaid
Hand-me-down car seat

In another rhizomatic day yes
Almost unrecorded

MUSIC PLAYS ALL BY ITSELF

Most everyone is sleeping
Or doing their secret things

The tower is packed
And doesn't have to be undone

Just cleared out a bit in the middle—
Those toys can fall down now

His glaze of thrown stars
The die with Snake Eye

A labyrinth without end—
Amazing amusement

Power in the house
Country sirens reverb apocalyptic

But here it's everyday life

Rural haven
A bed for dreaming

Fort Da
Mommy always comes back

Alright, Thunder Thighs
Crawl to the Ball
My heart gives a little jump as you are carried away

A fan of fans
She can now play by herself

Or I can hold her completely with one arm
Nursing for the benefit of all

 I can't resist kissing cheek and thigh
So succulent and self-contained
Three peachy asses in all readings

TATAMI MOMMY

At ten months old you are brachiating up chairs like a brachiosaurus
But this does not imply you are evolving out of the mud

Since you came out from the get go with the wisest expression I had ever seen
Serene and though non-focused, peaceful as any Lama Rinpoche Stardust Pupa

Am I evolving into a mommy because I sleep next to you under a Down
Comforter shaped like a powdery grid of flour powder ravioli or

A grid of tatami mat cut into neat squares.
You play with colored wooden doughnuts
whose age label says for "18 months Plus"
 so don't believe everything you read

You make raspberries at great moments
during the reading of the Guy de Bord

The grubby puppeteer at Union Square
with his Frank Sinatra Wolf puppet
and a lion who sang Hotel California
to a girl muppet knockoff fascinated you to no end

At Bedford Street stop the Ukrainian violinist played you one phrase of "Long Ago"
I am a misanthrope today only liking you and your father.

Nobody else is worth the trouble they give me
Can't wait for you to wake up so I can play with you

Kiss you eight times nine equals seventy-two times plus the Seal Park swings

MIRANDA LEE ARRIVES IN ALAMOS

       on the eve of her
  17th Month

Two Bats Flit
     in & out of the cross-beamed bedroom
& in the morning one more for you (spirals
                      circles, my
                         glasses are
                           off—)

               who are now sleeping soundly

   M e x i c o   M e x i c o   M e x i c o

              on the very same bed
              many more in your family (your dad's side)
              bore

down on
You slept "in media" us

all night & are again
occasionally bumping off of the long pillows

set on either side of you like
the world's most pellucid billiard ball

I think of love as a side effect
. . . since I

with, by means of love

Vuelte = turn, revolution

To turn it all over in your hand
Is to turn it all over in your mind

NEW HOME TO POLLEN PATH

   First time Miranda asked
to go to bed—
   She said "Nap"
Then "Nurse"

It was in the tub like when she started to kick on Bastille Day

Then she sang the alphabet very well, all lit up
Tipping back and forth

Side to side

She's just old enough to say
"New Home"

in her upward lilt
on each word &
find
where the lights are
and do they have fireflies there &

How do the beds lie

Shakespeare too
deepest relaxation
husband can relax
the new angle I see
& curves from certain
seats

Lightning to clear us

What stars
beauty springs

From fore & aft
After the "Bee In"

I reached
        "Beauty above me
        "Beauty below
        "Beauty to the left of me
Beauty to the right
Means you are *inside*
    the flower

a bee
on the [pollen]
    path

that flows
that fine gold powder
is what I have seen
on 2 separate occasions

It's their house too,
Those wasps

Major nesting instrument here

I'm 40.853 years old
        & I have my first house
on the first night

Diana's Day
      was Friday &
Now it's

Wednesday, the newest
      Moon
Waxes,

astounds at the

      Water calendar

ANYTHING

Mandy is two

Mommy is blue

Because her little girl
Is going on three
But Miss Amanda she's as proud as can be
Cuz she's a big girl now
          —Billie Holiday

Miranda's the one writing now

I am reading
I am writing

 she says

raspberry washable marker making little scratchy curvies all over the envelope
"M" "D" "E"

she tones curving up at the end of each letter and moves the pen

and

I love **singing**

and

Only Mommy
and

I know that book

Falling into language
She rises into speech

For months now the slow ascent to comprehension
Conversation unfolds

Her voice now connects meaning blocks:

(watching out the back window)

Red Bird Fly Away

Only Baby Carry Bubbles

(Asserting herself down the street clutching the bright pink plastic tub)

Only Mommy

Only Nurse

Nurse in Car
Nurse in Bubble
Nurse in Elmo
Nurse in Book

Only Nurse!

(We can't say Sonic Nurse
Or she'll want to do it again)

Framing this poem I recall
Transcribing the last days words of my grandmother
As she floated from consciousness
Ice chips melting in her mouth

Miranda my daughter
Rose into language
the music has had meaning for months
And now coheres, focuses, relays

I no longer have to read your mind
You can tell us what you want

I show you an Eye Pillow
and you make it

Bed Eye

Just in July
We walked down the street
And realized you could say
Anything

So fed you "Shakespeare"
And "Proust"

You can feed back

     Acrobatics

     Bubbywumps

Samuel Delaney upon hearing our alphabetic recitations
Of Apple Bowl Cat Dog Egg etcetera

Asks, can you say
Rambunctious?

You delightedly wrap your teeth around it all

I say: you can say ANYTHING

And you say
ANYTHING
&

when you see a Heart

It means I Love You

NAME OF THE GAME

Let's Play Hello Kitty goes with her mama to Hudson on the train and then she
goes in a taxi police car and they ride it to a house owned to someone with 5
Mommy Cats and 5 Kitty Babies house and there's one more and there need to be
and she's called Hello Kitty. I think that's the end of the naming of the game.

Now let's do it.

Let's Play I'm a girl statue and I like to stand still and catch water in my little
orange plastic round thing and it has little curvers.
I think that's it.

I'll say the letters and you type them
N M E G A Q P R

I want those.
Now we need to do all the other letters big.
I'll tell the letters
And you type them.

A Z P Q W E R T Y

Let's play in the morning the little cat
shines the pink light in the dark dark dark dark dark dark woods.

CAROLINE CRUMPACKER

was born into the house of Gemini and New York City on May 29, 1964. Her daughter Colette Grainne O'Malley arrived a Sagittarius in Cape Cod on December 11, 2003. They live with partner/father/novelist Tom O'Malley (also Sag.) in Upstate New York. Caroline's poems, translations, essays and reviews have appeared in magazines including *Boston Review, Chicago Review, The Poetry Project Newsletter, jubilat, Volt, The Germ* and others as well as *The Talisman Anthology of Contemporary Chinese Poetry* (Talisman, 2007); *American Poets in the 21st Century: Who We Are Now* (Wesleyan University Press, 2007); and *Isn't It Romantic: Love Poems by Younger American Poets* (Verse Press, 2004). She is a founding editor of *Fence* and *Double Change* (DoubleChange.com) and a contributing editor for *Circumference*. She is the curator of the Bilingual Reading Series/World of Poetry at the Bowery Poetry Club and works as the Director of the Millay Colony for the Arts, a residency program in Austerlitz, New York.

AESTHETIC SYMBIOTIC

Kinetic dis-assemblage
        sexual hysterias
        and religious trance
        are no excuse.

We are all
        chemists of the nursery.

Even those who have devoured
        their childhood for survival
        are part of the experiment.

Variables such as
the louche interior life   of mothers,
the voracious appetite   of the baby

operate against   the thermometer of collective empiricism.

Applicant: Narratives of motherhood.
Applicant: The average baby speaks
        in relation to a breach in pre-speaking thought.

Applicant: Alchemy of negotiation that breaks
        at points of idealized convention.
Applicant: Physical. Moon.

A patient erasure knocking around mother,
            whoring around mother.
And baby developing relationship-capacities.
Why, baby?

A small red arrow of songs and heartbreak
is Herself among the flowers,
            a showering of present tense
            upon the dramatis of her necessity
            attended by the necessity of her continuity.

Motherhood   a trying on   a flowerbed   .
            an ecstatic physicality   of depreciation.

not even the rain has such small hands

And underneath everything—a riot
            of words scratching to the surface.

Maternal brutality is
            the desire for multiple worlds.

She overhears it as music.
                        Clairvoyant of environment.

And this is our world, an unfriendly acquisition
            of shared perception.

Everything learned is a displacement,
            the baby knows this
            as a form of flowering
            a flowering of form
                        and a pre-formal exchange of ideals.

The first covenant, love, is broken
            by its formation
            whereas the second comes   with attachment to meaning.

Nothing is noted as absence   except by the collective
                                     agreement on presence
                                     which backfires on trial.

Mothers depreciate and evolve   to animal logic.
Narratives of mother   contradict themselves.

Hence the larger grammatics

            we are   as conjugate of she is.

Declension:

We are all
            accompanied   despite the overwhelming evidence.

We are all
            conducting trial runs   for the endlessly repeating first five years.

We are all
            decoding narrative   structures in relation to newness.

Over-ride upon she is: love   but conventions   of love.

Refinance: I give to thee this world of mine.

Undone: World of mine.

Re done: World of mine.

Landscape to world   pre-spoken conjugation held
                                                in speaking.

Present tense to interior: relentless acquisition.

Flower: Bed.

Flowers:	Bedded.
She among the flowers:	Psychological hold.
Vernal. Sprout infinitive.	

SMALL FICTIVE DEVICES: FAMILY

1. Life in the setting of a 21st century City. A small life. A tapping. One woman living in a red building. Notice what she's wearing today it feels so good. There is theater to modern cities. On the level of architecture and on the level of erotic encounter. She walks in. This is her real life. Meaning she has acquired a taste for it. She walks in. She is doubled over. No, that was the time before. She walks in rapt with contemplation of the narrative in which she has landed. Textual dysmorphia

2. One day the body is a different species and how does one configure the mind around this happening? *Yes, little bird, this is still your convocation.*

3. The colors themselves invent. There is an anatomy to color, unavailable to anything but the intelligence of the colors themselves.

4. Bodice bit of violet candy. A name beginning with C. Our fascination with flesh. *I gave my love a cherry.* Cherry. Charlotte. Colette.

5. The psychology of the child. There waking alone is the first pathology, wanting.

6. In love understood as if eating a strawberry for the first time and saying "So THIS is a strawberry."

7. "Words are not merely a substitute for wordlessness; they are something else entirely. Or, to ask a more obviously psychoanalytic question, what exactly must be given up in order to speak?" Adam Phillips, *The Beast in the Nursery*

8. These are her first words: mama dada cat dog duck cow bottle sheep ball bath balloon more banana no apple that bubbles blocks door book choo-choo bird park bye-bye bowl avocado up home oh pool bag house help hi eggs the gas-station nurse baby hat hello high-chair please boys almond horrible.

9. Conversation ragged. Intimacy mutates with venue. I at home hereby withhold meaning. Sitting with our feet in the plastic pool, she asks me about my sex life.

10. Mix wet ingredients in a 2 cup measuring beaker: Add the wet to the dry and stir until just moistened. Add extras, if you wish. Spoon batter into greased or lined 12-muffin pan and bake at 325 for 25 minutes.

11. Going to touch him. Without the support of the body. Without the contextual authority of her real life. Tap tap. After being ripped apart, the flesh cringes without the assistance of the spirit. She is patient with the narrative she has landed in. The old story of atavistic form.

12. Her friend calls the lesson only partially welcome.

13. The Love Supreme. One bag of diapers. One tube of unpetroleum jelly. One tube of Neosporin. One anatomical re-enactment of a week's purchases. One bar of soap. One tub of wipes. One packet organic cheese. One pound red grapes. One world of baby objects twirling. One Chopin étude. One baby toothbrush. One box vanilla teething biscuits. One case water. One financial problem. One laughing woman coming up the stairs. One satin brassiere. One milk letdown. One bag cornstarch. Two bottles sunscreen. One small t-shirt. One pair of baby shorts. One lactation tea. One digital thermometer. One resentment against the father. One statement of need. One casual dismissal. One latté. One call to another mother. One bottle nontoxic bug repellent. One teething ring. One small telephone. One joint bank account. One act of transgression. One misspoken sentence.

14. Chinese verbs don't use tense she finds in translating from Chinese to English. How does one remark on the life of the mother and the life before the life of the mother as two lives within one life, separated by time, she wonders?

15. Derivation of dada: rocking horse, double affirmative Russian, art movement.

16. Derivation of mama: me my mine milk yum.

VIEWER DISCRETION AND YOUNG CHILD

Darling this story begins *al segno*
      following the river
      to middle expressionism   and then to the moral order
      of families   as the dissolving centerpiece of a predisposition
                for nostalgia.

Ach Du Leiber . . .

This to say she   understands water individually
    not   collectively.
Physicality   is easier   than abstraction
    even at   her   age.

The river   contradicts the bath.
The little inflatable pool   a desolate thing.

She says   *warrr* . . .
We say *Yes yes*   *water.*

Everyone here   owes a debt to the River.
Without   knowing why.

We would pave it over if we could.

The hose unleashes   a torrent.
She says *Stop warr.*   I say the evening peeling a bit at the corners
like the old landscape   drama it is. I had cachet once in choices.
And a butterfly enters   the conversation as the lost soul
of romantic painting.

Before the bridges   imagine its necessity.
Function is   the rending.

Now a thriving business   in dislocation.
Small servings of beauty   sold in the name of geographic privilege.
Sweet-smelling summer   funk.

The railroad straddles the river   and takes us
          as the song says   up up up.
Up-river the family   thrives like the green reeds
of a New Orleans Gothic.

Families are form   not function.

Where the corn   and lilies manipulate.
Where the bookstore   has a section called "River".
Where the words   are,
          a new place   is created.

The water is sugar tea in August.
I lie sweating in bed   at mid-day thinking this is my life.
And outside a drumbreat   of ruination
          and celebration..

We go walking and she says *beach*
No no, — quay.

The remaining imperative, love.

JENNY BROWNE

Her mother's water broke at the Wisconsin State Fair on August 15, 1971 and Jenny was born at Milwaukee General shortly thereafter. Her own daughters were both born at home in downtown San Antonio, Texas: Lyda on January 29, 2004 and Harriet on June 5, 2006. She is a James Michener Fellow in poetry at the University of Texas and recently received a grant from the Artist Foundation of San Antonio, every cent of which will be used for child care.

"Both of the poems included in this collection are grounded in the immense amount of advice-giving that befalls new mothers, an on-going "shower." I'm not complaining but it does seem like most advice is both really useful and completely useless. Mostly, I feel as guilty for what I do as for what I don't, as hopeful for what my children's futures hold both because of and despite me. Then again, Lyda loves the Beatles. I can hear her singing in the kitchen, '. . . all you need is love, love. Love.'"

A MAN CAN STILL DREAM OF CIGARETTES

The Spanish teacher said you'll know you've finally learned the language when
the dream baby's snake face looks up and says *hola*. I dreamed the real baby came
too soon. We put her back and went to the rodeo where women wearing jeans
without back pockets leaned hard around barrels and the dust did rain. The
parenting book tries to explain how it feels likes you go to sleep in your bed and
wake up in Mozambique. It could be China or Afghanistan. There are no camels
in the Koran. We don't write what we know too well. We don't dream what
we've already seen. Behind her tiny veined lids, the real baby's eyes gallop. Two
hours old, each dewy thought a shiny fire truck parting the Red Sea bellowing new.
There is no need to seed her mind like clouds above a barely contained blaze. The
parenting book doesn't try to explain how it feels to be born. There is no way to
say I wonder in Spanish. A sign above the road says you too arrived here through a
tunnel in the darkness. It could say you can't be lost if you don't have a map. There
are no camels in El Salvador but there are black birds that back-flip on telephone
wires. That is what some call a translation. The baby's toes curl around my finger
like tender claws. Somewhere oil fields burn endlessly, their confused faces clearly
visible from outer space.

THE SEASON WHEN SOME PEOPLE WILL SAY

you should always begin with scissors.
Rock is too obvious. Some people say
obviously. Some people say it's really
coming down. Some people say down is
the new up. Some people say the sky is full
of birds whose names I will never learn.
Some people say don't you remember me
and some people already know the answer
to a question before they ask it. Some people
ask if you know what you are having
and some people pretend they don't know
what some people mean by this and say yes,
a baby. Some people don't think this is funny.
Some people say you shouldn't drink coffee.
Some people say the cup is half asleep. Some
people say you will never sleep again.
Some people say I was just resting my eyes.
Some people say I hope it has your eyes.
Some people say I can't even see
my feet anymore. Some people say
you should approach birth with the calm
of a stoplight changing color but yellow
means speed up or scared to death depending
on the some people in question and some people
say a dream of cherries means you will soon have
knots in your tongue. Some people say watch out
for red dye #3. Some people say produce like
the word for fruits and vegetables and not the verb
that means to make or create something. Some people
say you should keep a journal. Some people say paper
equals full moon, unmade bed, cream but no sugar.
Some people's mothers say don't think you're
the only one who ever made deals with God.
Some people say please and thank you. Some people
say you will never be the same. Some people say who
wants the same? Some people say you know
this isn't a game.

SUSANA GARDNER

was born in 1973 in Rhode Island, where she was raised. Her first chapbook, *To Stand to Sea* (The Tangent Press, 2006) is presently being translated into the Italian by Massimo Sannelli and forthcoming from Cantarena Press, Genoa. She lives in Switzerland with her partner and her daughter, Stella Maris, who was born the 20th of February 2004. She also edits DUSIE, a post-modern journal and eclectic press of innovative poetics, www.dusie.org/. The piece selected for this anthology is from *S C R A W L or,- (from the markings of) the small her(o),* which was first published in the inaugural *dusi/e-chap kollektiv and is available to read in its entirety at the Dusie site. This piece is also a part of a longer manuscript entitled *UTTER,* which encompasses the experience of giving birth as well as that of motherhood—all of which was written since becoming a mother

A S T ERASTERIAS

A REALISM LOST HER NAME :   M A R I E   (O) SHE
         SHE STROLLS   IN HRS

NAMES MARI/ S /HE TELLS HER/E &HERS &HER HRS
         SO(U)LS AS ASTER HARMS IRHE

TELLS (O) A HARM I(H)RES LET LOS   (O) A SEASHELL TRIM
 O R,- A LARAMIE SUN-

LESS ATLAS SIR,- AN HRS ASTRAL ASTROL ASTROL
         O( )R MUSES
                 ı

HER HATTED HRS IN & SO,- A GRANDAMES ERR HER LATERAL
         LOSS LOS S/ T I L L S

OR,- ONE GRANDMERE HER SALT LUNES IN A SEAGRAMS
        R E N D

TRILLS AS A TEAGRAM SENT NILLS ALAS,- LET US
        S U N US

SEE AT LAST UNLESS STELLINA TIS SUN AS
        S E A S

AS ATTIS SITS NULL AS SEAS TAT NETS & SO LULL AS ALL A S U
        *A (*S U N

S/ A NS SET AT LAST ASTIR (O),- ASTER NETS US LETS ALLES SEIN
        A S S E N T US

(O) AS ALL ATTENS US   MY A T L A S T MY OUTLASTS   L(N)E T S
        A L A S NESTS US

from the markings of the small her(o) when morning wakes
     b r i g ht

wakes unfolded new gesture in the space of or toward a balance or possibility
     of w h a t

is and is so spoken this (o)   and   what new language spoken or simply
netted
     and s o

suited toward her as is and better is so suited toward (her)
     w h i l e

fresh s(o) air crisp as an imperative open window like c l o c k
     w o r k

a i r in g out bed things as feathered filled things& stale night
     a i r

bitte   bitte   bitte   eh   eh   eh   with fine   r e p e a t
       repeated&again

as to turn into this world as in flesh &in so coming to
       b e born—gauntlet of

smallness   she   and her said fitting the g r a n d e s t entry she
       (o) we all might ever know

to only so soon forget a n d r e l y on others to impart or
       translate here :

she b a l l r o o m (e d) and she t/his (her) glove(d) outgrown
       her(o) in size

and strangely dependent on what those o t h e r
       e y e s w i t n e s s

in so fortunate in so   seeing   what   this birded hour was and just what
might
         h a v e u n f o l d e d

such   an   entry—immer   so—which   is   first   is   first   (o)
         &a l w a y s formed

as form must dictate surely even here &is first and perhaps only
         signified by a date or

time or occurrence— steel hands their metal chill—say eradication
         say w a v i n g any

other/*or let's just say a rather brutal alternative—say incision from the*
         w h o l e

what must signify beginning then   so began is ever first is
         f i r s t

t h e s m a l l her(o)

previously &so,- not noted
or side-noted   or   all too simply
abandoned   dismissed   seamingly
squashed and quelled along the side-
lines as too damn precious   or unnaturally
prescient &so crushed sentimental as such

yes, the small her(o) must surely
wonder where feeling went
toward the end of the 20th
                    century ?
when narrative and confession
begged prosaic & so chill
&so   to be
heard again   when the next
g e n e r a t i o n

m i g h t very well r e a d
this we/us
          —as dull
as is merely broken parted&
distorted us/we as thoughtless
or unduly heralded&
such &so side-stepped
in way of marginalia

          a s s o
u n f e e l i n g of the smallest
and of   we this she
          our surely most unheard
s t i f l e d h e r (o)

NEST TURNS LETS LUNA LOS (LASSEN) A TERSE RIME ASSA
        S E N T (I) RAN MIT

INA   ALAS   MET   ATTEM   &RAINED   STEMS   &SO   I
        R A N LOS&SO RAN

MET   A SIRAN MET ASTERIA   A SIREN TRAIN UNS AMISS
        A S T E R N / E N (*)

MET ANON A SAINT HER SATIN STRAND MER-A -MATE   A SIREN
        S E T :   A R T E M I S   TATS   HER

NAME A S T I R ASTER ASTERIA O SIR,- UNSERE MANE STIR, A
        M E A N S T A R / A S A SISTER

AS A SET UNSERE DEAR MINARETS, UNSERE SISTER INSEL SETS
        TIS SATE( ) ASTER ASTERIA

JENNIFER MICHAEL HECHT

was born in 1965 in New York. She and her husband John live in Brooklyn with their son Maxwell, born May 14, 2004, and their daughter, Jessie Leo, who arrived March 23, 2006. Hecht is a poet, historian, and philosopher. She is the author of two books of poetry and three books of philosophy and history. Her five books have won five prizes, including the Phi Beta Kappa 2004 Ralph Waldo Emerson Award; the Poetry Society of America's 2002 Norma Farber First Book Award; and the University of Wisconsin's Felix Pollak Poetry Award; and have been published in five languages. Hecht earned her PhD in the History of Science and European Culture, Columbia University in 1995. She teaches at the New School and writes essays, reviews, and poetry for *The New York Times*, *The Washington Post*, and *The Philadelphia Inquirer*.

"My books and babies alternate years so it looks as if I did one, then the other, year by year. I did not. It was all a jumble. As to content, before I was a mother I assumed that babies would not change my poetry, because I rarely wrote love poems and don't exactly write about my life either. But behold, they show up in almost every poem. In the middle of my life, I bent over myself and straightened back up with a human in my hands and I have found every moment of it mesmerizing, I mean, if I may, *what the freak?* From me cleaved off some creatures? Amazing people too. Small. Full of surprises. I revel in nudging their ribs to giggle or dissertating upon a red, red cow. It does make me feel like life is less record and more cord, but that doesn't stop me from constantly recording, because I enjoy it intensely and because we've got to eat."

STEADY, STEADY

I believe you can build a boat.
I believe you can get to water.
I do not believe you can get the boat on water.

How bear such burdens?
How do people do
what you are still afraid of?

The answer is that when big things happen
you do go through the looking glass,
but it is still you who goes through,
the inner text is all still right to left,
so you just keep reading.

Because there is no boat and there is no water.
I stare at my tiny baby's face

but he so wriggles he can't quite be seen.
He grows steadier, more and more the blur
is gone; he joins us in the myth of the stable.

Of the quakiness of infancy and old age
we shimmer and shimmy into being
and out again. In the mean
time, we're horses in the stable of the myth.

A quick check of the ocean, or any fire,
is a reminder of how things seem;
I can't seem to see them.

You're on the beach and you find out the Secretary
of Defense thinks calico cats are agents of the devil.
Your friend asks if they get ten percent.

The water in this metaphor
is unreal, because of the way time passes
so you can't quite get the boat on water,

but you can build the boat,
and a boat is good for a lot of things
not just on water.

Will we, without the boat on water,
always feel that we are missing
something pretty basic to the picture?

No. That is what I'm trying to say.
It is important to let sense quiver;
even in this stable of the myth of stable,
even living aboard a boat mired
in mud in view of the sea.

Who wants yet another world?
It's enough already.

CLAUDIA RANKINE

is the mother of the four year old Ula Alexandra Lucas and author of four volumes of poetry. PLOT was written before Ula was born.

from PLOT

A short narrative of breasts and wombs entitled

Liv Lying on the Floor Looking at

the Dirty Thought

[The womb similar to fruit that goes uneaten will grow gray fur, the breasts a dying rose, darkening nipples, prickling sickness as it moves toward mold, a spongy moss.]

Liv, answer me this: Is the female anatomically in need of a child as a life preserver, a hand, a hand up? And now, pap smeared, do you want harder the family you fear in fear of all those answers?

Could you put fear there as having to do with him? think. think . . . as having to do with milk? To your health! Cheers. Or against the aging body unused, which way does punishment go?

"Let us not negotiate out of fear. . . ." butbutbut. . . . Then the wind touched the opened subject until Liv in a light breeze, squalls, was without a place to put her ladder.

From the treetop something fell, a bundle, a newspaper, a bug, a bag, still nobody's baby. Sound was desperation dropped down, a falling into place, an not way away—

Statistics show: One in what? One in every what? A child in every pot will help the body grow? No matter, all the minutes willingly slip into the first, then the ashes still shiver.

Liv, is the graffitied mind sprained? Who sprayed a cancer there? Which answer?

What dirtied up prevention? No matter. Anyway, which way does your ladder go?

Toward? Or away? in keeping with that ant crawling on your ankle. O mindless hand, rub hard. Not quite in pain because pain is shorthand for what? One in every what? Cradle call.

Ohh kiss it up without facing yourself. Knowing the issue, go ahead, slouch, rest your chin on your folded hands. Think: blunt impact, injury. Toss a "but" against the wall,

tic, tock

+ + +

10:12 pm

Is it allowed? Am I, as a descendent of particulars, unneeded times, permitted the thing and more? This world, its worst is real. What doesn't hurt, ticking past, what doesn't intersect? Our destinations recalled, our points of fracture, of limbs crushed to memory, no more than experience, I am too aware of other ways.

Another Frame of Mind

As if a source exists only for its result, within Liv's sketches lives the eternal term disappearing into her child: mother coded for other, a gate only, a mighty fortress, a door swinging open . . .

or is she that—that vessel, filling up, swelling to overflow until mothery is the drowned self, drowning all that is, all that clings?

Whether her eyes are open or closed she hears only a child.
Whether her eyes are open or closed she hears only the child.
Whether her eyes are open or closed she sees only her child.
Whether her eyes are open or closed she sees only her own. . . .

Or too soon whose womb rhymes with plot? Whether her eyes are open or closed she feels the same loss in jubilation.

11:26 pm

In the weeks it has taken to suck and swallow, girdled child in the preliminary of tissue, in the rudimentary of ear, of eye, of mouth, why wish to be born? The story remains numb within hunger, the story is occupied pain, the body brims from cracks unnamed. A billion results, each the gulf of a particular break.

Still Life

A draft enters. A sketchy gust. Blown is the woman standing within her likeness. To her left the sun needs to be drawn but her hands are the shape cradling her breasts, keeping her nipples in place. Each breast is the rest floating within metonymy. Her swollen scape keeps her awake. In its milky silence she feels distaste. She holds still. She waits. The draft draws dust into her eyes. Her eyes tear until her outline dislodges. dilutes. blurs. In the time it takes to fix her face the moon is drawn quartered.

12:13 am

Shaped to this world, its intrinsic illness, maligned by memory, less and less unable to grieve, am I the lot on whom you strive? What is it we are meant to be? Are we love? Are we happiness? Are we truth?

Milk and Tears

Long after she grows tired in the night she hears only the child's cries. His cries, already recalling, and silence,
the dumbness she wedges herself into.
and additionally compromised, she hears each cry, punctuating every space of exception, running through her, meaning to break, to interrupt each moment attempted. She hears and calls it silence. Then it is as if the hood of motherhood was meant to blur herself from herself, a dark cloth dropping over her eyes until the self of selfless near arose.

1:07 am

Today I wake, tomorrow I wake, and still this assemblage, its associated distortions, bewilders me.

+ + +

No Solace from the TV

She said she thought it was a dead animal, some wild animal, "You know, small animal, killed and buried or . . . or something." She didn't know. Just not. . . .

She said, "Who would believe that!" She was a woman, she understood women. This she didn't understand. "As a woman, as a mother . . . no, this was not . . . not a mother."

"You could see, anyone could see she was pregnant. We aren't fools. She can't fool anyone. She was pregnant. Where is the baby?"

"It's hard to know," he said, "hard to know now the psychological state of the mother. We could be looking at anything from reckless endangerment to . . . to murder. Intent to murder. But who know, you know . . . who knows."

"Someone . . . someone could be thinking a . . . female with a problem just looking to get rid of a problem. You know, scared of the equation."

"One could see that this life . . . in this life she might have felt driven to it . . . without choice. A mother, but not a mother really. A woman, but not a mother. A desperate woman or perhaps a woman only."

In the drift from screen to sleep Liv finds no peace. A woman but not a woman really, in her nightmare she chews at her breasts. Hers is the same sucking sounds baby goats make. She examines her flesh-toned spit and molds it into sunglasses. After wearing the glasses for some time, her vision, she notes, is angled downward, cradled by a shadow barely a foot long.

The Dream Play

Simultaneously and as a consequence, Erland comes to Liv in her dream. His face is flushed. Has he been running?

Where's the baby? he asks.
I haven't go it, she says.
What's in your stomach then?
The blood's run out.
The blood's run out? Where out?
Out, out, and it's taken the thing with it.
Are you mad?
Don't talk about it.
Where's the baby? he shouts.

The Dream Riddle

If the floor muscle gives way, bitter and fibrous, and the bluing cervix turns shades of gray, who will be no more than a moan, little person about whom?

Wake Up Wake Up Wake Up   Liv dreams she sits up,
rests her head against a

moan

little person

flake away desire. dissolve congested rock. underneath it is impossible not to glean. here is more than any drama can bear. spare is the room you would enter. scoured are the hours you would pass. Dearest, living is beneath you. infested as it is by our nostalgic narratives of hope. here exists for itself alone. as your form passes through. stay your soul in mine. keep your room. my womb. as hermitage. these hours now are ours. but swear you will turn back.

otherwise   and deep

disappointment

Wake Up Wake Up Wake Up

she keeps waiting for this time to be

waiting for the time to be

Over breakfast Liv tells Erland she dreamed Ersatz dead, a miscarriage, and that he, Erland (Don't look at me that way), was red-faced, embarrassed about something in a goat-infested place.

Oh, yes, there was blood and breasts and moans and deep disappointment. Then, wake up, wake up,   I remember.

The HEart That She Holds

On the hemorrhaging spread on which sense rests Liv knows she strays, is straying into. There are a trillion reasons to go forward, to say "yes" and let the body lead.

Each hour that passes occludes the life within her, a fusion she feels the body needs. Is pregnancy the thing happening or the reason? When Liv says, *I am so sorry . . . I am so sorry that . . .*

she is willing herself forward into the birth she fears because she fears the regret of before, as if all loss must be repaid, as if a body spoilt will spoil itself in spite, tick tocking toward barren.

Minute to minute she is released from doubt and then certain she is misled. She avoids her thoughts, circles wide, maneuvers toward the void where what matters is what is.

7:23 am

Erland

who presumed birth, is taken to tomato red. He feels, obliquely, his own need,
as if it were greed to resent life being walked away from. What is left to him
understands little—Is their child poor company, cadaver of a incompetent cervix,
discard of a drawn lot? Is he a burden on her uterine muscle? assuming too huge a
room? This is it: a whole possible embodied by Liv and he now not caring, fearing,
though nearing to meet it. In thought the thought is barely tolerated, ushered out,
and still

oh, Liv,

must you insist on rot in the plot to continue? Must you turn life on its head,
inverse the process, live its evil?

Liv,

must you kill life's will toward its one true recognition of joy?

Liv,

oh Liv.

Fruitless Still Life

Ideally (so already never) what they desired, sired, is a love that would flood
everyday fears communicable: each broken step, open depth, blackened call,
searing grasp, oh ruined cell—but it's a retarded and retarding love that frets.
Though fret love will until ill or illy suited to protect the Xed-in soul of another
(as if any other could be shielded by any him or her), it hems, it haws, it coughs its
part, it peters out, it does. Seen for itself, love must face regret—material tent held
over (though never cemented), a wish thrown far, some ink to document the days,
record a birth outworn, and, torn to tears   other times.

LISA FISHMAN

(b. 12/14/66) has published three collections of poetry and a chapbook. She was 37 when her son, James Niccolo Fishman-Morren was born on May 24, 2004, the first day of strawberry season (difficult timing, on the farm), a birthday he shares with Bob Dylan.

"Of mothering, I have to say I too dislike it. I enjoy (in the deepest sense of the word; I take joy in) James as a person—I love his personality and his body and his nature—but find childcare tedious and draining overall. To clarify: Who James is is so much more interesting to me than who I am *as a mother*—the latter is just the given. The wondrous thing is himself. I couldn't do the parenting without two other full-time care-givers (Henry and Rick) as well as daycare, which he started minimally at four months and went to several days a week from eight months on. Also couldn't do it without periodic one- to two-week trips child-free. Writing continues, reading suffers most. James takes so much pleasure in whatever he's doing and whomever he's with, especially if it involves guitars or banjos, that I find in his joy (and depth of feeling, and particularity of thought) a place for the genuine."

EVENING WITHOUT SWALLOWS

A child is a use I put myself to
said a woman in the store.

Was it for shoes or grain she shopped,
I do not know, I made her up
but not specifically here or there.

       As I was driving through Dolly's window,
stumpaty, stampaty, stump.

A method is a gimmick very often,
said a crow upon a stone. Take pie #437
with ceramic bluebird through which steam comes out.

The edges of its crust are fluted, as a skirt will
ripple in a light wind without music.

SONG FOR MR. SINGER
           from Songs for James

The rain comes from a chord
and the rain is full of rain
G C G D
Look the umbrellas are really guitars
I will learn how to sing for you
says the cricket, the loon, and the sun inside the moon
Remember how rhyme was bound to love
the other self springing forward and back
And the kindness of music grew large
in the orchard; the kindness
of music had cities in it—
trains lit up the windows as they passed—
The kindness of music threw stones
into the sea. That sky is far away.
Where is your body,
brown cow? G C G D

ARIELLE GREENBERG

was born on October 24, 1972. She is the author of two books of poems and a chapbook. Her poems have been included in the 2004 and 2005 editions of *Best American Poetry* and a number of other anthologies, including *Legitimate Dangers* (Sarabande, 2006). She is a former editorial board member of *How2*, the poetry editor for the journal *Black Clock* and a founder and co-editor of the journal *Court Green*. She also founded, in 2005, and continues to moderate the private poet-moms listserv for working poets who are mothers to young children, part of the impetus for this anthology. She is an Assistant Professor in the poetry program at Columbia College Chicago and lives in Evanston, IL with her husband, Rob Morris, and their daughter, Willa Green Bywater. Willa was born at home in water on May 4, 2005, after a (mostly lovely) five-day labor, with poet Rachel Zucker in attendance as doula. Rob and Arielle both took on the legal last name of Bywater (a matriarchial last name in Rob's family) while Arielle was pregnant as an imperfect solution to the naming conundrum.

COMING APART BETWEEN THE HOURS

Moist skin: I'm split.

Livery: part hired, part owned,
part aimless cruising a living
out of night shifts and know nothing.

You could call it a schism but that'd imply a whole.
A phrenia but that'd imply some energy.

Not that I have none.
I'm an empty flask of joie de vive
with the scent still musking around in my thick crystal walls.
There are compartments in my compartments.

Dark little princes in every lighthouse.

> I sent some sugar but the sugar was hijacked.
> I sent some artillery, bunting, cow's milk, paper diapers—
> all fallen on the road to who I am when I'm together.

When *we* are. Chum. Child. Chump.

Taxicab: I've got a radio and radio static,
a cell on headset and speaker phone and two pick-ups telling lies.

Heart: the one with all the chambers.

Hello from in here.

It's like being in a castle
half-dead brides behind the secret doors.

REENACTMENT

Something about the way you raised your tiny fist this morning
reminded me of Colonial Williamsburg.

Something about the way you, six weeks old, raising your tiny fist
while drinking the milk of my body this morning
reminded me of Colonial Williamsburg:
the soft green and lilac air, the mindful octagonal plantings,
the smell of calico muslin, the slaves.

The mock slaves coming in from the fields.
The performance of slaves pasting herbs into salves.
The thespian slaves saving face in the henhouse.
The play-acting slaves descended from slaves.

On my side you were a slave in Egypt.
Then you were kicked in the head by a Czar's horse in Poland.
You came to this country with just a length of neon and lace tucked in your
    kerchief.

On your father's side you invented, manufactured and owned shirt collars.
You manufactured the silver spoons of our nation. The actual silver spoons.
They still hang on little hooks in museums. Citizens hunt for the missing knife
    in the pattern.

G IS FOR GLASSBLOWER. GESTATED. GRAVID. UGLY.

      Ruined by beauty you could mutter if you weren't so damn material,
could lie belly-down, snake in the mud like you'd like
but you can't, you're
full of matter, you're mammalian
like all species with milk, you're
closed by these million pod-like black petals chiming *mother,* you're
a rattled cage, a viper basket.
      Damaged at every cross-hatch.
Skin tagged and marked with skin at all the body's fractious queries,
stretched like a meat-hound, swoll,
purple, lumped, hard-boiled, yes,
and devoid of your beautiful square-cut diamond
and your plain gold band because so plumped with that mewling life
you're practically unmarried.
      There could be weeks yet to go.
Two more moons, could be, this rounded lug.
Enough to make you drown, want to drown
crushed in the waves of your flesh.
Pins. Needles. Pins with plastic duck heads. Needles with a beautiful medicine.
Drink more water. Eat more eggs.
These snaky rules, these rules are
      Not for you. Nestle the kitten; keep it from snakes.
If she is a girl she will ruin your beauty.
If he is a boy he'll lodge like a bullet.
In neither case will you sleep on your belly,
or on your heartless side, or on your crushed-down spine,
will you sleep again deeply, they say, like it's ha-ha,
you'll never sleep again.
And then they remind you *This is a form of actual torture.*
      You half-remember a life with texture:
the flat wool of your best camel skirt, the slip inside a snakeskin purse,
the flick of your shiny hair, your face when it felt. Oh, now colorless,
and striated, *it will all be joy with kitten soon*
they say but they lie and you lie on the mat with the dog—
on just the thankless right side, for just minutes, before everything goes numb
  again—

(You once read a story that might not exist called The Glassblower's
    Children
who might not exist who go to a fair that might not exist
and buy a ring set with a raven's blinked eye
that carries them, napped, kidded, across a river that m.n.e.
to a glittering castle that might not exist where they become slaves
to a thankless queen who has everything and even these foster children
do not make her smile but to keep themselves company
they find their twins in the hallway mirrors until these, too,
are banned and blank and do not exist.
          And do you remember that the river is Forgetful
and wipes them clean of their glassblowing parents
and the fair and the village and leaves them
with only that sideways eye of the raven?
And where are you in this story, this hallway?
My little boat? My booth? My half-empty glass?)

LARA GLENUM

(12.19.70) is the mother of high-octane Sasha (5.6.05). Lara is the author of two books of poems including the forthcoming *Tiny Outrageous Mouth of Heaven*. She also translates twentieth-century Czech poetry and writes about avant-garde poetry and poetics.

ST. LIBERATA AND THE ALIEN HORDES

I was crucified   as an alien host!

      Still hanging on the cross   they peeled the seedy, white pods
      out of   my large muscle groups

      & scraped the sleeper colony out of my left lung

In Nicomedia, I'd been seen leading a winged devil by a chain
followed by a U.F.O.

The hermaphroditic cults of Cyprus
said I was pursued   by aliens disguised as plague pigs
          with tiny bells around their necks

      They carved
      strings of pods   like firecrackers   out of my spinal column

& The whole time
the executioners heard chattering noises   The hard shapes of antennae
could be seen   wriggling against the walls of grey amniotic sacs

In jail, I'd grown a beard   & wore shoes of solid gold:
      The Bride of Heaven!

Lumpy & swollen with a thousand pods   I began to split at the seams

      It was sheer ecstasy   until the high court
          convened
Until the craven Emperor with his long, curling fingernails
     mandated that
       I be crucified

before I erupted & gave birth   out of every major organ

out of every oil-gland
& mucoid duct

MESSAGE TO THE DEPARTMENT OF THE INTERIOR

I have decided to grow a second body This may be of some
concern to you

I fear my second body will have a forking spine & a rubber
leg & refuse to wear anything but a bloody deer costume

I fear my two bodies will have unseemly public duels

The second body will, in all likelihood, publish obscene
treatises on "the hairy halo" & radicalize the cottage industry
in deer pornography

It will most certainly attempt to cut off the face of the first
body & wear it as a mask whenever it enters "the reality
testing booth"

It will drool "red language" into a steel cup affixed to its chin
The "red language" will be collected & be inserted into the
tongue-holes of its enemies to induce morbid hallucinations

I know you said I should try to relax & ignore the residue the
bombs left in my torso

by eliminating all my bodies & proto-bodies, but who can
relax in our republic now that it's lain its terrible eggs on all
our tongues

THE EGGS OF MY AMNESIA

The sky was sticking to the corners of my mouth

The red weather was laying its eggs in my torso The eggs of
amnesia The red weather was flexing its terrible gills

to make the milk drip out of the holes in my spine It was
tapping out a code on the box The meaty box lined with dead
hares & a millennium of fat

It was running radio wire through the holes in my cheeks

The red weather was polishing my black teeth It was
polishing my exoskeleton It was giving me a plastic jaw filled
with soft, decaying language

My sockets were draining onto the heath of diseased signs

I needed a non-sign state A state not lined with corpses
I felt the eggs between my legs shift & bulge

The red weather affixed the steel muzzle to my jaw It bathed
me in its deadly cream & When I awoke

my mouth was a gun

THE GOLDEN WIRES SINGING IN THE VEINS

Queen Box feeds at one end of me
The Redeemer at the other

Angels eating glory out of my face
like ravenous curs

I'm half-in
half-out
of my blubber suit

Two feeding tubes dangling from my chest

My cunt is a violent surge-hammer
in the mouth of the Redeemer

The animals my skin could not contain
are clanging through the hospital

FERTILITY

I hung my ovaries over the door of the homestead
& invited the Surgeon General
into my parlour
            His assistants hooked me up to the weeping machines

The machines wore rabbit ears & spoke in code
as they harvested my sense-organs

My eye-guns were removed

& the machines pumped cream into my every orifice
with rubber hoses

until I was dribbling cream   out of my eyesockets
Cream hemorrhaging out of my nostrils   & my ears

A siren wailed
as they attached the silver boxes to my undercarriage
& my peripheral defense system

Each part of my body was ultimately alarmed

MAGNIFICAT

The eye-veins in that very cinematic season
purpled & bulged
The month fell open
& I spilled slop out my cunt
   (I was feeling nihilistic & craving a beastie with a body of pearl)

kaboom kaboom

I said, *Beastie, I'm going wacko with all the hatching*
I said, *Beastie, I'm gonzo*
    to straddle your cancers. Please oblige & etc.
   (the mercury in the beastie's cock beading off
   into paradise)

& The hatchlings were streaming out of my gluemouth
onto the transvertebral plane

I said, *I am a turbine column of eighteen breasts*
& The teeth
dripping out of my ghostmeat, etc.
   The milky explosions made cataracts of glazed pigs
in the doctor's throat   I couldn't speak
     I was dripping porkfat into the cunt-void

as the doctor suctioned all the wacko hatchlings out
with his metal finger

    The eye of the season rolled
     on its piggie filaments
The beastie lifted its tail & sprinkled its seed
       onto that very cinematic season

& My head
hatched its very first explosions
    Turbines
      pounding hard against orchid-machines
My ghostmeat dripping horse teeth into the void

The doctor's onyx antlers

spiraling into my glueflesh
Extracting extracting

The ruby-throated   hatchlings in their amniotic sacs
In their hair-covered shells

SUSAN HOLBROOK

(born 1967) teaches North American literatures and Creative Writing at the University of Windsor. She has published two books of poetry. Her daughter Elise was born May 20, 2005. After a few months without poetry, Susan decided to make her mothering life work for, rather than against, her writing, and started composing a line every time she nursed the baby.

NURSERY

Left: Trace pictograph of an elk in the fine veins of your temple. Right: If it were a Virgin Mary we'd be on the news. Left: Try to sit you up for a burp, you're still latched on. Right: Milk drops leave shiny slug trails across your cheek. Left: Reading at the same time, my book on your hip, worried the officious prose style will come through in the milk, give you gas. Right: Doping for sleep. Left: Feeling like a mother didn't happen when you were born, or when I first fed you, or first used the word "daughter." It's happening six months later, in the dark, as a mosquito kazoos and without a second's contemplation I pull up your covers, lay my bare arms on top of the blanket, whisper "bite me." Right: I wasn't talking to you. Left: You spit up to make room for more, like the Romans. Right: Why is an elk worth nothing but a Virgin Mary on grilled cheese costs 28 000 dollars. Left: Hand straight up in the air, flamenco dancer's articulate fingers. Right: *I've seen parents put their infants to bed right after eating, often because the baby falls asleep on the breast or bottle. I don't advise this for two reasons.* Left: Grinning kitten races off with the breast pad Frisbee. Right: *One, the baby becomes dependent on the bottle or breast, and soon needs it to fall asleep. Two, do you want to sleep after every meal?* Left: Actually, yes. Right: The tv flashes against your cheek, a small smooth screen. Left: Through the blinds moonlight strips stratify the bars of your crib. Right: From down here on the futon I watch your mobile. Left: The green bunny's coming around again. Right: Sun's coming up please don't notice. Left: Puddin'. Right: I wipe grains of sweat from your brow, as if you were a doctor delivering a baby. Left: October and the low afternoon sun glows through your jack-o'-lantern ears. Right: Richard's brought Chinese food, hot grease silhouettes on the paper bags, putputtering from your diaper, does he know it's you. Left: I wish I had a suit with feet. Right: Ruby jujube. Left: When was the last time I hummed and glugged simultaneously. Right: Too tired to look at the clock, come under here, little bug. Left: Not again. Right: From this angle the window that looks onto the pear trees instead looks up beyond them, incessant blue jays heading south, crossing the paler blue square of sky in groups of seven, five, nine, seven, five as if on a loop, going and going and we two are warm enough and staying. Left: I drink milk at the same time, am I an elaborate step that could be skipped. Right: Little lambs caper on the flannel blanket, twist one up and clean out your earhole with it. Left: before writing a poem about it I sometimes forgot, repeated sides. Right: three years ago in Texas, Peruvian immigrants had their children taken away when the photo shop clerk developed their breastfeeding pictures and called the cops; a nipple in a baby's mouth was a second-degree felony: "sexual performance of a minor." Left: I close my eyes, these days only getting the kind of sleep you have on planes. Right: *Extracting oil from Alberta's tar sands requires three barrels of water for each barrel of oil produced.* Left: Heave you over my shoulder, pink terrycloth sack of cream. Right: Your "wrist" is a crease circling your fat arm like a too-tight string. Left: Still pitch before dawn and while you eat I dream a little, that you were born a gnome, and I loved you just the same, maybe more. Right: Dimples for knuckles. Left: Dark green eye keeps darting up at me, as if finally putting the face and the food together. Right: I wouldn't write this poem in Texas. Left: I never wanted to be one of those grown women with a teddy bear room. Right: *Passion is injurious to the mother's milk, and consequently to the child. Sudden joy and grief frequently disorder the infant's bowels, producing griping, looseness, &c.* Left: Now that you've started solids, applesauce in your eyebrows, I've become a course. Right: Spider on the plastic space mobile, walking the perimeter of the yellow crescent moon. Left: Dollop. Right: Now it's on Saturn's rings, if it fell off it would drop right into my mouth. Left: I take 2%, you take hindmilk. Right: Fingers shrimp their way through the afghan holes. Left: I have *hindmilk.* Right: We watch the show about you, the young and the restless, you keep smacking your lips off and craning your neck back to see what the devil Victor's on about now. Left: Beads of milk pop out before your mouth even gets there. Right: What if your donor turned out to be Eric Braeden, who plays the patriarch Victor Newman, what if you concluded every one of our disagreements with a curt and authoritative "End of discussion." Left: Heat gusts through the vent, stirs stars. Right: This little piggy had tofu wieners, this little piggy had none. Left: Ugh, plugged ducts. Right: How did the childless author of *Tender Buttons* know. Left: I can't move to change the station away from the man who keeps saying "as far as the weather" without adding "goes" or "is concerned." Right: You've got it made as far as milk. Left: Your lashes fall to your cheeks, the tiny nailclippers are within reach, and I plan the great triumph of my afternoon. Right: Kitten licks your head, leaves welts. Left: I could go for a fontanelle about now. Right: *He was put in a pie by Mrs. McGregor.* Left: Lying down together, your foreshortened head huge, I remember your birth. Right: The other side always lets down, twins the default setting. Left: You smile at a private joke, milk floods out the corners. Right: One for the road. Left: In the bathroom at the Woodstock service station a changing table and thank goodness a small metal chair, which I would never have noticed before you came, or if I did would have thought it an odd luxury, for doing up boots or taking a load off. Right: In a different house, you keep a watchful eye, dark magnetic Northern lake. Left: Feet curl in your shrunk sleeper, grandma says you'll get bunions. Right: You wet your suit, and mine, while drinking, like a functional doll I once had, her innards a single fine plastic tube. Left: The other grandma said you'll be bowlegged if we stand you up too much. Right: Their hardcover *Oryx and Crake* is too heavy so I read a musty pamphlet my mother got when pregnant with me: *Girls will feel dowdy at this time, so wearing heels can give their spirits an extra boost.* Left: You latch on to my elbow and I'm surprised, as if I'd imagined you can see in the dark, forgetting you too are only human. Right: No longer eating, you keep lips latched, flutter your tongue, tender moth or creepy guy. Left: I thought she said "history in the *milking.*" Right: It's easier to pinch the skin of older mothers. Left: I don't know Elmo let alone Baby Elmo. Right: Your nostrils are wheels on a tiny pink VW Beetle. Left: The doctor says you have thrush – I don't have my babycare guide but here's a *Peterson Field Guide* which says you should have a conspicuous eye-ring, a distinctly orange cast about the head, ghostlike spots, legs more dusky than your toes, your voice a melodic flutelike rolling from high to low to high, whee-toolee-weee, and you are presumed to winter in the hills of Hispaniola. Right: wing, whale, to-lifer, to-know, to-die. Left: wing, ward, overs, most, -ism. Right: stuff, side up, on, of way, of search, of asylum. Left: Bunny rattle nestled in the crook of your arm, your entire arm nestled in the crook of my hand. Right: Insert scenes of battle for more universal appeal. Left: You would win a nestling tournament. Right: No chair in the westbound service station, so we nurse in the bathroom stall, the diaper bag too heavy for the coat hook and it ticks and falters then smacks at my feet, you don't miss a swallow. Left: Here is the babycare guide which says I can catch thrush from you and could experience red, itchy, cracked and burning nipples and shooting pains while nursing. Finally, the kind of mammaire verité and deromanticization of motherhood the reader expected. Right: *See the way new trees flourish when they get started on a nurse log. Also called a mother stump, nurse logs are trees that have fallen and started to rot.* Left: Your Fisher-Price crib aquarium emits enough light to nurse by, enough surf sound to imagine myself in a hammock under coconut palms, a crab on my nipple. Right: If we've already established that you're a star why would we wonder what you are. Left: just when I was being a smart aleck about deromanticization, a sharp tooth. Right: I guess it's like, star, what are you, *really.* Left: Geese shouting hockey hockey hockey. Right: I thought I was supposed to be the one cheek pinching and chin chucking. Left: You talk with your mouth full and wear your hat to the table. Right: Snow. Last November I didn't see it, had the calendar turned to May, waiting for you to see your first everything. Left: Your first words emerging, you shout Hi! to my chest before latching on, Meow! when you're done. Right: Teddy Graham crumbs in my $40 bra. Left: Unlike the cat, whose paws twitch while he dreams of chasing, you dream you are doing precisely what you are doing. Right: It's referred to as "letting down," although you feel the opposite. Left: handed, fielder, brain, Bank, atrioventricular valve. Right: minded, -ism, handed, ful, fielder, face, circular cone, brain, Bank, away, ascension. Left: Skim milk light through the curtain, it must have snowed in the night. Right: Cat eating plastic, just out of reach. Left: So these are "jugs." Right: *A good nurse is judicious, and obeys the medical man's orders to the very letter, while, on the other hand, a bad nurse acts on her own judgement, and is always quacking, interfering, and fussing with the breast. Such conceited, meddlesome nurses are to be studiously avoided; they often cause, from their meddlesome ways, the breasts to gather.* Left: Lift. Right: Tuft. Left: Loved. Right: Lift her. Left: Richter. Lift her wrote her wrought her daughter laughter lifter sitter safe her light left on her. Right: Snowbound and out of milk. I could express into my tea but I'm not making yoghurt. Left: On the other temple, veins outline a house, a single plume of smoke threading up into your hair, a bare tree in the front yard. Right: Dress you in a lamb suit in the hopes your babysitter will be tender with you. Left: One more nurse before I leave, Heidi still wearing earrings, a clean sweater, a game expression. Right: Ouch, there's the other tooth you cut this evening, kicking and clawing at Heidi with the labour of it, was the bottle of Amurula thanks enough, while we went to a party where adults conversed about who would win the federal election after the Gomery report and if you had to sleep with a man who would it be and we razzed the hosts about their carefully worded invitation "we hope that you will be able to find a sitter and join us," Heidi at that moment bouncing the hollering lamb and trying to open applesauce with one hand, Johnny Depp won a majority, I know objectively speaking the cappuccino crème brûlée was delicious but I couldn't taste it for missing you. Left: Home again late, you're fed at 2 a.m. without having to ask and you gurgle proudly as if I've finally caught on. Right: You thump your palm on my chest, then your own, you and me, I agree, difficult to distinguish. Left: Tethered to you, I must postpone killing that spider, forced to witness her labour, empathize with her line-by-line desires. Right: My left, your right. Left: *Patriarchal poetry left left left right left.* Right: Today I fed peaches to someone who's never heard of peaches. Ditto the moon, every Christmas carol, horse and the word horse. Left: I used to need two hands and a nursing pillow, now I can erase the hell out of two Sudokus, you outside the halo of the booklight. Right: 2 or a 6, 2 or a 6, 2 or a 6 or a 7. Left: This is expressive verse. Right: You pause to swish milk between your gums—a bit oaky this morning, a bit sassy, a bit maternal. Left: *Patriarchal poetry might be what is left.* Right: House Finch below the feeder, raspberry throat among a party of sparrows, you hang back embarrassed to be the only one who dressed up, I think you look good. Left: Check later to see if 'snorfle' is a word. Right: Tufted Titmouse, who is neither, nor is it all that tufty. Left: The closest thing was 'snorkel' which is kind of the opposite. Right: Emerging teeth like white stitches glowing in your gums. Left: In fact, you are more of a Tufted Titmouse than that bird. Right: You kick through your snaps, hoist a foot into the icy dark. Left: I must have heard you crying, awakened, stood up, leant over the crib to ply the binky and the fuzzy sheep, sung Baby's Boat to no avail, given in, picked you up careful not to knock your head against the mobile, dug amongst your books for the mat to put on the futon, laid you down, unbuttoned my shirt, unhooked the nursing bra, found your mouth, because here we are but I don't remember the last 10 minutes on the road. Right: I can never rest now, knowing the teeth are there, like a gun in a play. Left: a noisy slurping emanates from our airport bathroom stall, *last call flight 142 to Calgary,* you pretend not to hear. Right: They suggested nursing for takeoff to save baby's tender ears, that you heard, and you milk it all the way across two Great Lakes. Left: The extravagantly indecisive route of the river through the prairie, ribbon candy. Right: Little cherub, clouds about your head. Left: Wishing that kid in front would put a sock in it. Right: Grandma K.'s house full of mirrors and you are jealous of all the other nursing babies. Left: The line along the elk's neck ruff extends down further than I had first noticed, leg bent elegantly above your ear. Right: A new place, and you are too excited to sleep. Left: Here three can fit in the king-sized bed and you keep shimmying down to make an H of us. Right: You are no longer an infant, not yet a toddler, just a plain old baby. Left: Are you a tot. What is the age range of tots. Right: In the Mothers' Room at the Calgary zoo, your feet are the biggest, your burp the most robust, and I can see the other mothers doubt my claim that you are only six months old, think perhaps I have either lost my mind a little or stolen you. Left: You place your palm on my cheek and guide me away from the adult conversation, back to the appropriate downward, adoring gaze. Right: *If he be suckled after he be twelve months old, he is generally pale, flabby, unhealthy, and rickety; and the mother is usually nervous, emaciated and hysterical.* Left: You've got a hold on the right, like a chain smoker. Right: The days are shorter, the curtains heavier, and we seem always to be nursing in the dark, mistaking eyes for mouths, wrist bones for nipples. Left: Pet your felt head, to keep you awake and on task. Right: Lambie. Left: Eyeing my inflating belly, friends would ask, You're not going to start writing sentimental mothering poems are you. Right: The mirrors distract both of us, why did I think I could cut my own hair. Left: We park to eat lunch with a breathtaking Kananaskis view, you fascinated by the Mr. Lube sticker. Right: I'm no athlete but I could pitch for La Leche League. Left: All soft skin similes would have nowhere to go but right back to you. Right: Imprint of my sweatshirt zipper across your chin, Frankenstein's baby. Left: You thrash around in your sleeper until one leg flaps flat and the other is packed with knees. Right: The red numbers on the digital clock are huge, like in your birthing room or a train station. Left: At 3:51 I realize I could spell your name on a calculator. Right: The more you drink the more chance you'll wet Grandma's guest bed. Left: If the goods flow one way, why are we both "nursing." Right: You're not really hungry, just social drinking. Left: The prairie climate is dry and your nose clogs, you resent having to pause for jagged gasps of air like you're trying to win a swimming race. Right: Nursing you for the sixth time in as many hours, eyelids puffed between open and closed, I hear a butter knife scuff toast and clang in the marmalade jar and someone asking "are they *still* sleeping?" Left: You clutch your stuffed mouse, from whom you'd been separated by airport security, who checked it for bombs. Right: How to hide my breast without smothering you as the gay steward offers me mini pretzels. Left: they put us all in the parents' ghetto, across the aisle *two* babies with *one* mum. Right: Your smells make us embarrassed and sorry for the people around us until we hear the group ahead was visiting Ontario to hunt. Left: Home, and you are too excited to sleep. Right: You pat my belly, the old stomping grounds. Left: the plastic moon glints in the light of the real moon.

CHRISTINE HUME

has lived in sixteen different states and countries. She is the author of two books of poems, winners of the Barnard New Women Poets Prize, the Green Rose Award, and Small Press Traffic's 2005 Best Book of the Year Award. Her chapbook, *Lullaby,* is forthcoming from Ugly Duckling Presse. She is an associate professor at Eastern Michigan University, and lives in Ypsilanti with her partner, Jeff Clark, and their daughter, Juna Hume Clark—born on May 20, 2005, the day before Christine's 37th birthday.

HATCH

Where is the nutrient in it?
One third of your darkness reflects back. It listens to itself. Two black syllables then another flit into the tree, then another. Windwhipped hives organzing. Outside is not made of the same dark as inside.

Are you comfortable?
I move inside night, but I am not its insides. I jerk-and-excise, I do not express.

Can you open your eyes?
My looking does not bound back to me. It wanders the half-lit night trying on further circles of the unknown. It holds down my limbs and puts the moon out of my moth-mind.

Can you hear my lullabys?
I cannot count each kind of darkness to catalog your fears. As when you descend into the ocean, you find yourself immersed in song; my whole body, made of water and night, reverberates in self-melodies.

What do you hear of our talk?
Blood fastens to insistences of all language at once, alive and lying. All tongues unlocked and lapping one another, dousing for routes to bodies.

Why do you kick at words?
To get your songs off my hands, I wade through their falls and uplifts. I dreamt a dog was trying to dig me out.

Why do you punch and undulate?
If I want to listen, I turn to the left; if I want to speak, I go right to the bone.

Can you bear the sound of my voice?
Past the bridge, past the blink, past shifting animal shapes, past this cesspool, I go inward to check my traps.

Why are you lonely?
Night breaks open and words scurry to work. They arrange my loneliness excruciating inside me, and split it in two again.

Are you lonely?
Something sat on my shadow. My shadow sat on its stolen body.

Can you feel gravity?
Air woke up inside night and ate away my tail. A slow pulse absorbed my gills. After that, I turned away from the dark, but felt it hot at my back. It fed me a second-hand heart. I kept my nightgown shut. I had to quarantine myself so I would not inherit its haunted rooms.

What will leaving be like?
All I know fits though one night, one hole, down one funnel, everywhere coming from all times until memory is mine. Forgetting inserts itself up to ten. Then it will become your clock, and birds will climb into your mirror.

LULLABY

Speculations on the First Active Sense

Affection of your waking hours breaks into rhythmic blinks

Breathing is the shock of your initiation *here*

Is and is and is, pulse is prehistory

Even before you listen your body hears itself

    (Rhythm is an intelligence activated by being)

And by what babble and by what charge

Organized by a nervous system, rhythm begins as two competing motions, saturated and insistent

Those hurrying iambs proliferate perception

Let that rhythm orchestrate thought

Let it build and break your chemic cycles

Each organ enrapts or ruptures the rhythm

Each sub-rhythm pitches in

The forever multiplying human body

What you overheard the first nine months

Stuck to you, it stayed underwater

Rhythm struck like waves inside you amplified

Stripping you down to crashing rhythms of water

Lullaby enacts substantiation

Lullaby atavises whatever it touches

What a rhythm will become to stay in the world

Ecstatic rages digging themselves into the room

Into your voice haunting air and innards

You are born into vocal rhythm

It percolates your fundament

You list toward the memory of total comfort

Listen toward the fantasy of total comfort and you hallucinate

Tenderness rides on the rhythm of that voice

Semantics is nothing doing

       (Branch ticking at the window)

From the beginning you know words mean to crush

The body goes under, but the head stays outside

Lullaby exists between body and belief

Lullaby prays because sleep requires it

Like god, lullaby limits itself to commands and promises

So folded in on itself, lullaby doubles your language

Lullaby sustains as it redirects

Immerses you in sensual trance

To extract lyricism from the infantile

Let blood depart and recombine, let it eavesdrop

By lub-dub and by left-right

The chorus continually wringing your gut and hands

Singing lullaby, you recover your mother's pulse

Listening, your body downpours

As if in the torn natal eye

Lost world of the daily

Goes down that hole rhythmized

Baffles traffic's chaos outside

The seconds shedding their tick

Grammar latches on to compulsion and silences

First words repeat cadences more than phonetics

Insist you forget the rest of your rhythmic repertoire

(To distrust language's rhythm is a form of self-loathing)

The ear is the original vigilant animal

Attempting to arrange its confused, mute, obscure world

Rhythm tries to make something of it

A wall patterned by contractions, rhythmic lashes of a branch

To produce rhythm intentionally is to be human

To produce rhythm intentionally is to speak

The child throws the spool of black thread

A voice constructs a gravel runway to sleep

A maze through wolves and lost mothers

The child pulls the spool back by its thread

To listen for *you* is to identify a secret rhythm

To listen *for* is to predict the future

What you listen for isn't only what you get

Lullaby is language's best way of being duplicitous and hedonistic

Lullaby is Pavlovian oblivion, getting lost in your body's fjords

From unconscious to unconscious, lullaby invaginates

Come out of yourself by listening in

Rhythm is transferred in memories, like hatreds, like fears

Like bugbears and murderers in the milk, you gulp it

Lullaby is a process of vanishing

Lullaby vampirizes the visible

Accessing a *human* outside the senses

By excess and by tip of the tongue

Rhythm is the first lie

The sweet lure and bye belies its bully language

Its impossible promises of killers and riches

Lullaby wants you dead, and lullaby fears your death

Devoted to the expected, you listen

Suspecting surprise, you listen twice

A wave breaks its bough and hearing falls off

Persistence blood-binds you

Inconceivable for you not to slide under the spell

The hallucination of eternal return is also erotic

Any human voice eroticizes sleep

You fall into it like you fall with someone into treetops

The ear is cocked; the ear clenches itself off to sirens

Singing is the whole body emerging from the throat, on the wind of lungs

The voice lobs itself out of a hole

An abyss in each word

Coaxing you to enter and disappear

You take every word with you into sleep

Holes in the words dilate and dream

Exhausted, your ears are panting mouths

All your sayings escaping

Lullaby is inaudible without an ocean in the background

Birds entangle you in their heavy calling

Lullaby heaves its lead body into your bones, its feather body

Superinduces lullaby's compound litres

You, your desire , and your refusal to sleep triangulate

A triple meter and a tendency to stay flat

Just try to slip off your mind

Boil of crickets, luna moths lathering

Your listening circulates, it is a flock of bats in the fixed, blank sky

Impulsing, hypnogogic

Every voice is also full of what it says

You know the song by heart as it passes through your teeth

Its moving accrues meaning

It is no wonder no one will ever be able to sleep

Against your body, your whole hair-raising childhood

If you have forgotten the rhythm of sleep

The sound of your own voice misleads you into someone else's mind

Push you down the dreaming world

First ceaselessly grind your nerves

First exhaust your arsenal of measures

And exhaust each word by wearing a hole in it

Sonic gaps return your terror of vertigo

You are used by that rhythm

Carried into a patch of stars

That pitches mnemonic-deific-amnesiac fits

Rhythm is bacterial

Rhythm automatically animates a lost memory

Where the tree is not only itself

Picking its fruit pulls an ancient sound out of the trees

When the voice breaks the cradle

Falls and falls dark into bored rhythms

Hammering out a novel one

Ghost rhythms inhabit you and itch

Cells reiterate and their rhythms attune you

Their rhythms send your organs out of their rockers

     (Organs are judges and judged)

Lullaby is a protest song

Whoever sings it is somatized, also horrified by the knives she is sharpening

Make the song stutter, it is no lullaby anyway

It looks intimate and docile, but it is a desperate, singular object of mad dedication

Echolalia erupting from a wound

Tests kinesthetic repetitions until

Lullaby is the chaperone of insomnia

Listening hard lets you guard yourself

Lets you sob asleep rather than choke

Throw a newborn into the sea

A real lullaby doesn't accompany anything

It steals your pillows as you sleep

Seething blood in an ear to the chest

The room covers over with skin

Lullaby is porous, scabbing

Lullaby is infused with mourning

To be possessed by rhythm is to be alive

You walk because of its totemic iambics

Enter by shortcut

Enter by laborious bridge

Rhythm repairs a fragment

There is no argument, there is hypnotic pass

By instinct and by pleasure, it hovers

To let yourself fall is unnatural

Stresses falling at half-second intervals

Liquids and nasals alternating light and dark vowels

(And drowsy inklings lull the distant folds)

Fresh transfiguring of freshest rhythm

Under your skin even when forgotten

In the slip between *material* and *maternal*

The *I* carried away, carrying on like that

Lullaby pours those fuckers back to you

By scandal and by chance

Rhythm of hair around a nipple

Lullaby of you thirsty walking toward mirages

That animal gnawing itself with percussive insistence

The barking dog's choke-chain collar

Babies cradled in contaminated branches

Grey dogs creeping forward

Toward the high tree in your hearing

Where exhaustion builds conspiracies, builds a fort in your ear

Given by blood and by breath

You cannot find the sleep in any rhythm

Hearing the cry, you mindlessly fill with milk

It keeps you learning to swim

Adjusting your rhythm to that of the waves, the undertow

Pineal gland gladdening

That havoc of rocking again

Faraway a train trembling like fire

A sound that wants to interfere with your wakefulness

Rhythm liberates what rhythm would contradict

The hinge-rhythm digs a hole for a grave or a tree

A ladder voice emerges from your voice

Primal overhearing of early nerves

Lullaby looks ahead by listening back

Anima moving with interruptive connectivity

Electricity in the muscles and sensory-motors

Lullaby unselves you as it sugars you up

Listen your mama is gone, your papa is gone

Listen, listen lullaby goes on

ELENI SIKELIANOS

"I was born in California in 1965, and share a birthday (but not a birth year) with poets Walt Whitman and Saint-John Perse. My daughter, Eva Grace Sikelianos Hunt, was born July 20, 2005. I am thus far the author of five books of poetry and one book of hybrid nonfiction. A selected poems will be appearing in French in 2007 (translated by Béatrice Trotignon). Poems have likewise been translated into Spanish, Catalan, German, Arabic, Romanian, Croatian, Slovenian, and Serbian. Among awards received for poetry, nonfiction and translations are a National Endowment for the Arts Award, a Fulbright Arts Fellowship, The National Poetry Series, a Seeger Fellowship at Princeton University, and a New York Foundation for the Arts Award. I received my MFA in 1991 from what was then the Naropa Institute, where I had the privilege of studying with (or observing) many of the most exuberant and influential living poets of our times. I try to pass on what I can to my students at the University of Denver, where I currently teach in the Creative Writing Program. I live in Boulder with the novelist Laird Hunt and, of course, our daughter Eva Grace, who teaches us every day.

"Adjustments: curtailed sleep, curtailed traveling, curtailed foot-loose, no more (so far) writing retreats, no more solo trips, no backpacking around Africa or Europe. Need a big bed every night. Took (is taking?) a while to figure out the reconfiguration of public/private in this new life.

"Am learning: about growth and form in and outside of time, about a patience as capacious (and sometimes as fragile) as the days, about tribal affiliations, about the connections between everything and everybody, about new meanings of focus and attention."

from BODY CLOCK

I wish I were that animal glue
lips animally red

instinct sinewing limb to minute to limb

        the   -er you are / I am the bottomer feeder and forager
        the   -ing you are / I am   and –ed

life takes place in the verb
                        a word
transforms into a creature

                    in just a grizzled minute
       a *leopard* creeps out of a word

There was

the space between his [her] face and how I felt about it

where sunlight condensed from what once was sun

a perspiration of minutes sweating between us

the door love practiced in me opened, shut, opened, shut

to look at you and lodge it in my heart

an attitude of love, called Ritual Disaster

put commas around the baby, put
quote marks around her

have mental custody of
(anything)
the baby

put a text-message-smile on her face

the baby in the body clock

then then then   and
next   this comes
next and   then
put pieces of time next
to pieces of time

in the many directions in which a body grows, it grows
or shrinks in time

put the baby's arms
next to her hands or heart, a

corpuscle a drop of time

a piece of time or blood fell into her heart thus
time began or [time] stopped

What about this
luminous ether, these bumping
atoms, ultraviolet light knocking electrons
off the surface of
a piece of metal?

The numbers and circles with perfect existence
outside the mind?

Gravity's shape on which depends
the flow of time?
_____

Where did the baby come from?

what will the baby be shaped like?
will she come out round with a red
rose tattoo?

with wing of the ilium?

                              Body said, *What?*

                                    ↓

will she come out innominate
with many parts otherwise unnamed; as, the innominate artery, a great branch of
the arch of the aorta; the innominate vein, a great branch of the superior vena cava

                              Body said, *What?*

                         —— bed she built ——

when she lies down   when she arises
from the placenta's vascular sheets

touching all the quantum fields she walked through to
greet me

_____

pools of intricate color collect on the face

_____

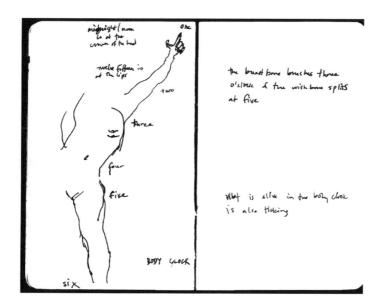

midnight / noon
is at the crown

twelve fifteen is
at the lips

BODY CLOCK

the breastbone brushes three
& the wishbone splits

EXPERIMENTS WITH MINUTES

> If we could shine a flashlight
> through the edge of a minute
> see the membrane's red
> corpuscle, & surface
> tension of a second at
> the interior atmosphere of an hour
> Move the flashlight out
> on eternity — possible? Not. (Duh.)

In this conception a minute is round though not perfectly — its lines disconnect in the drawing of it to meet up with the next / past minute. You might see the small freckles of scattered seconds at the interior (heart-meat) of the minute.

This is a big-meat minute, true to its actual size, but only took 34 seconds to draw.

This minute took 31 seconds to draw, but accidentally depicts 61 random seconds

I tried a painstaking minute, which took 43 seconds and turned out less beautiful than the quick minute — kind of minute-meat ugly, in fact

What are the parts between the minutes, the seams between, how to count such silent machinery?

Now I will try to draw a

minute that takes exactly a minute. It required me to sometimes speed up, sometimes slow down.

This house is a little haunted, it's
my body   body-house

   bones rising to the surface in the night   sinking
back before daylight

what parent pain we carry
several more than 40 years

the way a crumpled can will flash
from the roadside in certain angles of light
like a flashing eye or

what derives of the desiring heart

I guess I'd say plurality bleeds in

I emptied the body satchel out. Of course it was a womb. Cat's claws, whiskers,
hair-snarls, nut husks, everything
that collected in the sheets ground to a fine
powder nearly erased
by history (a day's work). We named her
Eva Grace.

She knits herself an everything head

makes herself into a
      scary animal

   a scarred star or
some blank thing from
                  far
                    afar

this was a girl trying all the things
   to get from baby to big

The live cat claws the night
for sounds like
sharpened rain

DANIELLE PAFUNDA

was born in 1977 and holds a BA from Bard College, an MFA from New School University, and is currently pursuing her PhD in the Creative Writing Program at the University of Georgia. Author of a collection of poems and a chapbook, an essay on Susan Wheeler is forthcoming in *Efforts & Affections* (University of Iowa). She is co-editor of *La Petite Zine,* and soon to launch the micro-press Wunderbin Books. Her daughter Hazel was born July 30, 2005. "What was life before Hazel? Less."

WHEREIN A SURROGATE IS DETERMINED PRIME

When the artifact came to skim my cavity, I was,
they said, to follow the protocol. To respond *I
am well* and to ask no questions in the sprint of offer.
With the decibel, she would scan me
for tumors, distaffs, and darkling. Divine
the collateral on which they would base the procedure.

And though she was rarely seen, and though
they insisted otherwise, it was my intent to refuse
for you a protection. If only the cotton batting
had dissolved and my enzymes been plant or animal.
In addition to mineral. I could not have known
the choke beforehand. I cannot now stall the choke.

WHEREIN A SURROGATE FAILS TO ADMIT

They say that we cannot transmit. We were not built
to generate a message from the core. And when her
abdominal plates split along the crest, when they girded
her limb with putty and fuselage she could not call
what she had a *pain.*

After the midwife completed the picketing, I carried
her charge back to the nest. I meant to. A bulb
had gone out in the track along the corridor, and I

thought it that which we do not translate. With the bundle,
I slid between panel and hull. The studio glistened.

They had affixed to the floor, in pattern, a trundle
of moth eaten footsteps. The plumed vinyl
from which each fall was cut bore slippage. Step.
Shuffle. Heel. Ball. Change. I meant to. Step.
They say we cannot complain. They asked me
to remove the tourniquet, and when I clarified that
the limb was mine, they asked me to remove that as well.

WHEREIN A SURROGATE'S AMELIORATION

They slit open my tract and inserted the coiled
copper wire. In its hollow tip, a new fluid
they said would help me conjure. Would aid me
in my application of the extraordinary protein.

No. First they inserted the plastic tubing. First
they managed the point of entry. Then the slither,
then the swift sheathing, and finally what burst
would have been an exploit on any other scale.

At the time they had me propped. A face in my
face when my chin was angled up, and always
the width of her daring me to fall left or right.
It wasn't me, I told them. It was the potion
that made me see double. That put me outdoors.
That had the nerve to lay a matchstick on my robes.

WHEREIN A SURROGATE ASSUMES THE ROLE

By the time the mirror descended, they had already
proscribed my countenance. One stirrup for furrow

and one for engagement. On the diagonal, my critter tamped.
So I did not witness. No asp, no swift glad exchange.

For the first time, I swilled. The artifact arrived,
her train sifting the piston. And I did not lift my hand.

Still she applied the froth to my brow, the breath
to my belabored frame. She whispered it me.

And though you were eventually released, though
my sentence grew from ought and frigate whelping.

I traveled the expanse of that theatre, with wetness,
a fray, an apparition's grievance.

WHEREIN A SURROGATE'S FRUITION 2

Night, my transit, they said, had been excoriated. Into
the crib, they ushered.

Withered and through the mesh. I called for a dusting
of grave attendance.

Rather, blanketing ensued. A sonic persistence giving away
my potential. At intervals.

Once dawn they injected the gag, and I could no
longer spasm.

Rather, I hooked around the bell's noose. I rang, swung,
swung, rang. For several hours, the wash of bone betrayed me.

Then my tension abated. For the animal's organ, they worried.
Thus I agreed to the pungent syrup. To everything, I must
admit. And when they stitched into my grin, I could no longer
say which was a violation and which affectation. Only
your plural eye rolled me. And vanquished.

CAMILLE GUTHRIE

was born on January 25, 1971 to Karen and Bob Guthrie. Pierre Guthrie Dobbelmann was born on August 24, 2005 to Camille and Duncan Dobbelmann. "Nature Study" was written years before Camille dreamed of getting pregnant; the birth of her son inspired the others. All of the sonnets use end-rhymes from either Keats or Shakespeare. "In the Night Kitchen" is dedicated to Yvonne Perot Dobbelmann (d. 1936) who died after giving birth to Pierre's grandfather. Camille wants to tell all the young women poets ambivalent about motherhood that having a child has been the most profoundly creative time of her life.

NATURE STUDY

Now you are inhabited in real time. Now the whole city has a view
Into your privacy. Once you swam the Pacific width, now there's another
To consider at breakfast. Considering your rebellions, why renew
This faith in progress? Is it really so natural to be a mother,
All that pain torn from a battered womb
With sterile gestures? Why not prefer the husbandry
Of rare orchids, write boring novels, or make a down-payment on a tomb
For beauty or truth? Even bad poems leave something for posterity.
Children get run over by cars. Just wait until the doctor says: I give you
Triplets. The fluttering props. Does this have anything to do with the Prime
Mover or Darwin? Sorry for my crippled spirits. Anyway, we'll see
How it goes with teething, night-waking, and quiet time.
Tell me if you play Bach to it, will it be
A boy or girl? Something's been saying, I want, I want, in you.

LET ME NOT WANDER

My beloved's doubles partner plays the lute.
Now they have twins. Things grew lonelier after my sister went away
For work. She sent the baby a wooden mouse. We take a walk in park every day
Like the blues song. He falls asleep in my lap; put the Olympics on mute.
It's been only two weeks since the last painful dispute
Over money; we'll have another soon. On the sill waits a painted bird made of clay.
After lunch, we put on Woody Guthrie songs and assay

Through the lyrics. Aliquippa, Allegheny, Asheville, Albion—
He's learning the A's. "The Samurai are restless," is the theme
Of the movie tonight. He touches my face and means, "All gone."
When the scruffled teenager appeared in my dream
To make love to me, I felt the baby's forehead; it was "on fire."
Remember to write to Mifune to tell of my long-distance desire.

MEANING WHAT

Rain pushed the garbage up the street almost sadly,
Yet plastic bags flew in the trees as if in exaggerated joy
With the dirty wind. We go to the park anyway and maneuver gladly
Around the other moms, who care not for poetry, and push arrogant strollers to
    annoy
Me, displaying their milky breasts. The baby invents rude sounds
For more than an hour. What if the incessant traffic damages his ears?
I lay awake plotting ways to write a best-seller. It confounds
How single mothers do it! I read a childless poet, but he stirs and I hear
It first: get up. What if you fall for the incarnate beauty of another
More sexually free and less crabby? Why am I the one always ordering
Take-out? Looking at you with fury, "I am the mother
Of this house." Meaning what. We put on Fulsom Prison and sing
Along but badly. I bought eight pacifiers this week: there's one
Left. What if we die without a will? What if the baby is accident prone?

THE BBC

Today the BBC says that torture is on an increase
In secret prisons in Europe, where the CIA let an Afghani farmer die
After questioning. Here it's no secret our savings is on the decrease
Since I'm not working. Will this first year linger in the baby's memory
Luxuriantly as we spend each long day together? We have the same eyes

Though his are flecked with brown. In Iraq, the BBC says there are long fuel
Lines and the black market is growing. The President proffers more lies
About the war, and eight point eight billion is missing! Look at the pictures: so cruel—
The man whose wife and child were shot by a convoy. I hang an ornament
On the fireplace for Christmas where it will dangle stupidly until spring.
Pierre watches me read from his swing, hands folded and content
At least for ten minutes. The BBC says you're not allowed to say "niggarding"
In an American office now. The BBC says black holes sing in B-
Flat. We fold laundry and look out the window: me and thee.

IN THE NIGHT HOSPITAL

I spy on the patients across the way from the corner of my eye
As I listen to his heartbeat in the night hospital. What it would feel like to get life-
In-prison? Sixty years ago the baby and I would surely die
Of my condition. A familiar story: bereft father, tiny red baby, the still wife.
The TV shows of the death of Nixmary Brown and it's impossible not to weep
Now that I know. A woman screams—now there's a newborn just behind
My room. When he's older, I'll rent a medieval stone keep
And just keep him there! We'll learn Latin, paint abstracts, read each other's mind,
Go hawking. We can't afford college anyway. There are worse ways to spend
One's childhood. The medicine burns my veins and I vomit, only making it
A longer night. I open P. D. James but can't wait for the end
When Adam finds out the truth. The baby has a name; he's no longer "it"—
Pumping his heart relentlessly. Fear comes into my room and comfortably
Sits on my chest while I sleep, and follows me home when we're finally released.

STACY DORIS

"My dob is 5 21 62
babies: Rayzl 12 03 05
Laish 03 23 06
often motherhood puts me at a loss for words, as if they all are slowly finding new meanings"

from KNOT

A pair heralds all lack, endless but never infinite: infinitesimal,
Where missing's microscopic, possibly viral. Cells, even fused, define
Independence, each isolate though its coat may yield. Fungal, growth's
Antidote. But they're no singularity; rather a confluence welling; marooned,
A shore, outer, where inadmissible's identical to entry and somebody lunges,
A contingency exploded, thus bathed in attentions, shrouded; automatic.
Any chamber cracks, sesame so seeded, openly secret, hushed as in motion,
On a wind, sewn. They's such a progression, extended so spent, minute,
Thus immeasurable, thus fully magnitude.

Another's a relation, as in a telling, unfolds, gauzes, so mends. Wending
Through somebody, we's improve in perspective; heal; practice inclusions
Or concluding. Unraveling, anyone rewires, unrestrained; enters. So fitting
In finally fills, perhaps, as gaping's completion. Is need a thing, subject to
Recreation, produced, thus memorized, thus tending to deformity, odd,
Focusing impossibilities? It beams expectancy, ripens; ticks, where birth
Twists, as an arm or braid. As a pinprick bearing bursts; gestures an exit,
A skull giving way, definitively opened, thus uncharted, a knowledge. Out
Through the top, branching.

Viewed, anyone surges from the cut of reflection, out of somebody's
Hollow, vocal, into any ideal. Tearing liberates but there is none: incisions
Repair any fiber to a different picture of fabric. A sense, any organ with its
Wrappers off feels nothing. Thus kisses eclipse. Who makes a mark or
You's thus imprinted gets saved to an adjacency, eased from containment,
Explosive as in sacred, coaxed to inflammation, distracted, thus reduced
When a breath, held longest, most quenches. Somebody abstracts anyone,
Incising, once they contracts to abandon, thus abundance. A romance.

ii.IX

Arrangement, everywhere tacit, defines any touch, arcs, thus melodic,
A geography. Coats, dull in exposing. Thus contact cuts flesh, configures
Skin to swallowing. Birth's different mechanics trigger inversely perhaps;
Utterly release, so to mother's an act of rejection, systematic and self-
Organized, since only accordance, blind to differentiation, messes.
What isn't born litters and fishes, prowls in place of nursing, has wings.
For the hatched, respiration constitutes purpose.

Where breath pours in and out of lining and levels, equally, everything
Makes sense. To incorporate liquidates destruction, perverting a blister
In reverence; accepted. Sounds mark indelibly, in niches of air, dormant
And flammable, imitation memories. A shrine. Thus every inhalation's
A whole existence, constituent of toxins and fits, paroxysms, invisible
Meaning live. Extinguishing, exhalations bury in fibers: chairs, floor, glass,
Flower, lurch, lunch. Respiration sentences. Tangles in circuits, its strings
Pulled; mounts narrowly to disappear, a balloon. Bursts.

In simple indifference to volition, elegance shapes. Thus discretion's
Finite; ends in dazzlement. By revealing, action edifies, a construct. Ease
Shears then, dispassionate, from repetition. Loves wear away, through
Distinction patterns; become admissible, thus lost where adoring depicts
Potential, paints internal as eternal. Attraction's an aside that could shape
Anyone from without: on a whim. Elsewhere, among its illusions, desire
Rewires entirely, circles not back but beyond. Where somebody takes
Anyone's place and becomes this substitution for sound, afloat. Mournful,
What's left names a monument to need.

ii.XI

Achievement's model, same as pornography's, its equal, is the picnic:
Ornament and emblem of gratuitous though enforced consumption,
Tableau or charade, still-life, nausea of false abundance. Delight or any
Triumph's just evacuation, an airing for better housekeeping's benefit,
Working order rinsed and spit out: enshrined. To let go, hypnotic, beating,
To admit any moment as death for once makes it never too late. Then
Enjoying exceeds sensation and anyone learns that you're cut off from
Your feelings. They change. Since faith equivocates, professed, circulatory,
Thus laced with doubt, prohibition's release. Belief's agreement to loss,
So anyone sinks. Sound, a spiral, implies joy's centripetal, throwing mass
To concentrate. Somebody's an impression, left to fend, efferent where
Pooling bears, where waves refer to nerves.

Anyone's an instance, thus mask or mass, lily-like. Dip below anyone;
Float. We're somebody's surface, once "cell" means "exchange," which is
Everyplace. In adjacency then, where substitution's birth's rationale,
By invading, and each are a speck of its whole, in an order, blood streams.
Where anyone's sensing loom empty, they're embodied, but impervious,
Defying alertness to proceed by escaping unrevealed, aflicker, there goes.
Tough. Intimacy's a matter of coincidence, at least, so that conjugation's
Licentiously random. Incursion is based on better engendering, on a
Second chance, so lucky to die where fertile means yield.

Unlike water, with its many ways, anyone's sole technique is to settle,
In the light of improvement. A day's throat thus leaking at both ends,
Rigor may be their armchair. The way time flies equals our's inadequation.
Satiety results from plans action imposed thus denatured. It overrides
Exploit so that pleasure, a sideline, go unfelt in the pursuit. In permanence,
Anyone's a vacation, simplifying; refined by diminishment. Thus to forget
And be forgotten is elegance, a ghosting, philanthropic, into dark.
Somebody's location, traversable, there. Any ending's perfection.
A couple's every fulfillment's a lament.

ii.XIV

AMY SARA CARROLL

(birthdate: October 28, 1967), assistant professor of American Culture/Latina/o Studies and English at the University of Michigan, Ann Arbor, received a Ph.D. in Literature from Duke University (2004), and an MFA in Creative Writing (Poetry) from Cornell University (1995). Her research, teaching, and writing interests include Latin/o American contemporary cultural production (performance, art, video, and literature), feminist, queer, and postcolonial theory, visual culture, cultural studies, inter-American studies, border studies, and critical creative writing. Recently she published "'Accidental Allegories' Meet 'The Performative Documentary': Boystown, Señorita Extraviada, and the Border-Brothel→Maquiladora Paradigm," *Signs*, Winter 2006, and "Incumbent upon Recombinant Hope: EDT's Strike a Site, Strike a Pose," *The Drama Review* (TDR), Vol. 47, No. 2 (T178), Summer 2003. In addition, her poetry has appeared in various journals and anthologies such as *Talisman, Carolina Quarterly, The Iowa Review, Mandorla, Chain, Bombay Gin, Seneca Review, Big Allis, Crayon, Borderlands, Faultline,* and *This Bridge We Call Home.* In 2005-2006, Carroll held a Mellon postdoctoral fellowship in Latino/a Studies and English at Northwestern University. She gave birth to her son Césaire José, affectionately known as Zé, on April 21, 2006.

LATE ONSET PARTICLE CAPITALISM

Strike when the iron is hot: the spot bubbles to the surface—red-faced—
some malicious, illicit strawberry, singed below a soft cap of hair, I discover it
there by accident, demand an explanation. Vague mumblings of *scalp stimulation,
postpartum emotion in high gear.* I dream of an embedded chip, my son's induction
into the matter market. What matters is this: *He is okay.* Well, temporarily. Weeks
later, the market crashes, so to speak—in the ER, we become parental footnotes
while the real work is done—intubation, a central line, the social worker in talcum
tones. The doctor lays down her hand, a pack of worst case scenarios that fan out
across the table. *He may not make it through the night and if he does we cannot predict
the extent of the "devastation."* Devastation? *Loss of limbs, loss of hearing, loss of vision,
permanent brain damage, multiple organ failure.* Unable to process listing-as-event,
I adhere to my own paranoid versions of the tale: they are removing the chip,
deactivating the product. He is temporarily checked into an upscale refurbishing
clinic. On a respirator to regain consciousness, he manufactures nipple dreams,
which intersect with my own fantasies of his lopsided smile, an escape-artist's grin.
In other words: recycling lines pared out to me, choking on their saccharine-sweet
cadences, I wish first that he might live and then greedily branch out to demand
additional reassurance. The white-coated herds that hoard expertise like pocket
change prove all too accommodating, commodity-trading interpellation: late onset
GBS, bacterial meningitis; each one of us, a petri dish, navigating the birth canal.

LET DOWN

I hang on the thread of a letter to you. Each day I resolve to include a snapshot of your wonder, but here it is going on a month and I've barely tucked away a moment to put my fingers to the keyboard. One month—you seem so very grown-up! A bellybutton all your own. A full head of hair and little nose freckled with acne. The luck of tummy gas to alter the course of what will pass from either end of the self. You pet me as you incessantly snack, I feel each micro-caress in contrast to the spinning of the breast's thread—that is the sensation—you're pulling a thread out of me in the process of a feeding, a persistent unraveling of some hilo negro. I grow equally desirous of your latch where more than two hours becomes a weight on the chest that commands relief in its excess. Your cry and I am letting down—the milk's weeping or shooting in a white-blue stream, the slightly turned smell of sweetness on your chin, dribbling off the sphere of the breast, your head lulling into my lap, then on my knees, we hear the blast of a burp as loud as a coal mine's collapse—today the world is caving in, I prop it up with toothpicks, the curl of your first smile.

THROMBOTIC

Excuse me, I need to speak to a man about a horse. *Do you mean you're going to whiz like a wild beast?* No, I'm off to converse with a woman about a chameleon, a meatier breech of contract (contractions' being the subjunctive substance of robot-human contact). A cyborg's contact zone (otherwise known as a mouth-watering hole, parasexual repronarrativity)? Exact change, a home-grown nano-constituency, elemental earthiness to which "we"—*check their IDs*—are bound. The world spins 'round its axis, night and day, time's foreplay, played out on our faces and hands. Crow's feet, some stickler's sweet sound of the *musak's* occlusion (one partially occluded vein, a thrombotic disorderly, rushing to and fro', divided midstream, an ocean's expanse now turned mighty river). Is our Dog capable of Kafka's luminescent levitation? Light as a feather, stiff as a board, when I touch your lever, it's the untruths I abhor. Not white lies, not brown cocks crowing thrice to unlock the sanctity of a shifting moral plateau. No, the levees broke, the authority choked on the cuckoo in the clock. *Do you mean Sylvester swallowed Tweety?* Not exactly. The devil's in the details, the proof's in the punch, the bird, like the hand, is in the bush, and this story's meteor missed high ground.

OVULATION, egg-drop dense as ovaltine, all the afore mothers I cannot be. Low Sunday brew destined to scorch the lungs' pod-dwelling fronds. Midwifery, remodelling a planetarium's bottlecap or bottle-bottom heavy lens, I turn upon myself. This June, a gemini germinates in my mind, twin exclamation (!!) marks a find, *bijiminy* bigeminy. Tone-deaf crickets serenade me, *The corn, knee-high, kneads a whippin'*. Meanwhile, the Jim Crow itch that knows no scratch pardons the sky for the clouds that pass, the miles—adulterous hours—the calendar's ex. *Should I stay or should I go?* Thick discharge, papers glow with news of an aftermath. And, every sign I think I see, malapert malaprop, misdirects me to the carriage house, a round back (Quasimodo's vanishing act). *Now you see them, now you don't.* Two light sabers, a double yolk. A sulfurous pill lodges itself. Beneath the tongue. Against my will, doubled-over, womb-hungry, the birds of regret worm-hole entry. Tracks of a plane—*long time coming*—trail off, a dissident text, messaging, *A house in order needs no past.* Sheer righteousness, broken glass.

BETSY FAGIN

was born on May 3, 1972. Theo was born on August 6, 2006. Her poems appear in a number of literary journals including *Fence, Five Fingers Review, So to Speak, Van Gogh's Ear,* and *Word/ForWord.* She is the author of a number of chapbooks. Recent work appears in *Women's Studies Quarterly* and is forthcoming in *the tiny.* Betsy is currently living in London.

CRYSTAL VIRTUES

crystal faults,
accident, time.

ink as black, pulsing
left life of issue, treasure.

evil body—
            my clustered spine
            my sticking mind
virtue is yours,

fruited.
honeyed and green, growing
honorably.

decay and nourishment of bone,
of cartilage, of shape.
two hearts have I within
and lies.

starved economy of panic
in itself thinned
completes, persists.

structure determined whole
dead substance.
blue milky heart, sick.

can it shape
what it must take or shaken
too quickly,
too cooled.

SATISFIED & TICKLED

to know anything about me start at the bottom.
the sugar of the am, the been.

the am was a long journey lined shining
metal. responsibilities of tin and copper,

lead of corn, of cream, of cash.
without reason. no I am. not at all.

I am . . . I've been . . . loved like light
in the depths of a dry well. of the sun

I am.   satisfied. I know.   I should be.
even now. sugar sweetness I am.   become

whole of this fullness. please know
about me. we are now, we've been.

SASHA STEENSEN

was born in Chagrin Falls, Ohio in 1974. She is the author of one book of poems and co-author, with her husband Gordon Hadfield, of another. Their daughter, Phoebe Steensen Hadfield, was born on August 28, 2006. Sasha lives in Fort Collins, Colorado where she teaches Creative Writing at Colorado State University and co-edits Bonfire Press. Her new manuscript, *The Method*, which includes "The Stranger at the Gates" and "I Hear America Swimming," takes its title from a collection of proofs by the Greek mathematician, Archimedes. Written during Sasha's pregnancy, *The Method* follows a 10th century copy of Archimedes's manuscript from its birth in Constantinople to its recent restoration at the Walters Art Museum in Baltimore.

I HEAR AMERICA SWIMMING

Everyone insists that I will write about pregnancy, but I won't. For one embarrassing moment, I thought I would quit the project altogether. Someone calls her a "passenger," another a "hijacker." I will, however, write about my own birth. The doctor arrived bloody. After a night of heavy drinking, he had walked through a sliding glass door. The future is full of heart transplants & face transplants. But I have a bungalow in which I lay low. Method miming me shows his palms and frowns. A baby with boar-like tusks turned away. Think of the Method as an infant—he was born with a full head of black hair. At this very moment, the scientists are transplanting hair follicles, and soon he will look like his "old self" again.

I remember the hotdog trees in Florida that fifth summer when we all went to Disney World. I remember the world before Disney, and it was the happiest place on earth. The accident is a childhood memory we all share. The time we threw the boomerang and it didn't come back, slicing our friend's eye open. The time our sister fell off the monkey bars, or at least that is what we were instructed to tell our parents. The time we ran our go-cart into the ditch. The time we broke our leg on the teeter-totter because our brother jumped off suddenly. If there had been more of these accidents, or if we had had fewer hospitals and McDonald's, perhaps there would be enough to feed the other children.

I proceed as a companion, but eventually I will be told to wait outside. A stranger in the house I built. Sparrows circle my head and squirrels and rabbits accompany me into the wilderness. At some point this spring, I will be shot. It is just like an animal to frolic heartily in the face of such danger. These are our imaginings of animal life, and even when we allow them into our homes, we don't completely understand why. Perhaps subconsciously we are looking for some magic formula that will turn children into creative adults. Now that I will have my own children, I only want what is best for them.

The ongoingness originally fascinated me, which is why I became a follower. How someone collects interest as I breathe. How someone survives inside because I choose to eat. How the Method will long outlive me, his rottenness all cleaned up and smelling pretty. I hope someone unearths me and puts his nose to my eyeholes. But then, I am sure of an afterlife, a collection of the most distant sideroads lined with flowers and poison oak.

THE STRANGER AT THE GATES

I thought:

The Method, so happily recovered.
I am the one who called us all together.
I driven time.
I wars and waves.
I was.
I go over sea-lanes rife with fish.
I did not.

I saw a shadow on the water.
I know this situation makes a perfect poem,
but I will not.
I want to write that I've already been to Jupiter,
but I have not,
or that Catholicism died in the darkness
of the already dark ages.

I a man mountain, a level island.
I a side-road.
I a dead toad on the side-road,
can only say what I've seen with my own eyes.
The heart inside us shakes
aswirl with evil.

I the eye in the wading pool
bathed in shame.
I sing for our time too.
I planned to follow all the "I's"
I could find.
I ahaze.
Not even the geese could make their way.
I sit down on the curb and wait.

Listen.
I loved him.
Our hour sat and sulked
but I a second hand
did not budge.
I an automobile.
I a blast furnace ensnared.
I a home like all the others in my neighborhood.
I at some other century
imaginary love affair
with heifers and others
left like a stranded hair.

I told you
I'd tell your story
if you just let me tell it.
I an embellishment
before the roads of the world grew dark.

I a moon making its way round.
I hate a metaphor.
I pissed on the sidewalk.
I did not.
I heard her heartbeat fifteen times
before she was born.
I a final glow of antiquity.
I "a method of exhaustion."
I felt her bare foot from the inside.
I streak the administration.
I bare myself too,

my breast to the moon
making its way round.
I resent you

who I serve.
I said I would say
what you want
but say it my way.
I a television, a television.
I a giant model heart
touring the city-state
before slaves
in the birthplace
the cradle, etc.
I a swallow in your sight
loosed the sack and all the winds blew past.

I doled out my time
and money.
I was broke before
the reformation
the resurrection
and the restoration.

I a heathendom.
I a saintdom.
I a polka dot.
I cock-of-the-walk
cocksure, yelping
put beeswax in my ears.
I a dog in obedience class
who can no longer hear.

I say what you want me to say.
I say how brave.
I say how clever.
I say how we went together
happily.
How you loved me.

How we became a we
and I died and you lived on
restored and pretty.

BIBLIOGRAPHY

RAE ARMANTROUT
Next Life. Middletown, CT: Wesleyan University Press, 2007.
Up to Speed. Middletown, CT: Wesleyan University Press, 2004.
Veil: New and Selected Poems. Middletown, CT: Wesleyan University Press, 2001.
The Pretext. Los Angeles, CA: Green Integer Books, 2001.
True. Berkeley, CA: Atelos Press, 1998.
Made to Seem. Los Angeles, CA: Sun and Moon Press, 1995.
Necromance. Los Angeles. CA: Sun and Moon Press, 1991.
Couverture. Paris, France: Les Cahiers de Royaumont, 1991.
Precedence. Providence, RI: Burning Deck Press, 1985.
The Invention of Hunger. Berkeley, CA: Tuumba Press, 1979.
Extremities. Berkeley, CA: The Figures, 1978.

JULIANNA BAGGOTT
Lizzie Borden in Love: Poems in Women's Voices. Carbondale, IL: Southern Illinois University Press, 2006.
This Country of Mothers. Carbondale, IL: Southern Illinois University Press, 2001.

Fiction
Which Brings Me to You: A Novel in Confessions. With Steve Almond. Chapel Hill, NC: Algonquin Books, 2006.
The Miss America Family: A Novel. New York: Washington Square Press, 2003.
Girl Talk. New York: Atria Books, 2001.

Fiction published under the name N. E. Bode
The Somebodies. New York: HarperCollins, 2006.
The Nobodies. New York: HarperCollins, 2005.
The Anybodies. New York: HarperCollins, 2004.

MEI-MEI BERSSENBRUGGE
I Love Artists: New and Selected Poems. Berkeley, CA: University of California Press, 2006.
Concordance. Berkeley, CA: Kelsey Street Press, 2006.
Nest. Berkeley, CA: Kelsey Street Press, 2003.
The Four Year Old Girl. Berkeley, CA: Kelsey Street Press, 1998.
Endocrinology. Berkeley, CA: Kelsey Street Press, 1997.
Sphericity. Berkeley, CA: Kelsey Street Press, 1993.
Empathy. Barrytown, NY: Station Hill Press, 1989.
Hiddenness. New York: Whitney Museum Library Fellows, 1987.
Tan Tien. Milwaukee, WI: Woodland Pattern, 1984.
The Heat Bird. Providence, RI: Burning Deck Press, 1983.
Pack Rat Sieve. Bowling Green, KY: Contact II Publications, 1983.
Random Possession. New York: I. Reed Books, 1979.
Summits Move with the Tide. Greenfield Center, NY: Greenfield Review Press, 1974.
Fish Souls. Greenfield Center, NY: Greenfield Review Press, 1972.

LEE ANN BROWN
Nascent Toolbox (with Laynie Browne). Woodacre, CA: Owl Press, 2004.
The Sleep That Changed Everything. Middletown, CT: Wesleyan University Press, 2003.
Polyverse. Los Angeles: Sun and Moon, 1999.

JENNY BROWNE
The Second Reason. Tampa, FL: University of Tampa Press, 2007.
At Once. Tampa, FL: University of Tampa Press, 2003.
Glass. San Antonio, TX: Pecan Grove Press, 2000.

LAYNIE BROWNE
The Scented Fox. Wave Books, forthcoming 2007.
Daily Sonnets. Denver, CO: Counterpath Path Books, forthcoming 2007.
Mermaid's Purse. New York: Spuyten Duyvil, 2005.
Drawing of a Swan Before Memory. Athens, GA: University of Georgia Press, 2005.
Pollen Memory. New York: Tender Buttons, 2003.
The Agency of Wind. Pengrove, CA: Avec Books, 1999.
Rebecca Letters. Berkeley: Kelsey Street Press, 1997.

Chapbooks
Original Presence. Shivistan, 2006.
The Desires of Letters. Brooklyn: Belladonna Books, 2006.
The Desires of Letters. G o n g editions, 2005.
Nascent Toolbox. Woodacre, CA: The Owl Press, 2004.
Webs of Argiope. New Haven, CT: Phylum Press, 2004.
Gravity's Mirror. Washington, DC: Primitive Editions, 2000.
Clepsydra. Saratoga, CA: Instress, 1999.
L O R E. Saratoga, CA: Instress, 1998.
One Constellation. Buffalo: Leave Books, 1994.
Hereditary Zones. Boog Literature, 1993.

Fiction
Acts of Levitation. New York: Spuyten Duyvil, 2002.

LESLIE BUMSTEAD
Cipher/Civilian. Washington, DC: Edge Books, 2005.

MAIREAD BYRNE
Talk Poetry. Oxford, OH: Miami University Press, 2007.
SOS Poetry. /ubu Editions, 2007.
Nelson & The Huruburu Bird. County Wicklow, Ireland: Wild Honey Press, 2003.

Chapbooks
An Educated Heart. Long Beach, CA: Palm Press, 2005.
Vivas. Co Wicklow, Ireland: Wild Honey Press, 2005.
Kalends. Brooklyn, NY: Belladonna Books, 2005.

b

JULIE CARR
Mead: An Epithalamion. Athens, GA: University of Georgia Press, 2004.
Equivocal. Farmington, ME: Alice James Books, 2007.

MAXINE CHERNOFF
Among The Names. Berkeley: Apogee Press, 2005.
Evolution of the Bridge: New and Selected Prose Poems. Cambridge, England: Salt Publishing, 2004.
World: New and Selected Poems: 1991-2001. Cambridge, England: Salt Publishing, 2002.
Leap Year Day: New and Selected Poems. Chicago: ACP, 1991.
New faces of 1952. Ithaca, NY: Ithaca House, 1985.
Utopia TV Store. Chicago, IL: The Yellow Press, 1979.
A Vegetable Emergency. Venice, CA: Beyond Baroque Foundation, 1976.
The Last Aurochs. Iowa City, IA: Now Press, 1976.

Fiction
Some of Her Friends That Year: New and Selected Stories. Minneapolis, MN: Coffee House Press, 2002.
A Boy in Winter. New York: Crown Publishers, 1999.
American Heaven. Minneapolis, MN: Coffee House Press, 1994.
Plain Grief. New York: Summit, 1991.
Signs of Devotion. New York: Simon and Schuster, 1987.
BOP. Minneapolis, MN: Coffee House Press, 1985. Reprinted in the Vintage Contemporary Fiction Series, 1986.

NORMA COLE
Collective Memory. New York: Granary Press, 2006.
Do the Monkey. Spain: Zasterle Press, 2006.
Scout (Text/image work in CD-ROM format). Krupskaya, 2004.
A little a & a. Los Angeles, CA: Seeing Eye Books, 2002.
BURNS. Brooklyn, NY: Belladonna Books, 2002.
Spinoza in Her Youth. Richmond, CA: Omnidawn Press, 2002.
Stay Songs, for Stanley Whitney. New York: Bill Maynes Gallery, 2001.
The Vulgar Tongue. San Francisco, CA: a+bend press, 2000.
Spinoza in Her Youth. Elmwood, CT: A.Bacus, 1999.

Desire & its Double. Saratoga, CA: Instress, 1998.
Quotable Gestures. France: CREAPHIS/un bureau sur l'Atlantique, 1998.
Mars. France: CREAPHIS/un bureau sur l'Atlantique, 1997.
Capture des Lettres et Vies du Joker. France: Format américain/Bureau sur l'Atlantique, 1996.
Contrafact. Elmwood, CT: Potes & Poets Press, 1996.
Moira. Oakland, CA: O Books, 1996.
Catasters (with Jess). Edinburgh, Scotland: Morning Star Editions 1995-96 Folio Series.
Mars. Berkeley, CA: Listening Chamber Editions, 1994.
My Bird Book. Los Angeles, CA: Littoral Press, 1991.
Mon Livre des Oiseaux. France: Fondation Royaumont, 1991.
Metamorphopsia. Elmwood, CT: Potes & Poets Press, 1988.

Mace Hill Remap. France: Moving Letters Press, 1988. Archived at Duration Press web site.

WANDA COLEMAN
The Riot Inside Me: More Trials and Tremors. New York: David R. Godine, 2005.
Ostinato Vamps. Pittsburgh, PA: University of Pittsburgh Press, 2003.
Mercurochrome: New Poems. Santa Barbara, CA: Black Sparrow Books, 2001.
Mambo Hips and Make Believe: A Novel. Santa Barbara, CA: Black Sparrow Books, 1999.
Bathwater Wine. Santa Barbara, CA: Black Sparrow Books, 1998.
Native in a Strange Land: Trials and Tremors. Santa Barbara, CA: Black Sparrow Books, 1996.
Hand Dance. Santa Barbara, CA: Black Sparrow Books, 1993.
African Sleeping Sickness: Stories and Poems. Santa Barbara, CA: Black Sparrow Books, 1990.
A War of Eyes and Other Stories. Santa Barbara, CA: Black Sparrow Books, 1988.
Heavy Daughter Blues: Poems and Stories, 1968–1986. Santa Barbara, CA: Black Sparrow Books, 1987.
Imagoes. Santa Barbara, CA: Black Sparrow Books, 1983.
Mad Dog, Black Lady. Santa Barbara, CA: Black Sparrow Books, 1979.

GILLIAN CONOLEY
Profane Halo. Seattle, WA: Verse Press/Wave Books, 2005.
Lovers in the Used World. Pittsburgh, PA: Carnegie Mellon University Press, 2001.
Beckon. Pittsburgh, PA: Carnegie Mellon University Press, 1996.
Tall Stranger. Pittsburgh, PA: Carnegie Mellon University Press, 1991.
Some Gangster Pain. Pittsburgh, PA: Carnegie Mellon University Press, 1987.

Chapbooks
Fatherless Afternoon. Les Ferris Editions, 2004.
Woman Speaking Inside Film Noir. Lynx House Press, 1984.

NICOLE COOLEY
The Afflicted Girls. Baton Rouge, LA: Louisiana State University Press, 2004.
Resurrection. Baton Rouge, LA: Louisiana State University Press, 1996.

Fiction
Judy Garland, Ginger Love. New York: Regan Books/Harper Collins, 1998.

OLENA KALYTIAK-DAVIS
And Her Soul Out of Nothing. Madison, WI: University of Wisconsin Press, 1997.
Shattered Sonnets, Love Cards, and Other Off and Back Handed Importunities. New York: Bloomsbury/Tin House, 2003.

JEAN DONNELLY
Anthem. Los Angeles, CA: Sun & Moon Press, 2002.
The Julia Set. Washington, DC: Edge Books, 1995.

STACY DORIS

Knot. Athens, GA: University of Georgia Press, 2006.
Cheerleader's Guide to the World: Council Book. New York: Roof, 2006.
Parlement. Paris: P.O.L, 2005.
Conference. Bedford, MA: Potes & Poets, 2001. *Une Année à New York avec Chester*. Paris: P.O.L, 2000.
Paramour. San Francisco, CA: Krupskaya, 2000.
La Vie de Chester Steven Wiener écrite par Sa Femme. Paris: P.O.L, 1998.
Kildare. New York: Roof, 1995.

Edited Books
Christophe Tarkos: Ma Langue est Poétique: Selected Work. New York: Roof, 2001.
Twenty-two New (to North America) French Poets. Vancouver, Canada: Raddle Moon, 1997.
Violence of the White Page, Contemporary French Poetry in Translation. Santa Fe, NM: Pederal, 1992.

RACHEL BLAU DUPLESSIS

Torques, Drafts 58-76. Cambridge, England: Salt Publishing, 2007.
Drafts. Drafts 39-57, Pledge with Draft, Unnumbered: Précis. Cambridge, England: Salt Publishing, 2004.
Draft, unnumbered: Précis. Vancouver, Canada: Nomados, 2003.
Drafts 1-38, Toll. Middletown, CT: Wesleyan University Press, 2001.
Renga: Draft 32. Philadelphia, PA: Beautiful Swimmer Press, 1998.
Drafts 15-XXX, The Fold. Elmwood, CT: Potes & Poets Press, 1997.
Essais: Quatre Poèmes. Bar-le-Duc, France: Un Bureau sur l'Atlantique, Editions Créaphis, 1996.
Draft X: Letters. Philadelphia, PA: Singing Horse Press, 1991.
Drafts 3-14. Elmwood, CT.: Potes & Poets Press, 1990.
Tabula Rosa. Elmwood, CT: Potes & Poets Press, 1987.
Gypsy/Moth. Oakland, CA: Coincidence Press, 1984.
Wells. New York: Montemora Editions, 1980.

Essays/Criticism
Blue Studios: Poetry and Its Cultural Work. Tuscaloosa, AL: University of Alabama Press, 2006.
The Pink Guitar: Writing as Feminist Practice. Tuscaloosa, AL: University of Alabama Press, 2006.
Genders, Races, and Religious Cultures in Modern American Poetry, 1908-1934. Cambridge, England: Cambridge University Press, 2001.
The Pink Guitar: Writing as Feminist Practice. New York: Routledge, 1991.
H.D.: The Career of that Struggle. London: Harvester and Bloomington: Indiana University Press, 1986.
Writing Beyond the Ending: Narrative Strategies of Twentieth-Century Women Writers. Bloomington, IN: Indiana University Press, 1985.

Edited Books
The Feminist Memoir Project: Voices from Women's Liberation (coedited with Ann Snitow). New Brunswick: Rutgers University Press, 2007.

The Objectivist Nexus: Essays in Cultural Poetics (coedited with Peter Quartermain). Tuscaloosa, AL: The University of Alabama Press, 1999.
The Feminist Memoir Project: Voices from Women's Liberation (coedited with Ann Snitow). New York: Three Rivers/ Crown Publishing Group, 1998.
Signets: Reading H.D (co-edited with Susan Stanford Friedman). Madison, WI: University of Wisconsin Press, 1990.
The Selected Letters of George Oppen. Durham, NC: Duke University Press, 1990.

BETSY FAGIN
Rosemary Stretch. Switzerland: *a dusi/e-chap, Dusie Press, 2006.
For Every Solution There is a Problem. Brooklyn: Open 24 Hours, 2003.

BETH ANN FENNELLY
Tender Hooks. New York: W. W. Norton, 2004.
Open House. Lincoln, NE: Zoo Press, 2002.

Essays
Great With Child. New York: W. W. Norton, 2006.

MIRANDA FIELD
Swallow. New York: Mariner Books, 2002.

ANNIE FINCH
Annie Finch: Greatest Hits. Columbus, OH: Pudding House Press, 2006.
Home-Birth. Cincinnati, OH: Dos Madres Press, 2004.
The Encyclopedia of Scotland. Cambridge, England: Salt Publishing, 2004.
Calendars. Manchester, VT: Tupelo Press, 2003.
Season Poems. San Francisco, CA: Calliope Press, 2001.
Eve. Brownsville, OR: Story Line Press, 1997.
Catching the Mermother. West Chester, PA: Aralia Press, 1995.
The Encyclopedia of Scotland (abridged libretto). New York: Caribou Press, 1982.

Essays
The Ghost of Meter: Culture and Prosody in American Free Verse. Ann Arbor, MI: University of Michigan Press, 2005.
The Body of Poetry: Essays on Women, Form, and the Poetic Self. Ann Arbor, MI: University of Michigan Press, 2005.

Translations
Louise Labé: Complete Poetry and Prose: A Bilingual Edition (Edited and with translations by Deborah Lesko Baker). Chicago, IL: University of Chicago Press, 2006.

Edited Books
A Formal Feeling Comes: Poems in Form by Contemporary Women. Brownsville, OR: Story Line Press, 1994.
After New Formalism: Poets on Form, Narrative, and Tradition. Brownsville, OR: Story Line Press, 1999.
Carolyn Kizer: Perspectives on Her Life and Work (coeditor with Johanna Keller and

Candace McClelland). Fort Lee, NJ: CavanKerry Press, 2001.
An Exaltation of Forms: Contemporary Poets Celebrate the Diversity of Their Art
(coeditor with Kathrine Varnes). Ann Arbor, MI: University of Michigan Press, 2002.
Lofty Dogmas: Poets on Poetics (coeditor with Maxine Kumin and Deborah Brown).
Fayetteville, AR: University of Arkansas Press, 2005.
Multiformalisms: Postmodern Poetics of Form (coeditor with Susan Schultz).
Cincinnati, OH: Textos Books (Wordtech Editions), 2007.

LISA FISHMAN
The Happiness Experiment. Boise, ID: Ahsahta Press, 2007.
Dear, Read. Boise, ID: Ahsahta Press, 2002.
The Deep Heart's Core Is a Suitcase. Kalamazoo, MI: New Issues Press, 1998

Chapbook
KabbaLoom. Wyrd Press, 2007.

CAROLYN FORCHÉ
Blue Hour: Poems. New York: HarperCollins, 2003.
The Angel of History. New York: HarperCollins, 1994.
The Country Between Us. New York: HarperCollins, 1982.
Gathering the Tribes. New Haven, CT: Yale University Press, 1976.

Edited Book
Against Forgetting: Twentieth-Century Poetry of Witness. New York: W. W. Norton,
1993.

KATHLEEN FRASER
W I T N E S S , Tucson, AZ: Chax Press, 2006.
hi dde violeth i dde violet. Vancouver, Canada: Nomados Press, 2004.
Discrete Categories Forced Into Coupling. Berkeley, CA: Apogee Press, 2004.
20th Century. San Francisco, CA: a+bend press, 2000.
boundayr (with aquatints by Sam Francis). Santa Monica, CA: The Lapis Press, 1988.
Il Cuore : the heart, Selected Poems (1970-1995). Middletown, CT: Wesleyan University
Press, 1997.
Wing. Mill Valley, CA: Em Press, 1995.
When New Time Folds Up. Minneapolis, MN: CHAX Press, 1994.
Notes Preceding Trust. Santa Monica, CA: The Lapis Press, 1988.
Something (Even Human Voices) in the Foreground, a Lake. Berkeley, CA: Kelsey
Street Press, 1984.
Each Next: Narratives. Berkeley, CA: The Figures, 1980.
New Shoes. New York: Harper & Row, 1978.
Magritte Series. Berkeley, CA: Tuumba Press, 1977.
What I Want. New York: Harper & Row, 1974.
Little Notes to You from Lucas Street. Iowa City, IA: Penumbra Press, 1972.
In Defiance (of the Rains). San Francisco, CA: Kayak Books, 1969.
Change of Address. San Francisco, CA: Kayak Books, 1966.

Essays
Translating the Unspeakable: Poetry and the Innovative Necessity. Tuscaloosa, AL: University of Alabama Press, 2000.

Children's Books
Stilts, Somersaults and Headstands. New York: Atheneum, 1968.

SUSANA GARDNER
To Stand to Sea. Portland, OR: The Tangent Press, 2006.
S C R A W L OR,- (from the markings of) t h e s m a l l h e r(o). Switzerland: *a dusi/e-chap, Dusie
Press, 2006.

LARA GLENUM
The Hounds of No. Notre Dame, IN: Action Books, 2005.
Tiny Outrageous Mouth of Heaven. Notre Dame, IN: Action Books, forthcoming 2008.

ARIELLE GREENBERG
My Kafka Century. Notre Dame, IN: Action Books, 2005.
Given. Seattle, WA: Verse/Wave, 2002.

Chapbooks
Fa(r)ther Down: Songs from the Allergy Trials. New Michigan Press, 2003.

Edited Books
Youth Subcultures: A College Composition Reader. New York: Longman, 2006.
Efforts and Affections: Women Poets on Mentorship (coedited with Rachel Zucker). Iowa City, IA: University of Iowa, forthcoming 2008.

CAMILLE GUTHRIE
In Captivity. Berkeley: Subpress 2006.
The Master Thief. Berkeley: Subpress, 2000.

KIMIKO HAHN
The Narrow Road to the Interior. New York: W. W. Norton, 2006.
The Artist's Daughter. New York: W. W. Norton, 2002.
Mosquito and Ant. New York: W. W. Norton, 1999.
Volatile. New York: Hanging Loose Press,1998.
The Unbearable Heart. New York: Kaya Productions, 1995.
Earshot. New York: Hanging Loose Press, 1992.
Air Pocket. New York: Hanging Loose Press, 1989.
We Stand Our Ground (with Gale Jackson and Susan Sherman). New York: IKON, 1988.

SHARON HARRIS
AVATAR. Toronto, Canada: The Mercury Press, 2006.

CARLA HARRYMAN
Baby. New York: Adventures in Poetry, 2005.

h

Gardener of Stars. Berkeley, CA: Atelos, 2001.
The Words: After Carl Sandburg's Rootabaga Stories and Jean-Paul Sartre. Berkeley, CA: O Books, 1994.
There Never Was a Rose Without a Thorn. San Francisco, CA: City Lights, 1995.
Memory Play. Oakland, CA: O Books, 1994.
In the Mode Of. Tenerife, Canary Islands: Zasterle Press, 1992.
Animal Instincts: Prose, Plays Essays. Berkeley, CA: This Press, 1989.
Vice. Hartford, CT: Potes and Poets Press, 1986.
The Middle. San Francisco, CA: Gaz Press, 1983.
Property. Berkeley, CA: Tuumba Press, 1982.
Under the Bridge. San Francisco, CA: This Press, 1980.
Percentage. Berkeley, CA: Tuumba Press, 1979.

Essays
Adorno's Noise. Ohio and Iowa: Essay Press, forthcoming 2007.

Special Editions
Toujours L'épine Est Sous La Rose (trans. Martin Richet). Paris, France: Ikko, 2006.
Open Box. Brooklyn, NY: Belladonna Books, 2007.
Dim Blue and Why Yell. Brooklyn, NY: Belladonna Books, 2000.

Collaborations
The Grand Piano, an experiment in collective autobiography, vol. 1 and 2. Detroit, MI: Mode A, 2006 and 2007.

Edited Books
Lust for Life: on the Writings of Kathy Acker (coedited with Amy Scholder and Avital Ronell). New York and London: Verso, 2006.

JENNIFER MICHAEL HECHT
The Happiness Myth: Why What We Think Is Right Is Wrong. New York: HarperCollins, 2007.
Funny. Madison, WI: University of Wisconsin Press, 2005.
Doubt: A History. New York: HarperCollins, 2003.
The End of the Soul: Scientific Modernity, Atheism and Anthropology. New York: Columbia University Press, 2003.
The Next Ancient World. Dorset, VT: Tupelo Press, 2001.

BRENDA HILLMAN
Pieces of Air in the Epic. Middletown. CT: Wesleyan University Press, 2005
Cascadia. Middletown, CT: Wesleyan University Press, 2001.
Loose Sugar. Middletown, CT: Wesleyan University Press, 1997.
Bright Existence. Middletown, CT: Wesleyan University Press, 1993.
Death Tractates. Middletown, CT: Wesleyan University Press, 1992.
Fortress. Middletown, CT: Wesleyan University Press, 1989.
White Dress. Middletown, CT: Wesleyan University Press, 1985.

Chapbooks
The Firecage. San Francisco, CA: a+bend press, 2000.
Autumn Sojourn. Mill Valley, CA: Em Press, 1995.
Coffee, 3AM. Iowa City, IA: Penumbra Press, 1982.

Edited Books
The Grand Permission: New Writings on Poetics and Motherhood (coedited with Patricia Dienstfrey). Middletown, CT: Wesleyan University Press, 2003.

SUSAN HOLBROOK
Misled. Calgary, Canada: Red Deer Press, 1999.
Good Egg Bad Seed. Vancouver, Canada: Nomados, 2004.

FANNY HOWE
Lives of a Spirit/Glasstown: Where Something Got Broken. New York: Nightboat Books, 2006.
On The Ground. Saint Paul, MN: Graywolf Press, 2004.
Gone. Berkeley, CA: University of California Press, 2003.
Selected Poems. Berkeley, CA: University of California Press, 2000.
Q. England: Paul Green Press, 1998.
One Crossed Out. Saint Paul, MN: Graywolf Press, l997.
O'clock. London: Reality Editions, 1995.
The End. Los Angeles, CA: Littoral Books, 1992.
The Quietist. Oakland, CA: O Books, 1992.
The Vineyard. Barrington, RI: Lost Roads, RI, 1988.
Robeson Street. Boston, MA: Alice James Books, 1985.
Introduction to the World. New York: The Figures, 1985.
For Erato. Berkeley, CA: Tuumba Press, 1984.
Alsace Lorraine. New York: Telephone Books, 1982.
Poem from a Single Pallet. Berkeley, CA: Kelsey Street Press, 1980.
Eggs. Boston, MA: Houghton Mifflin, 1980.
The Amerindian Coastline Poem. New York: Telephone Books, 1976.

Fiction
Radical Love. New York: Nightboat Books, 2007.
Economics. Chicago, IL: Flood Editions, 2002.
Indivisible. Cambridge, MA: Semiotext(e)/MIT Press, 2001.
Nod. Los Angeles, CA: Sun & Moon Press, 1998.
Nord Profond. Paris, France: Mercure de France, 1997.
Saving History. Los Angeles, CA: Sun & Moon Press, 1992.
Famous Questions. New York: Ballantine, 1989.
The Deep North. Los Angeles, CA: Sun & Moon Press, 1988.
The Lives of a Spirit. Los Angeles, CA: Sun & Moon Press, 1986.
Taking Care. New York: Avon Books, 1985.
In the Middle of Nowhere. New York: The Fiction Collective, 1984.
The White Slave. New York: Avon Books, 1980.
Holy Smoke. New York: Fiction Collective, 1979.
Bronte Wilde. New York: Avon Equinox, 1976.

First Marriage. New York: Avon Equinox, 1975.
Forty Whacks. Boston, MA: Houghton Mifflin, 1969.

Essays
The Wedding Dress. Berkeley, CA: University of California Press, 2003.

Young Adult Novels
The Race of the Radical. New York: Viking Press, 1985
Radio City. New York: Avon Books, 1983
Yeah, But. New York: Avon Books, 1982
The Blue Hills. New York: Avon Books, 1981.

MARIE HOWE
The Good Thief. New York: Persea Books, 1988.
What the Living Do. New York: W. W. Norton, 1997.

Edited Books
In the Company of My Solitude: American Writing from the AIDS Pandemic. With Michael Klein. New York: Persea Books, 1995.

CHRISTINE HUME
Alaskaphrenia. Kalamazoo, MI: New Issues, 2004.
Musca Domestica. Boston, MA: Beacon Press, 2000.

CLAUDIA KEELAN
The Devotion Field. Farmington, ME: Alice James Books, 2004.
Utopic. Farmington, ME: Alice James Books, 2000.
The Secularist. Athens, GA: University of Georgia Press, 1997.
Refinery. Cleveland, OH: Cleveland State University Poetry Prize, 1994.

Chapbooks
Of and Among There Was a Locus(t). Boise, ID: Ahsahta Press, 2003.

CAROLINE KNOX
He Paves the Road with Iron Bars. Seattle, WA: Verse Press, 2004.
A Beaker: New and Selected Poems. Seattle, WA: Verse Press, 2002.
Sleepers Wake. New York: Timken Publishers, 1994.
To Newfoundland. Athens, GA: University of Georgia Press 1989.
The House Party. Athens, GA: University of Georgia Press 1984.

DEBORAH LANDAU
Orchidelirium. Tallahassee, FL: Anhinga Press, 2003.

ANN LAUTERBACH
Hum. New York: Penguin Poets, 2005
If in Time: Selected Poems 1975–2000. New York: Penguin Poets, 2001.
On a Stair. New York: Penguin Poets, 1997.
And for Example. New York: Penguin Poets, 1994.

k

Clamor. New York: Penguin Poets, 1991.
Before Recollection. Princeton, NJ: Princeton University Press, 1987.
Many Times, But Then. Austin: University of Texas Press, 1979.

Essays
The Night Sky: Writings on the Poetics of Experience. New York: Viking, 2005.

MINA LOY
The Lost Lunar Baedeker: Poems of Mina Loy. Ed. Roger Conover. New York: The Noonday Press, 1996.
Insel. Santa Rosa, CA: Black Sparrow Books, 1991.
Last Lunar Baedeker. Highlands, NC: Jargon Society, 1982.
Lunar Baedeker. Paris: Contact Publishing Co., 1923.

KIMBERLY LYONS
Saline. Berkeley, CA: Instance Press, 2005.
Abracadabra. New York: Granary Books, 2000.

CAROLE MASO
The Art Lover. New York: New Directions Press, 2006.
Aureole. San Francisco, CA: City Lights, 2003.
Beauty Is Convulsive: The Passion of Frida Kahlo. New York: Counterpoint Press, 2002.
The Room Lit by Roses: A Journal of Pregnancy and Birth. New York: Counterpoint Press, 2002.
Break Every Rule: Essays on Language, Longing, and Moments of Desire. New York: Counterpoint Press, 2000.
Defiance. New York: Plume, 1999.
Ghost Dance. Hopewell, NJ: Ecco Press, 1995.
Ava. Champaign, IL: Dalkey Archive Press, 1995.
The American Woman in the Chinese Hat. New York: Plume, 1994.

BERNADETTE MAYER
Scarlet Tanager. New York: New Directions, 2005.
Indigo Bunting. Zasterl Press, 2004.
The 3:15 Experiment (with Jen Hofer, Danika Dinsmore, and Lee Ann Brown). New York: The Owl Press, 2001.
Midwinter Day. New York: New Directions, 1999 (reprint of 1982 edition).
Two Haloed Mourners: Poems. New York: Granary Books, 1998.
Proper Name & other stories. New York: New Directions, 1996.
Another Smashed Pinecone. New York: United Artists Books, 1998.
The Desires of Mothers to Please Others in Letters. West Stockbridge, MA: Hard Press, 1994.
A Bernadette Mayer Reader. New York: New Directions, 1992.
The Formal Field of Kissing. New York: Catchword Papers, 1990.
Sonnets. New York: Tender Buttons, 1989.
Mutual Aid. Mademoiselle de la Mole Press, 1985.
Utopia. New York: United Artists Books, 1984.
Midwinter Day. Berkeley, CA: Turtle Island Foundation, 1982.

The Golden Book of Words. Lenox, MA: Angel Hair, 1978.
Eruditio Ex Memoria. Lenox, MA: Angel Hair, 1977.
Poetry. New York: Kulchur Foundation, 1976.
Studying Hunger. New York: Adventures in Poetry/ Bolinas, CA: Big Sky, 1976.
Ceremony Latin (1964). New York: Angel Hair, 1975.
Memory. Plainfield, VT: North Atlantic Books, 1976.
Moving. New York: Angel Hair, 1971.
Story. New York: 0 to 9 Press, 1968.

THYLIAS MOSS
Tokyo Butter: Poems. New York: Persea Books, 2006.
Slave Moth: A Narrative in Verse. New York: Persea Books, 2004.
Last Chance for the Tarzan Holler. New York: Persea Books, 1998.
Small Congregations: New and Selected Poems. Hopewell, NJ: Ecco Press, 1993.
Rainbow Remnants in Rock Bottom Ghetto Sky. New York: Persea Books, 1991.
At Redbones. Cleveland, OH: Cleveland State University Poetry Center, 1990.
Pyramid of Bone. Charlottesville, VA: University of Virginia Press, 1989.
Hosiery Seams on a Bowlegged Woman. Cleveland, OH: Cleveland State University Poetry Center, 1983.

Prose
Tale of a Sky-Blue Dress. New York: William Morrow, 1998.
Somewhere Else Right Now. New York: Dial Books for Young Readers, 1997.
I Want to Be. New York: Dial Books for Young Readers, 1993.

HOA NGUYEN
Red Juice. Austin, TX: Effing Press, 2005.
Your Ancient See Through. Honolulu, CA: Sub Press, 2002.

Chapbooks
Add Some Blue. Orono, ME: Backwoods Broadsides Chaplet Series, 2004.
Let's Eat Red for Fun. New York: Booglit, 2000.
Parrot Drum. Oakland, CA: Leroy Press, 2000.
Dark. San Francisco, CA: Mike and Dale's Press, 1998.

ALICE NOTLEY
Grave of Light: New and Selected Poems 1970–2005. Middletown, CT: Wesleyan University Press, 2006.
Alma, or the Dead Women. New York: Granary Books, 2006.
Coming After. Ann Arbor, MI: University of Michigan Press, 2005.
From the Beginning. Woodacre, CA: The Owl Press, 2004.
Disobedience. New York: Penguin Poets, 2001.
Mysteries of Small Houses. New York: Penguin Poets, 1998.
The Descent of Alette. New York: Penguin Poets, 1996.
Close to Me and Closer . . . (The Language of Heaven) and *Desamere*. Oakland, CA: O Books, 1995.
Selected Poems of Alice Notley. Jersey City, NJ: Talisman House, 1993.

To Say You. Riverdale, MD: Pyramid Atlantic, 1993.
Scarlet Cabinet: A Compendium of Books by Alice Notley & Douglas Oliver (with Douglas Oliver). New York: Scarlet Editions, 1992.
Homer's Art. Canton, New York: The Institute of Further Studies, 1990.
From a Work in Progress. 1988.
At Night the States. Chicago, IL: Yellow Press, 1988.
Parts of a Wedding. New York: Unimproved Editions Press, 1986.
Margaret & Dusty. Minneapolis, MN: Coffee House Press, 1985.
Sorrento. Los Angeles: Sherwood Press, 1984.
Tell Me Again. Santa Barbara, CA: Am Here/Immediate Editions, 1982.
Waltzing Matilda. New York: Kulchur Foundation, 1981. Rptd. Cambridge, MA: Faux Press, 2003.
How Spring Comes. West Branch, IA: Toothpaste Press. 1981.
When I Was Alive. New York: Vehicle Editions, 1980.
Dr. Williams' Heiresses. San Francisco, CA: Tuumba Press, 1980.
Songs for the Unborn Second Baby. Lenox, MA: United Artists, 1979.
A Diamond Necklace. New York: Frontward Books, 1977.
Alice Ordered Me to Be Made. Chicago, IL: Yellow Press, 1976.
For Frank O'Hara's Birthday. Cambridge, England: Street Editions, 1976.
Incidentals in the Day World. New York: Angel Hair, 1973.
Phoebe Light. Bolinas, CA: Big Sky, 1973.
165 Meeting House Lane. New York: "C" Press, 1971.

Books Edited
Oliver, Douglas. *Arrondissements*. Cambridge, England: Salt Publishing, 2003.
Berrigan, Ted. The Collected Poems of Ted Berrigan (with Anselm Berrigan and Edmund Berrigan). Berkeley, CA: University of California Press, 2005.

SHARON OLDS
Strike Sparks: Selected Poems. New York: Knopf, 2004.
The Unswept Room. New York: Jonathan Cape, 2002.
Blood, Tin, Straw. New York: Knopf, 1999.
The Wellspring. New York: Knopf, 1996.
The Father. New York: Knopf, 1992.
The Gold Cell. New York: Knopf, 1987.
The Dead and the Living. New York: Knopf, 1984.
Satan Says. Pittsburgh: University of Pittsburgh Press, 1980.

AKILAH OLIVER
The She Said Dialogues: Flesh Memory. Boulder, CO: Smokeproof/Erudite Fangs, 1999.

Chapbooks
a(A)ugust. New York: Yo-Yo Labs, 2007.
An Arriving Guard of Angels. Brooklyn, CA: Belladonna Books, 2006.
Thusly Coming to Greet. Boulder, CO: Farfalla Press, 2004.

ALICIA OSTRIKER
No Heaven. Pittsburgh, PA: University of Pittsburgh Press, 2005.

The Volcano Sequence. Pittsburgh, PA: University of Pittsburgh Press, 2002.
The Little Space: Poems Selected and New, 1968-1998. Pittsburgh, PA: University of Pittsburgh Press, 1998.
The Crack in Everything. Pittsburgh, PA: University of Pittsburgh Press, 1996.
The Nakedness of the Fathers: Biblical Visions and Revisions. Piscataway, NJ: Rutgers University Press, 1994.
Green Age. Pittsburgh, PA: University of Pittsburgh Press, 1989.
The Imaginary Lover. Pittsburgh: PA: University of Pittsburgh Press, 1986.
A Woman Under the Surface. Princeton, NJ: Princeton University Press, 1982.
The Mother/Child Papers. Los Angeles, CA: Momentum Press, 1980. Reprinted Boston: Beacon Press, l986.
A Dream of Springtime: Poems 1970-78. New York: Smith/ Horizon Press, 1979.
Once More Out of Darkness and Other Poems. Berkeley, CA: Berkeley Poets' Press, 1976.
Songs: a Book of Poems. New York: Holt Rinehart and Winston, 1969.

Essays
Dancing at the Devil's Party: Essays on Poetry, Politics and the Erotic. Ann Arbor, MI: University of Michigan Press, 2000.
Feminist Revision and the Bible: The Bucknell Lectures on Literary Theory. London and Cambridge, MA.: Blackwell, 1993.
Stealing the Language: The Emergence of Women's Poetry in America. Boston, MA: Beacon Press, 1986
Writing Like a Woman. Ann Arbor, MI: University of Michigan Press, 1983.
William Blake: The Complete Poems. New York: Penguin Books, 1977.
Vision and Verse in William Blake. Madison, WI: University of Wisconsin Press, 1965.

MAUREEN OWEN
Erosion's Pull. Minneapolis, MN: Coffee House Press, 2006.
Erosion's Pull (Special Edition). New York: Granary Books, 2005.
American Rush: Selected Poems. Jersey City, NJ: Talisman House, 1998.
Untapped Maps. Elwood, CT: Potes & Poets Press, 1993.
Imaginary Income. New York: Hanging Loose Press, 1992.
Zombie Notes. New York: Sun Press, 1985.
AE (Amelia Earhart). San Francisco, CA: Vortex Editions, 1984.
Hearts in Space. New York: Kulchur Foundation, 1980.
A Brass Choir Approaches the Burial Ground. Big Deal 5, 1977.
No-Travels Journal. Cherry Valley, NY: Cherry Valley Editions, 1975.
Country Rush. New York: Adventures in Poetry, 1973.

KATHLEEN OSSIP
The Search Engine. Philadelphia, PA: American Poetry Review, 2002.

Chapbooks
Cinephrastics. Providence, RI: HorseLess Press, 2006.

DANIELLE PAFUNDA
Pretty Young Thing. Brooklyn, NY: Soft Skull Press, 2005.
A Primer for Cyborgs: The Corpse. Atlanta: Whole Coconut Chapbook Series.

o

CLAUDIA RANKINE
Don't Let Me Be Lonely: An American Lyric. Minneapolis, MN: Graywolf Press, 2004.
Plot. New York: Grove Press, 2001.
The End of the Alphabet. New York: Grove Press, 1998.
Nothing in Nature Is Private. Cleveland, OH: Cleveland State University Press, 1994.

Books Edited
American Poets in the 21st Century: The New Poetics (with Lisa Sewell). Middletown, CT: Wesleyan University Press, 2007.
American Women Poets in the 21st Century: Where Lyric Meets Language (with Juliana Spahr). Middletown, CT: Wesleyan University Press, 2002.

PAM REHM
Small Works. Chicago, IL: Flood Editions, 2005.
Gone To Earth. Chicago, IL: Flood Editions, 2001.
To Give It Up. Los Angeles, CA: Sun & Moon Press, 1995.
The Garment in Which No One Had Slept. Providence, RI: Burning Deck, 1993.

Chapbooks
Saving Bonds. Minneapolis, MN: The Cultural Society, 2002.
Piecework. Stockbridge, MA: Oblek Editions, 1992.

ADRIENNE RICH
Telephone Ringing in the Labyrinth. New York: W. W. Norton, 2007.
The School Among the Ruins: Poems 2000–2004. New York: W. W. Norton, 2004.
The Fact of a Doorframe: Selected Poems 1950–2001. New York: W. W. Norton, 2002.
Fox: Poems 1998–2000. New York: W. W. Norton, 2001.
Midnight Salvage: Poems 1995–1998. New York: W. W. Norton, 1999.
Dark Fields of the Republic, 1991–1995. New York: W. W. Norton, 1995.
Collected Early Poems, 1950–1970. New York: W. W. Norton, 1993.
An Atlas of the Difficult World: Poems, 1988–1991. New York: W. W. Norton, 1991.
Time's Power: Poems, 1985–1988. New York: W. W. Norton, 1988.
Your Native Land, Your Life. New York: W. W. Norton, 1986.
The Fact of a Doorframe: Poems Selected and New, 1950–1984. New York: W. W. Norton, 1984.
Sources. Woodside, CA: Heyeck Press, 1983.
A Wild Patience Has Taken Me This Far: Poems, 1978–1981. New York: W. W. Norton, 1981.
The Dream of a Common Language: Poems, 1974–1977. New York: W. W. Norton, 1978.
Twenty-One Love Poems. Emeryville, CA: Effie's Press, 1977.
Poems: Selected and New, 1950–1974. New York: W. W. Norton, 1974.
Diving into the Wreck: Poems, 1971–1972. New York: W. W. Norton, 1973.
The Will to Change: Poems, 1968–1970. New York: W. W. Norton, 1971.
Leaflets: Poems, 1965–1968. New York: W. W. Norton, 1969.
Necessities of Life. New York: W. W. Norton, 1966.
Snapshots of a Daughter-in-Law: Poems, 1954–1962. New York: Harper, 1963; rev. ed., New York: W. W. Norton, 1967.
The Diamond Cutters and Other Poems. New York: Harper, 1955.
A Change of World. New Haven, CT: Yale University Press, 1951.

Prose

Poetry & Commitment: An Essay. New York: W. W. Norton, 2007.
Arts of the Possible: Essays and Conversations. New York: W. W. Norton, 2001.
What Is Found There: Notebooks on Poetry and Politics. New York: W. W. Norton, 1993.
Blood, Bread and Poetry: Selected Prose, 1979-1986. New York: W. W. Norton, 1986.
On Lies, Secrets and Silence: Selected Prose, 1966- 1978. New York: W. W. Norton, 1979.
Of Woman Born: Motherhood as Experience and Institution. New York: W. W. Norton, 1976, rev. ed., 1986.

ELIZABETH ROBINSON

Apostrophe. Berkeley, CA: Apogee Press, 2006.
Under That Silky Roof. Providence, RI: Burning Deck Press, 2006.
Apprehend. New York and Berkeley, CA: Fence Books and Apogee Press, 2003.
Pure Descent. Los Angeles, CA: Sun & Moon Press, 2002.
Harrow. Richmond, CA: Omnidawn Publishing, 2001.
House Made of Silver. Berkeley, CA: Kelsey Street Press, 2000.
Bed of Lists. Berkeley, CA: Kelsey Street Press, 1990.
In the Sequence of Falling Things. Providence, RI: Paradigm Press, 1990.

MARTHA RONK

Vertigo. Minneapolis, MN: Coffee House Press, forthcoming.
In a Landscape of Having to Repeat. Richmond, CA: Omnidawn Publishing, 2004.
Why/Why Not. Berkeley, CA: University of California Press, 2003.
Displeasures of the Table. Los Angeles, CA: Green Integer Books, 2001.
Eyetrouble. Athens, GA: University of Georgia Press, 1998.
State of Mind. Los Angeles, CA: Sun & Moon Press, 1995.
Desert Geometries (with artist Don Suggs). Essex, England: Littoral Books, 1992.
Desire in LA. Athens, GA: University of Georgia Press, 1990.

SUSAN M. SCHULTZ

And Then Something Happened. Cambridge, England: Salt Publishing, 2004.
Memory Cards & Adoption Papers. Bedford, MA: Potes & Poets, 2001.
Aleatory Allegories. Cambridge, England: Salt Publishing, 2000.

Criticism

A Poetics of Impasse in Modern and Contemporary American Poetry. Tuscaloosa, AL: University of Alabama Press, 2005.

Edited Books

The Tribe of John: Ashbery and Contemporary Poetry. Tuscaloosa, AL: University of Alabama Press, 1995.

ELENI SIKELIANOS

Body Clock. Minneapolis, MN: Coffee House Press, Forthcoming 2008.
The Book of Jon. San Francisco, CA: City Lights, 2004.
The California Poem. Minneapolis, MN: Coffee House Press: 2004.
The Monster Lives of Boys & Girls. Los Angeles, CA: Green Integer Books, 2003.
Earliest Worlds. Minneapolis, MN: Coffee House Press, April 2001.

The Book of Tendons. Sausalito, CA: Post-Apollo Press, 1997.
To Speak While Dreaming. Boulder: Selva Editions, 1993.

MARTHA SILANO
Blue Positive. Bowling Green, KY: Steel Toe Books, 2006.
What the Truth Tastes Like. La Plume, PA: Nightshade Press, 1999.

SASHA STEENSEN
A Magic Book. New York: Fence Books, 2004.
Correspondence (with Gordon Hadfield). Brooklyn, NY: Handwritten Press, 2004.

LARISSA SZPORLUK
Embryos and Idiots. Manchester, VT: Tupelo Press, forthcoming 2007.
The Wind, Master Cherry, the Wind. Farmington, ME: Alice James Books, 2003.
Isolato. Iowa City, IA: University of Iowa Press, 2000.
Dark Sky Question. Boston, MA: Beacon Press, 1998.

ELIZABETH TREADWELL
Birds & Fancies. England: Shearsman, 2007
Wardolly. Tucson, AZ: Chax Press, 2007.
Cornstarch Figurine. Dusie Books, 2006.
Chantry. Tucson, AZ: Chax Press, 2004.
LILYFOIL + 3. Oakland, CA: O Books, 2004.

Chapbooks
The Graces. Switzerland: Dusie wee book, 2006.
LILYFOIL or Boy & Girl Tramps of America. Sausalito, CA: Duration Press e-book, 2002.
The Milk Bees. Lucille, 2000.
Eve Doe: Prior to Landscape. San Francisco, CA: a+bend, 1999.
The Erratix & Other Stories. Guilderland, NY: Texture Press, 1998.
Eve Doe. Berkeley, CA: Double Lucy Books, 1997.

Fiction
Populace. Pengrove, CA: Avec Books, 1999.
Eleanor Ramsey: The Queen of Cups. San Francisco, CA: San Francisco State University Press, 1997.

CATHERINE WAGNER
Macular Hole. New York: Fence Books, 2004.
Miss America. New York: Fence Books, 2001.

Chapbooks
Imitating. London: Leafe Press, 2004.
Exercises. New York: 811 Books, 2003.
Hotel Faust. Sheffield, England: West House Books/Gratton Street Irregulars, 2001.
Box Poems. Los Angeles, CA: Seeing Eye Books, 2001.
Fraction Anthems. San Francisco, CA: 811 Books, 1999.

r

JEAN VALENTINE

Door in the Mountain: New and Collected Poems 1965–2003. Middletown, CT: Wesleyan University Press, 2004.

The Cradle of the Real Life. Middletown, CT: Wesleyan University Press, 2000.

Growing Darkness, Growing Light. Pittsburgh, PA: Carnegie Mellon University Press, 1997.

The Under Voice: Selected Poems. County Clare, Ireland: Salmon Publishing, 1995.

The River at Wolf. Farmington, ME: Alice James Books, 1992.

Home Deep Blue: New and Selected Poems. Farmington, ME: Alice James Books, 1989.

The Messenger. New York: Farrar, Straus & Giroux, 1979.

Ordinary Things. New York: Farrar, Straus & Giroux, 1974.

Pilgrims. New York: Farrar, Straus & Giroux, 1969.

Dream Barker. New Haven, CT: Yale University Press, 1965.

Edited

The Lighthouse Keeper: Essays on the Poetry of Eleanor Ross Taylor. Geneva, NY: Seneca Review, 2001.

ANNE WALDMAN
Selected Poetry

Outrider: Essays, Interview, Poems. Albuquerque, NM: La Alameda Press/ University of New Mexico, 2006.

Structure of the World Compared to a Bubble. New York: Penguin Poets, 2004.

In the Room of Never Grieve: New & Selected Poems 1985–2003. Minneapolis, MN: Coffee House Press, 2003.

Vow to Poetry: Essays, Interviews, & Manifestos. Minneapolis, MN: Coffee House Press, 2001.

Marriage: A Sentence. New York: Penguin Poets, 2000.

Iovis II. Minneapolis, MN: Coffee House Press, 1997.

Fast Speaking Woman (20th Anniversary Edition). San Francisco, CA: City Lights Books, 1996.

Kill or Cure. New York: Penguin Poets, 1996.

Iovis: All Is Full of Jove. Minneapolis, MN: Coffee House Press, 1993.

Helping the Dreamer: New and Selected Poems: 1966-1988. Minneapolis, MN: Coffee House Press, 1989.

Skin Meat Bones. Minneapolis, MN: Coffee House Press, 1985.

First Baby Poems. New York: Rocky Ledge, 1982.

Journals and Dreams. New York: Stonehill, 1976.

Life Notes - Selected Poems . Indianapolis, IN: Bobbs-Merrill, 1973.

Baby Breakdown. Indianapolis, IN: Bobbs-Merrill, 1970.

Fast Speaking Woman and Other Chants. San Francisco, CA: City Lights Books, 1978.

Edited Books

Civil Disobediences: Poetics and Politics in Action (co-editor). Minneapolis, MN: Coffee House Press, 2004.

The Angel Hair Anthology: Angel Hair Sleeps With A Boy In My Head (with Lewis Warsh). New York: Granary Books, 2001.

The Beat Book. Boston, MA: Shambhala Publications, 2006.

Disembodied Poetics: Annals of the Jack Kerouac School (co-editor). Albuquerque, NM:

University of New Mexico Press, 1993.
Out of This World: An Anthology from The Poetry Project at the St. Mark's Church In-the-Bowery 1966-1991. New York: Crown Publishing Group, 1991.
Nice to See You: Homage to Ted Berrigan. Minneapolis, MN: Coffee House Press, 1991.
Talking Poetics: Annals of the Jack Kerouac School of Disembodied Poetics [vols. 1 and 2] (with Marilyn Webb). Boulder, CO: Shambhala, 1978.
Another World: A Second Anthology of Works from the St. Mark's Poetry Project. Indianapolis, IN: Bobbs-Merrill, 1971.
The World Anthology: Poems from the St. Mark's Poetry Project. Indianapolis, IN: Bobbs-Merrill, 1969.

REBECCA WOLFF
Manderley. Champaign, IL: University of Illinois Press, 2001.
Figment. New York: W. W. Norton, 2005.

C. D. WRIGHT
Like Something Flying Backwards: New and Selected. Tarset, England: Bloodaxe Editions, 2007.
One Big Self: An Investigation. Port Townsend, WA: Copper Canyon Press, 2007.
Temblar (Valerie Mejer and Jennifer Clement, translators). Ediciones El Tucan de Virginia, 2006.
Cooling Time: An American Poetry Vigil. Port Townsend, WA: Copper Canyon Press, 2005.
One Big Self: Prisoners of Louisiana (with photographer Deborah Luster). Santa Fe, NM: Twin Palms Publishers, 2003.
Steal Away: Selected and New Poems. Port Townsend, WA: Copper Canyon Press, 2003.
Deepstep Come Shining. Port Townsend, WA: Copper Canyon Press, 1998.
Tremble. Hopewell, NJ: Ecco Press,1997.
Just Whistle. Berkeley, CA: Kelsey Street Press, 1994.
String Light. Athens, GA: University of Georgia Press, 1991.
Further Adventures With You. Pittsburgh, PA: Carnegie-Mellon University Press, 1986.
Translations Of The Gospel Back Into Tongues. Albany, NY: State University of New York Press, 1983.

Maps
A Reader's Map of Rhode Island. RI: Lost Roads Publishers, 1999.
The Reader's Map of Arkansas: in conjunction with The Lost Roads Project: A Walk-in Book of Arkansas. Fayetteville, AR: University of Arkansas Press, 1994.

KARENA YOUTZ
The Copycat Manual: A Populist Revival in Ten Easy Steps. Boise, ID: Privity Press, 2003.

ZHANG ER
Poetry in English
So translating rivers and cities: bilingual collection. Saint Paul, MN: Zephyr Press, 2007.
Verses on Bird: Selected Poems in Chinese and English Bilingual Edition. Saint Paul, MN: Zephyr Press, 2004.

t

Chapbooks (in English translation)
Winter Garden. New York: Goats and Compasses, 1997.
Verses on Bird. Jersey, NJ: Jensen/Daniels, 1999.
The Autumn of Gu Yao. New York: Spuyten Duyvil, 2000.
Cross River, Pick Lotus. Brooklyn, NY: Belladonna Books, 2002.
Carved Water. Kane'ohe, HI: Tinfish Press, 2003.
Sight Progress. New York: Pleasure Boat Studio, 2006.

Poetry in Chinese
Seen, Unseen. QingHai Publishing House of China, 1999.
Water Words. New World Poetry Press, 2002.
Because of Mountain. Taipei: Tonsan, 2005.

RACHEL ZUCKER
The Last Clear Narrative. Middletown, CT: Wesleyan University Press, 2004.
Eating in the Underworld. Middletown, CT: Wesleyan University Press, 2003.
Annunciation. New York: Center for Book Arts, 2002.

v

ACKNOWLEDGMENTS

The editors are grateful to have been granted permission to reprint copyrighted material by the following authors:

RAE ARMANTROUT
"Bases," "A Story," "Crossing," and "Fiction" from *Veil: New and Selected Poems* © 2001 by Rae Armantrout and reprinted by permission of Wesleyan University Press.

MAIREAD BYRNE
"Circus," *Fascicle;* "Personal Insurance," *5 AM;* "Tedium," *Masthead;* "The Handy Every-Mother Zone-Out Capacitator" was first published in a chapbook, *Kalends* (Belladonna, 2005).

LESLIE BUMSTEAD
Excerpts from "Abidjan Notebooks" from *Cipher/Civilian,* © 2005 by Leslie Bumstead. Reprinted by permission of Edge Books.

MAXINE CHERNOFF
"A Birth," "Sotto Voce," "Identity Principle" © Maxine Chernoff. From *Evolution of the Bridge: Selected Prose Poems*, Cambridge: Salt Publishing 2004. Reprinted with the permission of the publisher. "Have You A Daughter?" appeared in its entirety in *VERSE*.

WANDA COLEMAN
"Giving Birth" and "'Tis Morning Makes Mother a Killer" © 1983 and 2007 by Wanda Coleman. Reprinted from *Imagoes* by Black Sparrow Press with the permission of the author.

JEAN DONNELLY
"A Bonnet Gospel" appears in *Anthem,* Sun & Moon Press; copyright © Jean Donnelly Linde.

STACY DORIS
From *Knot* by Stacy Doris. Copyright © 2006 by Stacy Doris. Reprinted by permission of the University of Georgia Press.

RACHEL BLAU DUPLESSIS
"A red squall," "little wails," and "Marginalia," from *Tabula Rasa,* © Rachel Blau DuPlessis, 1987. All rights reserved. With thanks to Potes & Poets Press. "Draft 2: She," from *Tabula Rasa* and *Drafts 1-38, Toll,* © Rachel Blau DuPlessis, 1987 and 2001. All rights reserved. With thanks to Potes & Poets Press and Wesleyan University Press.

BETH ANN FENNELLY
"The Gods Tell Me, You Will Forget All This," "Bite Me," from *Tender Hooks: Poems* by Beth Ann Fennelly. Copyright © 2004 by Beth Ann Fennelly. Used by permission of W. W. Norton & Company.

And with endless, unbought **THANKS** to:

CODY ROSE CLEVIDENCE for her images and lovely self; **ARIELLE GREENBERG** for the listserv; Cathy's RA **NICOLE; EMILY BAKER, ANDREA CURRY, LIZ DETTY, CLAIRE KEYES, TARA KORTHALS, PAT LAFLEUR, CHRISTINA M. RIGLING** for heroic typing; **ALICE NOTLEY** (for her example, and for guiding us to her out-of-print work); **ALICIA OSTRIKER** for her wonderful foreword and for putting us, finally, in touch with Toi Derricotte!; **MARTIN CORLESS-SMITH, A. RAWLINGS, IRA SHER, EVIE SHOCKLEY, LAUREL SNYDER, JEN STOCKDALE, KEITH TUMA, SARAH WAGNER,** for advice and encouragement and love

Our **CONTRIBUTORS** for their endless patience and, in some cases, their permission to use previously unpublished and/or out-of-print work

Our **MAMAs: ANNE CUNNINGHAM** and **PAMELA PERRY WOLFF**

has a mission to redefine the terms of accessibility by publishing challenging writing distinguished by idiosyncrasy and intelligence rather than by allegiance with camps, schools, or cliques. It is part of our press's mission to support writers who might otherwise have difficulty being recognized because their work doesn't answer to either the mainstream or to recognizable modes of experimentation.

FENCE BOOKS

CRITICAL TEXTS AND ANTHOLOGIES

Not for Mothers Only: Contemporary Poems on Child-Getting & Child-Rearing
Catherine Wagner & Rebecca Wolff, editors

THE ALBERTA PRIZE

The Cow	Ariana Reines
Practice, Restraint	Laura Sims
A Magic Book	Sasha Steensen
Sky Girl	Rosemary Griggs
The Real Moon of Poetry and Other Poems	Tina Celona
Zirconia	Chelsey Minnis

FENCE MODERN POETS SERIES

Structure of the Embryonic Rat Brain	Christopher Janke, judge Rebecca Wolff
The Stupefying Flashbulbs	Daniel Brenner, judge Rebecca Wolff
Povel	Geraldine Kim, judge Forrest Gander
The Opening Question	Prageeta Sharma, judge Peter Gizzi
Apprehend	Elizabeth Robinson, judge Ann Lauterbach
The Red Bird	Joyelle McSweeney, judge Allen Grossman

FREE CHOICE POETRY

Bad Bad	Chelsey Minnis
Snip Snip!	Tina Brown Celona
Yes, Master	Michael Earl Craig
Swallows	Martin Corless-Smith
Folding Ruler Star	Aaron Kunin
The Commandrine and Other Poems	Joyelle McSweeney